Humanism, Anti-Authoritarianism, and Literary Aesthetics

Humanism, Anti-Authoritarianism, and Literary Aesthetics

Pragmatist Stories of Progress

Ulf Schulenberg

BLOOMSBURY ACADEMIC
NEW YORK • LONDON • OXFORD • NEW DELHI • SYDNEY

BLOOMSBURY ACADEMIC
Bloomsbury Publishing Inc
1385 Broadway, New York, NY 10018, USA
50 Bedford Square, London, WC1B 3DP, UK
29 Earlsfort Terrace, Dublin 2, Ireland

BLOOMSBURY, BLOOMSBURY ACADEMIC and the Diana logo are trademarks of
Bloomsbury Publishing Plc

First published in the United States of America 2023
Paperback edition published 2025

Copyright © Ulf Schulenberg

For legal purposes the Acknowledgments on p. vi constitute an extension
of this copyright page.

Cover design by Eleanor Rose
Cover image: Getty Images

All rights reserved. No part of this publication may be reproduced or transmitted
in any form or by any means, electronic or mechanical, including photocopying,
recording, or any information storage or retrieval system, without prior
permission in writing from the publishers.

Bloomsbury Publishing Inc does not have any control over, or responsibility for,
any third-party websites referred to or in this book. All internet addresses given in this
book were correct at the time of going to press. The author and publisher regret any
inconvenience caused if addresses have changed or sites have ceased to exist,
but can accept no responsibility for any such changes.

Library of Congress Cataloging-in-Publication Data
Names: Schulenberg, Ulf, 1966– author.
Title: Humanism, anti-authoritarianism, and literary aesthetics : pragmatist stories of
progress / Ulf Schulenberg.
Description: New York : Bloomsbury Academic, 2023. |
Includes bibliographical references and index. | Summary: "This book presents pragmatist
humanism as a form of anti-authoritarianism and sheds light on the contemporary
significance of pragmatist aesthetics and the revival of humanism"– Provided by publisher.
Identifiers: LCCN 2023001417 (print) | LCCN 2023001418 (ebook) |
ISBN 9798765102435 (hardback) | ISBN 9798765102442 (paperback) |
ISBN 9798765102459 (ebook) | ISBN 9798765102466 (pdf) |
ISBN 9798765102473 (ebook other)
Subjects: LCSH: Pragmatism. | Humanism. | Authoritarianism. | Literature–Aesthetics.
Classification: LCC B832 .S4439 2023 (print) | LCC B832 (ebook) |
DDC 144/.3–dc23/eng/20230412
LC record available at https://lccn.loc.gov/2023001417
LC ebook record available at https://lccn.loc.gov/2023001418

ISBN: HB: 979-8-7651-0243-5
PB: 979-8-7651-0244-2
ePDF: 979-8-7651-0246-6
eBook: 979-8-7651-0245-9

Typeset by Newgen KnowledgeWorks Pvt. Ltd., Chennai, India

To find out more about our authors and books visit www.bloomsbury.com
and sign up for our newsletters.

Contents

Acknowledgments	vi
Introduction	1
1 Humanism, Anti-Authoritarianism, and Form	13
2 "We Have No Duties to Anything Nonhuman": Richard Rorty's Anti-Authoritarianism	27
3 Pragmatism, Humanism, and Form	69
4 "… and the Practice Has to Speak for Itself": Wittgenstein, Pragmatism, and Anti-Authoritarianism	93
5 Marxism, Form, and the Negation of Aesthetic Synthesis	107
6 "Nothing Is Known—Only Realized": Postcritique, Bruno Latour, and the Idea of a Positive Aesthetics	139
7 "I Turned to the Poets": Humanist Stories of Progress	153
Conclusion	183
Notes	189
References	235
Index	245

Acknowledgments

I would like to thank my editor at Bloomsbury, Amy Martin, for her interest in and support of my project. I could also rely on the professional expertise of Hali Han. For helpful comments and suggestions I owe a debt of gratitude to Carl Jackson, Martin Rossiter, Geneviève Sollers, Annabelle White, and two anonymous reviewers. An earlier version of Chapter 3 was published in the *European Journal of Pragmatism and American Philosophy* XIII-2 (2021). Chapter 5 contains a few paragraphs that were taken from chapters 3 and 4 of my study *Marxism, Pragmatism, and Postmetaphysics: From Finding to Making* (Cham, Switzerland: Palgrave Macmillan, 2019). I wish to thank the editors and publishers for their permission to reprint these texts.

Introduction

One of the ironies of Hegel's philosophy of art is that after it declared the end of art, Nietzsche revitalized art by highlighting its significance in a radically detranscendentalized and naturalized world. According to Hegel, art reveals the absolute, and it does this by representing the absolute as spirit. In contrast to religion and philosophy, art expresses the absolute in sensuous form. In Greek art, as Hegel maintains, form and content were in perfect balance and harmony. In his *Lectures on Aesthetics*, he tells a narrative of decline. Whereas religion and philosophy, beginning in the East, have constantly gained in importance and complexity in their development and are finally capable of representing the absolute in modern times, art reached its peak in ancient Greece and since then has been in decline. Hegel's contention is that fine art "only achieves its highest task when it has taken its place in the same sphere with religion and philosophy, and has become simply a mode of revealing to consciousness and bringing to utterance the Divine Nature, the deepest interests of humanity, and the most comprehensive truths of the mind" (2004: 9). As far as "the spirit of the modern world" is concerned, as Hegel famously underscores, it "reveals itself as beyond the stage at which art is the highest mode assumed by man's consciousness of the absolute. The peculiar mode to which artistic production and works of art belong no longer satisfies our supreme need" (2004: 12). Art, it seems, is a thing of the past, since it no longer offers satisfaction of humans' spiritual wants. On Hegel's account, "thought and reflection have taken their flight above fine art" (2004: 12).[1]

Only a few decades after Hegel's narrative of decline, Nietzsche told a completely different story. As the French poststructuralists correctly pointed out, Nietzsche's philosophy was governed by a clearly anti-Hegelian gesture. The problem, however, was that the French theorists misunderstood Nietzsche when they advanced the idea that he offered a radical antihumanism.[2] This is part of the many deplorable misinterpretations and disorientations of French poststructuralism and deconstruction. From today's perspective, it seems much more fruitful and stimulating to interpret Nietzsche's naturalism as a form of humanism and philosophy of creativity that centers on what he in *Beyond Good and Evil* terms the "artistic refashioning of *mankind*" (2003: sec. 62; unless specified, all italics in quotations are in the original). In Nietzsche's narrative, there is no connection between art and the absolute (in the Hegelian sense) and art still plays a crucial role as regards the shaping of mankind's future. His philosophy is radically postmetaphysical in nature. It critiques the idea that something supernatural or transcendental might shape one's thoughts and direct one's actions.[3]

The modern antifoundationalist and humanist story of progress and emancipation, from Vico, Nietzsche, William James, and F. C. S. Schiller to Dewey and Rorty, demonstrates that our attempts at understanding the world should no longer be dominated by the appearance-reality distinction, the desire for the really real, the correspondence theory of truth, or by the desire to discover the universal conditions of human existence or the permanent, ahistorical context of human life. Nietzsche very much gave this story its form. His influence becomes obvious when one considers that theorists as varied as Dewey, Gadamer, Kuhn, Derrida, and Rorty have taught Nietzschean lessons: we will never achieve, and do not need, epistemological certainty; the immutability and purity of being have never been real; instead of a God's-eye view we have the subject who is always already in a perspective, who is always in a context and in history; and instead of trying to converge to the antecedently real and true and being adequate to the real, the human subject ought to understand the full implications of the development from finding to making.[4]

In *The Gay Science*, Nietzsche proposes that after the death of God "we still have to vanquish his shadow, too" (1974: sec. 108). He detects God's shadow in supernatural entities, immutable principles, theoretical abstractions, the need for epistemological certainty, the notion of an absolute ontology, and in the natural sciences' desire for truth and the really real. His naturalism also critiques forms of positivism and scientism. It is crucial to note that Nietzsche calls attention to the necessity of completing the "de-deification of nature" and of "naturaliz[ing] humanity": "When will all these shadows of God cease to darken our minds? When will we complete our de-deification of nature? When may we begin to '*naturalize*' humanity in terms of a pure, newly discovered, newly redeemed nature?" (1974: sec. 109). While Platonists and Christians established a firm link between God, eternal truth, and moral goodness, and justified this link by means of dualistic thought, Nietzsche strives to convince us that after the death of God we ought to accept the idea that humans are part of the natural world. They have the same ontological status as other creatures. However, because of their use of language and their creativity they have other possibilities of self-creation and self-overcoming. The notion of the death of God offers Nietzsche the possibility of developing his critique of European thought, from Plato and the Christians to contemporary forms of metaphysics, and his naturalism directs attention to the fact that modern culture, contrary to its self-understanding, is still governed by otherworldly ideals.

In *Beyond Good and Evil*, Nietzsche speaks of the endeavor "to translate man back into nature; to master the many vain and fanciful interpretations and secondary meanings which have been hitherto scribbled and daubed over that eternal basic text *homo natura*" (2003: sec. 230). This notion of "translat[ing] man back into nature" is central to Nietzsche's naturalism; it radically critiques the idea of a nonhuman authority in epistemology, morality, and art.[5] Nietzsche regards knowledge, art, and morality as means for the enhancement of life; they must not be placed in a transcendental realm where they appear as the exact opposite of life. Metaphysics and ontotheology have turned knowledge, art, and morality into a negation of the world we know or a desire to transcend this world of praxis. By contrast, Nietzsche's naturalism always returns one to the world of praxis, in which humans as natural creatures are situated at a particular time and place. In this "world of life, nature, and history" (1974: sec. 344), metaphysical and transcendental entities, principles, and abstractions, together with their binary oppositions, are critiqued and finally rejected in favor of that which has hitherto been anathematized.

Nietzsche's naturalism strives "to 'humanize' the world," so that we can "feel ourselves more and more masters within it" (1968: sec. 614). "Humaniz[ing] the world," for him, implies the attempt to demonstrate that language, logic, reason, morality, and the categories can only be derived from the contingent development of humans as natural and historical creatures and as creative self-fashioners under particular environing conditions. It is in Nietzsche that humanism and anti-authoritarianism for the first time fruitfully come together. This would have a profound impact on the antifoundationalist and antirepresentationalist story of progress and emancipation, which centers on the modern development from finding to making.

The intimate relation between humanism in the Nietzschean sense and anti-authoritarianism is at the center of this study.[6] The contemporary significance and potential of this relationship is best illustrated by pragmatist humanism;

that is, only pragmatism as humanism can teach one the full implications and consequences of the ideas that humans have no duty to anything nonhuman and that the only way for them to get beyond their practices is to creatively imagine better and more useful practices.[7] Once we have given up world-directedness and rational answerability to the world and have begun to think of normativity in terms of human beings' answerability to one another, we will be in a position to continue the secularism of the Enlightenment in a thought-provoking manner. Pragmatism, particularly in its Rortyan version, suggests that to think of progress without reliance on a nonhuman power means that one replaces the Kantian question, "What are the ahistorical conditions of possibility?," with the more useful question, "How can we creatively turn the present into a richer future without thinking of the world as a conversational partner?" When the notion of finding a timeless authority to which humans subject themselves, in a long process, is replaced by the idea that humans should strive to come to an agreement among themselves, and when talk about humans' responsibility to Reality, Truth, or Reason is replaced by talk about their responsibility to their fellow human beings, the change is dramatic and far-reaching. Anti-authoritarianism in its pragmatist version shows that humans, as creative and intelligent beings, have to dream up the point of human life. Appealing to a nonhuman standard in order to determine whether they have chosen wisely is no longer possible in a postmetaphysical culture that anti-authoritarianism helps prepare. No nonhuman authority can rank human practices, norms, agreements, language games, needs, or desires. Particularly Dewey and Rorty accentuate the necessity of developing a truly humanistic culture. At this moment, this is still a utopian human future in which the idea of responsibility to anything except our fellow humans would appear utterly unintelligible. Rorty only very rarely went so far as to claim that pragmatism might be capable of "contributing to a world-historical change in humanity's self-image" (1998b: 132).[8] Pragmatism's combination of humanism and anti-authoritarianism, I think, will play a crucial role in the endeavor to achieve this radical change. Pragmatists not only argue that the hope for a noncontingent, nonhistorical, and powerful ally unites Platonism, most religious notions of divine omnipotence, and Kantian moral philosophy; they also advance the idea that the quest for certainty ought to be regarded as an attempt to escape from the world of contingent and historical practices (which is the only world there is). From what I have said so far, it should be clear that one of this book's primary purposes is to contribute to a Rortyan "story of poeticizing and progress" (Rorty 1991b: 110).

There is a revival of humanism in the humanities. This resurgence is a multilayered phenomenon.⁹ As we will see, pragmatists such as James, Dewey, and Rorty have developed a particularly stimulating understanding of humanism. Their texts are governed by the attempt to call attention to the significance of making, poeticizing, creating, and imagining; that is, their stress on *poiesis*, imagination, and creativity tries to convince their readers that they ought to develop a new understanding of intellectual progress. Their antifoundationalist and antirepresentationalist stories of progress and emancipation emphasize the necessity of making the idea of a genuinely postmetaphysical culture look attractive. At the same time, however, pragmatist aesthetics has never offered an adequate appreciation of the importance of aesthetic form. In this study, I will do three things. First, I will contribute to an elucidation of the contemporary significance of humanism by explaining the potential of a pragmatist humanism. Second, I will advance the argument that pragmatist humanism is a form of anti-authoritarianism. Illuminating how humanism, pragmatism, and anti-authoritarianism are interlinked is one of my main goals. Finally, I will show that there is a possibility of bringing together the resurgence of humanism and a renewed interest in the work of aesthetic form by arguing that pragmatist aesthetics needs a more complex conception of form. Marxist theorists like Georg Lukács, Theodor W. Adorno, and Fredric Jameson have offered thought-provoking analyses of form. Hence, I suggest that a mediation between pragmatist aesthetics and materialist aesthetics promises interesting results and that the former can learn from the latter. Is there a possibility of stimulating pragmatist aestheticians' interest in the social nature or social register of aesthetic form? Will they ever grasp the meaning of Adorno's suggestion that "form—the social nexus of everything in particular—represents the social relation in the artwork" (1997: 255)?¹⁰ Like my previous books, the present study seeks to establish a transatlantic polylogue. It is an interdisciplinary work that brings together literary and aesthetic theory, philosophy, and intellectual history.

In Rorty studies, scholars like Colin Koopman, Alan Malachowski, David Rondel, and Christopher Voparil have called attention to Rorty's anti-authoritarianism. Rondel, for instance, claims that an anti-authoritarian perspective "was at the very heart of Rorty's philosophy, central not only to his more professionally abstruse views on truth, justification, knowledge, and rationality but also—and much more dramatically—to his histrionic retelling of Western philosophy's recent trajectory" (2021: 5). Voparil makes the interesting suggestion, which is also central to my argument, that "Rorty's antiauthoritarianism relates to his concern with human agency" (2022: 80). However, these scholars have only begun to illuminate the link between Rorty's humanism and anti-authoritarianism. Furthermore, explaining the importance of the relation between pragmatism, humanism, and anti-authoritarianism in Rorty's work should only be the first step. My study seeks to make clear how our understanding of the complexity of this relationship might shape the future of pragmatist studies. Grasping the significance of this link still is one of the desiderata of pragmatist studies. Another desideratum is to realize the significance of form for pragmatist aesthetics. In this study, I seek to confront these two desiderata and explain how they are connected and how the attempt to approach them can profoundly change our idea of what pragmatism and pragmatist literary and cultural criticism will be capable of offering in the twenty-first century.

In Chapter 1, I prepare the ground for my discussion of how humanism, pragmatism, and anti-authoritarianism are linked. I do this by analyzing the work of philosophers and intellectual historians such as David E. Cooper, Edward Craig, and Isaiah Berlin. Whereas the former two elucidate the anti-authoritarian tendencies in humanism, Berlin's *The Roots of Romanticism* is important for the argument developed in this study because it shows how a humanist notion of *poiesis*, the action of form-giving, and anti-authoritarianism hang together. In the final part of this chapter, I discuss Edward Said's conception of humanism. From the perspective of his Vichian humanism, Said wants to demonstrate that humanism is "the achievement of form by human will and agency" (Said 2004: 15). As I make clear, I intend to do the same, only from the perspective of a pragmatist humanism.

Developing his idiosyncratic brand of pragmatism, Rorty introduced a truly radical understanding of anti-authoritarianism. It does not go too far to state that the later Rorty's anti-authoritarianism is central to his version of pragmatism as humanism. In Chapter 2, I add a new perspective to the discussion of Rorty's endeavor to continue the project of the Enlightenment. This is done by asking two questions. First: What role does Rorty's anti-authoritarianism play for his antirepresentationalist story of emancipation? Second: To what degree does an analysis of his anti-authoritarianism help one understand his version of pragmatism as a form of humanism? Considering the answers to these questions together, I argue, will contribute to the attempt to highlight the contemporary significance of pragmatism and its story of progress and emancipation. One can appreciate the complexity of Rorty's anti-authoritarianism only when one understands why he highly values the Romantics, Nietzsche, Proust, and Dewey. In this chapter, I explain the significance of these authors. Furthermore, I discuss the importance of literature for Rorty's anti-authoritarian story of progress, and I also answer the question of whether his version of literary criticism offers something new. Finally, I seek to elucidate the meaning of Rorty's notion of a literary or poeticized culture. He intends this kind of postmetaphysical culture to be the final stage of the process of secularization. His anti-authoritarian and antirepresentationalist story of progress ends here.

At least since the 1960s, humanism has been attacked by structuralists, poststructuralists, deconstructionists, posthumanists, transhumanists, and other malcontents. In pragmatism, however, a particularly stimulating and thought-provoking understanding of humanism has persisted. As I have argued previously, this persistence of humanism is crucial, since one can grasp the unique contemporary significance of pragmatism only when one appreciates how pragmatism, humanism, anti-authoritarianism, and postmetaphysics are linked, and how this link has gained in importance after the exhaustion of anti- and posthumanist theories. Chapter 3 is divided into three parts. In the first part, I explain why pragmatism ought to be regarded as a humanist philosophy. In the second part, I discuss why most pragmatists, and especially pragmatist aestheticians, have been reluctant to consider the significance of aesthetic form. I advance the argument that Dewey's naturalist aesthetics does not offer a convincing conception of form and that it, moreover, is of no great use in the confrontation with modern artworks and with the objects of the historical avant-garde. In the final part, I argue that a pragmatist humanism that refuses to historicize the concept of form and ignores the radical formal and narratological innovations of modern art and literature weakens its own position and deprives itself of establishing a dialogue with continental aesthetics. Chapter 3 ought to be studied together with Chapter 5, since in the latter I seek to contribute to precisely this dialogue.

It has been repeatedly pointed out that there is an interesting parallel between the later Wittgenstein and the American pragmatists. Emphasizing the significance of social practices and action, both argue against the construction of philosophical theories. Moreover, the thought of both is directed against the human answerability to something nonhuman; that is, it criticizes the notion that there is a nonhuman authority whose commands human beings have to obey and whose constraints they have to confront. In Chapter 4, I answer the question of how a discussion of the later Wittgenstein and the pragmatists can clarify the meaning of humanism as anti-authoritarianism. How does the refusal to humble oneself before a nonhuman authority help one grasp the significance of humanism? It is important to note that while I concentrate on the similarities between Wittgenstein and the pragmatists, there are also important differences. In this chapter, I focus on two crucial differences. First, although he critiques traditional foundationalism, Wittgenstein offers a particular form of foundationalism in *Über Gewißheit* (*On Certainty*). Second, he does not completely reject the notion of certainty. Like the pragmatists, Wittgenstein questions any form of transcendent and transhistorical certainty. However, in contrast to the pragmatists, he directs attention to the significance of the quest for what might be called human or life certainty. This human certainty should be regarded as a nonintellectual taking hold of the world that is intimately linked to action, instinct, reflex, and spontaneous behavior. While Wittgenstein does not search for certain and immutable foundations of knowledge, he looks for nonepistemic foundations of our linguistic practices. In this chapter, I suggest that if the later Wittgenstein's position can be called pragmatism, then it is a pragmatism that is perhaps even more radically humanist than Rorty's.

The relation between pragmatism and Marxism has always been difficult and plagued by misunderstandings and willful deformations. These two philosophies of praxis have hardly ever been in a real dialogue. In Chapter 5, I argue that pragmatist humanists can learn and profit from materialist aesthetic theories. Pragmatist aesthetics has never developed a real interest in aesthetic form. By contrast, Marxist aestheticians like Lukács, Adorno, and Jameson have offered illuminating and far-reaching analyses of form and, in particular, of the social function or register of form. The chapter is divided into three parts. In the first part, I propose that Lukács, despite his metaphysical inclinations, can be useful for pragmatist aestheticians. The link that he establishes between narrative, form, wholeness, and totality might convince pragmatist humanists that aesthetic form is not necessarily synonymous with Kantian abstraction, stasis, necessity, and immutability and, moreover, that the form-content dualism is not just another version of the scheme-content distinction. In the second part, I advance the argument that pragmatist aestheticians can learn even more from Adorno. He introduces the term "the negation of aesthetic synthesis" in his critique of the historical avant-garde movements and their practice of montage. It is argued that pragmatist aesthetics can profit from his conception of form by developing a post-Adornian understanding of the negation of aesthetic synthesis. Pragmatist aestheticians might be inclined to keep the term but delink it from Adorno's critique of the avant-garde. By doing so, I submit, one can give it a positive connotation and apply it to innovative and formally demanding artworks that demonstrate that form-giving can be regarded as an anti-authoritarian act. The question of whether it is possible to establish a connection between the practice of form-giving and anti-authoritarianism is at the center of this chapter. In the final part, I argue that while the link between cognition, form, and totality governed Jameson's texts on postmodernism and postmodernity, the attempt to establish a relation between narrative, form, and totality has been even more important for him. In other words, Jameson urges one even more vehemently than Lukács to grasp to what degree narrative is intimately connected with aesthetic form. As I hope to show in this chapter, a consideration of the work of Marxist aesthetic theorists will teach pragmatist humanists a more complex understanding of aesthetic form, or it will help them to become truly interested in the practice of form-giving, the work of form, in the first place.

Undoubtedly, postcritique introduces one of the most interesting approaches in twenty-first-century literary and cultural studies. Proponents of postcritique are dissatisfied with the goals of critique. They want to achieve a paradigm shift in literary and cultural studies. Postcritics hold that critique is too dark, negative, gloomy, suspicious, and paranoid. Moreover, they think it is mechanistic, anemic, and governed by the imperatives of theory. Postcritics are interested in what would happen if the literary or cultural critic focused on the practices of making, creating, associating, mediating, assembling, translating, and connecting instead of those of detecting and subverting. At the beginning of Chapter 6, I discuss the work of Rita Felski. In *Uses of Literature*, she emphasizes the necessity of developing a "positive aesthetics." It is interesting to ask whether pragmatist aesthetics can contribute to the development of this positive aesthetics. Furthermore, the question must be posed whether this stress on the necessity of introducing a positive aesthetics also entails a revival of interest in aesthetic form. In the second part, I discuss Bruno Latour's actor-network theory. I argue that for him, like for most pragmatists, an analysis of form too easily degenerates into another version of formalism, and the latter is part of the Kantian baggage we have to finally get rid of. Since many postcritics have been influenced by Latour's ANT, they seemingly have been reluctant to engage in discussions of aesthetic form. I suggest that by ignoring the agency of form, which ought to be regarded as poetic agency, Latour and the postcritics are of only limited value for the pragmatist attempt to develop an aesthetics and literary criticism that will be capable of clarifying the intimate relationship between the agency and contingency of aesthetic form, on the one hand, and the contingency of social and historical networks, on the other.

The final chapter of this book functions as a coda. As I have mentioned, Rorty intends his literary or poeticized culture to be the final stage of the process of secularization. The question, "What can we learn from the poets?," is not only central to his postmetaphysical culture; it is important to see that pragmatist humanism as anti-authoritarianism urges one to confront the same question. In Chapter 7, I show that Rorty's poeticized culture and the idea of a pragmatist humanism have a nineteenth-century prehistory. I explain the complexity of this prehistory by discussing the work of Emerson, Whitman, William James, and Nietzsche. Doing so will further illuminate the contours of pragmatist humanism. Rorty holds that these authors tell humanist stories of progress. Furthermore, they are of great help regarding the attempt to answer the question of what one can learn from the poets. When one realizes the far-reaching implications of their ideas, I suggest, one might be inclined to state that they helped prepare the establishment of a Rortyan poeticized culture and that they can aid us in our endeavor to appreciate how pragmatism, humanism, anti-authoritarianism and postmetaphysics are interlinked. In case I will be capable of convincing my readers of the ideas that, first, pragmatism is a humanist philosophy and, second, pragmatist humanism is form of anti-authoritarianism, they will hopefully be interested in whether there is a prehistory of this kind of humanism. As a coda, the final chapter broadens the horizon and demonstrates that there is still work to be done if one strives to fully appreciate the complexity of pragmatist humanism. My discussions of Emerson, Whitman, James, and Nietzsche might stimulate my readers to develop an interest in the pragmatist-humanist aspects of these thinkers, and by doing so to deepen our understanding of the origins and thus the potential future of a pragmatist humanism.

As I argue in this book, pragmatist humanism, as a form of anti-authoritarianism, tells stories of progress. Maintaining that philosophy "is vision, imagination, reflection" (1917: 67), Dewey, like James before him, calls attention to the radical change of perspective that pragmatism requires. In his account, traditional philosophies

> worked out practically to identify truth with authoritative dogma. A society that chiefly esteems order, that finds growth painful and change disturbing, inevitably seeks for a fixed body of superior truths upon which it may depend. It looks backward, to something already in existence, for the source and sanction

of truth. It falls back upon what is antecedent, prior, original, *a priori*, for assurance. (1957: 159)[11]

This idea and practice of looking "backward" is characteristic of what Dewey termed the quest for certainty. It is incompatible with pragmatist humanism's future orientation.[12] Grasping the implications of the modern development from finding to making, as pragmatist humanists from James and Schiller to Richard Bernstein and Rorty propose, signifies that one understands that the radical change whose advantages pragmatism accentuates "involves a great change in the seat of authority and the methods of decision in society" (1957: 160). Pragmatist humanism's story of progress and emancipation is still unfinished.

1

Humanism, Anti-Authoritarianism, and Form

Here are two stimulating and far-reaching sentences: "Humanism is the achievement of form by human will and agency" (Said 2004: 15); "We have no duties to anything nonhuman" (Rorty 1998b: 127). In this book, I will argue that the attempt to bring these sentences together promises truly interesting results. Moreover, I shall advance the idea that the full implications of these two sentences become clearer when seen in connection with one of the central sentences in Adorno's late *Ästhetische Theorie*: "Kunst hat soviel Chance wie die Form, und nicht mehr" (1973: 213); "Art has precisely the same chance of survival as does form, no better" (1997: 141). There are many parallels between humanism and anti-authoritarianism; and as Rorty teaches us, they often overlap. When one regards pragmatist humanism as anti-authoritarianism, a discussion of humanism and form can shape one's understanding of the anti-authoritarian aspects of pragmatism. How can a pragmatist humanism, or pragmatism as anti-authoritarianism, use the idea and practice of form? What is a pragmatist understanding of form and the practice of form-giving? Practices and processes of forming are part of the modern history of making and thus central to the pragmatist story of progress and emancipation. However, so far pragmatists and pragmatist aestheticians have mostly ignored the work of form.[1] In other words, they have refrained from answering the question of what happens when one interprets the development from finding to making as partly overlapping with the history of the practice of form-giving.

As I argued in *Pragmatism and Poetic Agency: The Persistence of Humanism* (2021), for pragmatists as varied as James, Schiller, Dewey, and Rorty, humanism is an epistemological position and it is simultaneously governed by a Nietzschean emphasis on creative or poetic agency. *Poiesis* in the sense of Nietzsche's suggestion that "only we have created the world *that concerns man*!" (1974: sec. 301) is central to pragmatist humanism.[2] Nietzsche's philosophy of becoming teaches the pragmatists that the subject does not have to answer to the world; that is, it had better stop considering the idea of human answerability to something nonhuman. It is in Nietzsche that it, for the first time, becomes obvious how intimately interwoven humanism and anti-authoritarianism are. One cannot understand his attempt at a radical detranscendentalization and de-divinization without grasping the significance of this link.

The tradition of humanism that runs from Nietzsche to Rorty is anti-authoritarian insofar as it shows that with the death of God, the metaphysical need is not simply erased, and metaphysical and ontotheological categories and concepts still dominate humans' thoughts. However, in a postmetaphysical humanist scenario humans would realize that the strict separation between the natural and the extra- or supernatural, and the attempt to prioritize the latter over the former, has been man-made and hence can be reversed. If one is willing to see Nietzsche's naturalism as a version of humanism, then one is in a position to grasp that it teaches one that in a genuinely de-divinized culture, which is nominalist, historicist, and antifoundationalist, one must no longer strive to enter into a relation with a nonhuman entity or power. Instead of seeking metaphysical comfort in the confrontation with contingency and insisting on continuing to use terms and expressions like the really real, eternal truth, representation, discovery (or metaphors of finding), and being adequate, humans—and especially future philosophers—will gladly accept the instability and historicity of their vocabularies, the contingency of their ways of speaking and moral standards, as well as the unpredictability of the consequences of their actions. In a naturalized world there is no such thing as human answerability to the world, and this also implies that only as creators—or *homo poeta*—do we achieve full human maturity and dignity.

In this book, I will argue that a pragmatist humanism as anti-authoritarianism, particularly in its Rortyan version, tells a story of poeticizing and progress; that is, a story that centers on the poeticization of culture. For pragmatist humanists, the modern history of making is a story of poetic achievements that not only proposes that there is no permanent ahistorical metaphysical framework into which everything can be fitted, but that also seeks to convince us to no longer regard us as actors in a drama already written before we started inventing our practices. What happens, I will ask, when one finally appreciates that this antirepresentationalist and antifoundationalist story of progress and emancipation is intimately linked to the history of the practice of form-giving? Does this consideration of the work of aesthetic form urge pragmatists to give up their radical anti-Kantianism and question their aversion to Marxism (and thus Marxist aesthetics)? Since I hold that Marxist aestheticians, particularly Adorno, have submitted the most convincing analyses of form, I will advance the idea that pragmatist aesthetics will profit from a dialogue with materialist aesthetics (see Chapter 5).³

The primary aim of this chapter is to establish a conversation between philosophers and intellectual historians like David E. Cooper, Edward Craig, and Isaiah Berlin and literary theorists such as Timothy Brennan and Edward Said. Berlin and Said are particularly important for the argument that I develop in this book. I will argue that Berlin demonstrates how a humanist notion of *poiesis*, the practice of form-giving, and anti-authoritarianism are interlinked. Said's Vichian humanism is crucial, since it emphasizes that humanism is an ongoing practice. Moreover, it is characterized by its radical historicism and its attempt to highlight the significance of aesthetic form. My discussion of Said and form will lead to some remarks regarding the contemporary significance of Adorno's aesthetics.

According to Rorty, pragmatism strives to establish "the first truly humanistic culture" (2007: 135). Confirming his anti-authoritarian stance, he goes very far when he asserts that a "perfected society will not live up to a pre-existent standard, but will be an artistic achievement" (1999: 270). As we will see in the next chapter, Rorty's story of progress begins with the Romantics. As an intellectual historian, he never elucidates the significance of Renaissance humanism. It is one of the merits of David E. Cooper's *The Measure of Things* (2002) that it tells a more detailed history of humanism and its anti-authoritarian implications. This cannot be the place to offer a discussion of the significance of Renaissance humanism for our contemporary understanding of pragmatist humanism as anti-authoritarianism.⁴ However, I wish to underscore that Cooper is right in maintaining that "the famous humanist theme of the special 'dignity of man' is inseparable from that of creative agency" (2002: 42). Cooper's interpretation of the Renaissance humanists' texts is important for our purposes, since he puts a particular stress on the aspects of self-assertion and creative agency. He characterizes the humanists' antiessentialism and their notion of agency thus: "Far from having an 'essence', divine or natural, human beings are distinguished and in possession of a special dignity precisely because they enjoy no given, fixed place in the hierarchy of beings. They are agents, shapers, and the most 'extraordinary things' they are able to create are themselves" (2002: 43). Cooper undoubtedly does not advance the argument that authors such as Mirandola, Montaigne, Bruno, or Machiavelli were proto-pragmatists, but he demonstrates that their historicism and anthropocentrism prepared the ground for the establishment of a postmetaphysical and anti-authoritarian culture.[5] His contention is that the humanists' "heightened perception of history" convinced most of their readers and audiences "that the moral, political, and, indeed, religious systems of men were the products of artifice, constructions to be judged, not by their accord with 'natural law', but by their efficiency in doing the job they were designed for" (2002: 49).

Cooper thinks that humanism ought to be considered as the name of an epistemological or metaphysical tendency. Alternatively, it denotes a particular intellectual development. In modern times, this development culminates in Marx and Nietzsche. Cooper speaks of "the completion of a turn, by Marx, Nietzsche, and those they inspired, from the humanism of the Renaissance to a 'full-blown' humanism" (2002: 51). Later in his book, he states that "there is a relatively smooth path to be traced from the leading philosophical themes of Renaissance humanism to the Promethean tendencies of Marx's humanism and later humanisms, such as pragmatism and 'reactionary modernism'" (2002: 135). I think that Cooper's notion of "Prometheanism" adds a crucial aspect to the development of humanism from the Renaissance to Kant's Copernican Revolution and later radical humanists such as the early Marx, Nietzsche, and the pragmatists. "Prometheanism" goes further than the Copernican image of the world as our product, since it refers to the idea of a world shaped by distinctively human practices and hence vehemently underscores that creative or poetic agency is the locus of human uniqueness and dignity. In this context, Cooper calls attention to "the 'sculptural' rhetoric of Prometheanism—the talk of the world as carved or cut out, moulded or made by, human beings" (2002: 102). To what degree this "sculptural rhetoric" governs the texts of Nietzsche, James, and F. C. S. Schiller, I have explained elsewhere.[6]

Was man made in the image of God? Even early modern thinkers like Descartes and Galileo still believed in this image of God doctrine. At the same time, however, they became fascinated with the idea that the human subject might be capable of acting as its own authority. Theorizing the notion that the subject's powers at least to a certain degree were comparable to God's infinite powers and knowledge allowed the moderns to achieve an independence for the human intellect and begin the process of emancipation from the tradition of reliance on authorities, while not radically breaking with the traditional theological framework. The image of God doctrine still characterized the seventeenth and early eighteenth centuries. According to Edward Craig, the philosophy that was governed by this doctrine "laid heavy stress on a conception of man as first and foremost a spectator, an onlooker who could, and should, acquire insight into the order of reality as God had disposed it and so realise to some degree his potential for affinity with the divine mind" (1987: 224). By representing the cognitive powers of the human subject as quasi-divine and thus establishing a link between man and the creator, "the feeling is encouraged that the business of coming to know the world is conducted from an Olympian position outside the natural order" (1987: 225). From the position of Nietzsche's naturalism, this image of God doctrine appears nonsensical and deeply metaphysical. Furthermore, Dewey, in *The Quest for Certainty* and other texts, demonstrated the damaging consequences of this spectator theory of knowledge. After Goethe and Hegel, if one follows Craig, a different philosophical era began. In this new era,

> the view of man as the spectator of events in the natural world and out of it rapidly lost ground in favour of a more active conception that placed him firmly within it and saw his salvation in his power to change it. It was a period in which activity, practice and a closely related group of concepts came increasingly to be the tools that the philosopher first and instinctively grasped for to help solve his problems. (1987: 227)

Craig terms the general idea that stimulates this new orientation, that is, practical concepts invading the areas previously defined as purely theoretical and an understanding of the human subject as a being that actively creates its own world, the practice ideal or agency theory. According to him, the practice ideal, having been effective since 1780, "does almost amount to the invitation to accept a certain thesis, namely that we are the creators of our own environment, that the realities which we meet with are *the works of man*" (1987: 232). Craig defines the central concepts of the agency theory thus: "Activity, creation, the initiation of growth and change, the incorporation of other beings into one's sphere of potency, the imposition of order and form on one's material" (1987: 277). He correctly points out that all of these concepts can be used to characterize Nietzsche's philosophy.

Whereas Craig holds that Nietzsche helps one grasp the full implications of the humanist idea that the "works of man" shape the only world there is, the world of practice, Timothy Brennan offers a profoundly different understanding of this German philosopher. Brennan is right in underlining that "the body of ideas called humanism was never just a set of beliefs but a collection of contrarian intellectual practices" (2017: 2). Furthermore, the following definition of humanism can easily be brought together with the argument developed in the present study: "Humanism has to do above all—and non-negotiably—with secularity. Value belongs first with the only world humans really know, the one not given by nature or ruled by God, the one humans have fashioned by skill and effort" (2017: 1). Like Craig, Brennan elucidates the significance of agency, creativity, and making for humanism. Moreover, he emphasizes that humanism means that the only world that humans can really know is the one that they have made. This Vichian and Nietzschean insight signifies that humans have agency and the freedom to create. However, Brennan goes on by maintaining that humanists are not "against religion necessarily, [but] are secular only in the sense of being drawn to what transcendence pretends to supersede, viewing the metaphysical—in its classical sense—as reliant on the physical: a conceptual rendering of it" (2017: 1).

For our purposes, it is crucial to note that when pragmatist humanism combines humanism with anti-authoritarianism, as we will see in the following chapter on Rorty, it develops a more radical critique of metaphysics. The idea that metaphysics can be regarded as a "conceptual rendering" of the physical does not adequately describe the postmetaphysical standpoint of most pragmatists. Whereas pragmatist humanism as anti-authoritarianism sees Nietzsche as not only bringing together naturalism and aestheticism but also combining humanism and anti-authoritarianism and thus as introducing a radical version of humanism governed by the notion of poetic agency or *poiesis*, Brennan unfortunately does not see the necessity of questioning Foucault's idea, which he received from Georges Bataille, that Nietzsche was a radical antihumanist. Brennan writes: "It is not going too far to say that understanding the contemporary recoil from humanism is impossible without becoming familiar with Nietzsche's thought. Antihumanism derives from him more than from any other source—idea for idea, word for word" (2017: 6).[7] It will become obvious later on that I clearly prefer Rorty's reading of Nietzsche to that of French theorists like Bataille, Foucault, or Derrida (as always, the case of Roland Barthes is different because he is decidedly more protean and fickle than the others). The emphasis on Nietzsche's alleged "antihumanism" greatly contributed to the worst aberrations and disorientations of French poststructuralism and of what would later be called "Theory."[8]

It is interesting to read Isaiah Berlin's *The Roots of Romanticism* (1999) together with the texts by Cooper and Craig. Berlin's book is important for the argument developed in this study because it shows how a humanist notion of *poiesis*, the action of form-giving, and anti-authoritarianism hang together. Furthermore, Berlin's reading of Romanticism had a profound impact on Rorty's understanding of the significance of this period and phenomenon for the antirepresentationalist and antifoundationalist story of progress and emancipation. On Berlin's account, Romanticism is directed against the ideals of unity, harmony, and transhistoricity. It is a form of anti-Platonism. His contention is that the Romantics' critique was aimed at

> what had for the last two thousand years been the solid *philosophia perennis* of the West, according to which all questions have true answers, all true answers are in principle discoverable, and all the answers are in principle compatible, or combinable into one harmonious whole like a jigsaw puzzle. (1999: 67)

For pragmatist humanists, *The Roots of Romanticism* is valuable, since it contributes to the endeavor to highlight the complexity of the modern development from finding to making. Berlin repeatedly draws attention to the fact that for the Romantics processes and practices of form-giving often are governed by an anti-authoritarian gesture. He states that Romanticism for the first time introduces

> a crucial note in the history of human thought, namely that ideals, ends, objectives are not to be discovered by intuition, by scientific means, by reading sacred texts, by listening to experts or to authoritative persons; that ideals are not to be discovered at all, they are to be invented; not to be found but to be generated, generated as art is generated. (1999: 87)

When Berlin speaks of the Romantics' "passion for invented forms, ideals which men make" (1999: 87), or what he terms an "aesthetics of pure creation" (2000: 571) in "The Apotheosis of the Romantic Will," this also offers the possibility of regarding form-giving as an anti-authoritarian act. In this modern notion of aesthetic form, it does not appear as an abstraction, something static and general, but on the contrary as something concrete, idiosyncratic, and historical. Form-giving refuses to obey the commands of tradition, to which it is nonetheless inevitably connected. While this dialectical tension between form and tradition cannot be avoided, aesthetic form in Romanticism appears modern since it ought to be approached not as something already there that can be studied, but rather as something to be created, that is to say, made by radically questioning traditional authority. If one follows Berlin, the Romantics' strictly anti-mimetic art and antirepresentationalism are intimately linked with poetic or creative agency and the idiosyncratic acts of forming:

> There is no copying, there is no adaptation, there is no learning of the rules, there is no external check, there is no structure which you must understand and adapt yourself to before you can proceed. The heart of the entire process is invention, creation, making, out of literally nothing, or out of any materials that may be to hand. The most central aspect of this view is that your universe is as you choose to make it, to some degree at any rate. (1999: 119)[9]

It is noteworthy that Berlin sometimes seems more inclined than Rorty to underscore the Romantics' antirepresentationalism, antifoundationalism, and antiessentialism, and thus their anti-Platonist gesture in general. In other words, Berlin seems to hold that they are further down the road to a postmetaphysical culture than Rorty thinks or is willing to admit (remember that Rorty's narrative of the modern age culminates in pragmatism). Berlin, for instance, sees Fichte's theory of knowledge "as a kind of early but extremely far-reaching pragmatism" (1999: 89). He also elucidates the Romantics' severe critique of "objective criteria" and "objective truth," as well as their rejection of "any kind of general theory" (1999: 140, 144). From Dewey's *The Quest for Certainty* to Steven Knapp and Walter Benn Michaels's notorious neopragmatist manifesto "Against Theory" (published in 1982 in *Critical Inquiry*) and Stanley Fish's rhetoricized antifoundationalism, this attack on theory accompanied us throughout the twentieth century. At the end of his book, Berlin once more argues that Romanticism, in a truly modern manner, brings together antirepresentationalism, the notion of (endless) self-creation, and a radical understanding of *poiesis* and thus form-giving:

> Those are the fundamental bases of romanticism: will, the fact that there is no structure to things, that you can mould things as you will—they come into being only as a result of your moulding activity—and therefore opposition to any view which tried to represent reality as having some kind of form which could be studied, written down, learnt, communicated to others, and in other respects treated in a scientific manner. (1999: 127)

The attempt "to impose an aesthetic model upon reality" (1999: 145) would be central to Nietzsche's philosophy. The latter always returns to the idea of making, to humans' creativity, to *homo poeta*. Knowing is creating, and one should always consider "die ewige Lust des Schaffens," that is, the subject's "eternal joy of creating" (1982b, "Ancients": sec. 4). In numerous sections in *The Will to Power* Nietzsche works with the dualism finding versus making.

In his opinion, the "reverence for truth is already an illusion." Consequently, "one should value more than truth the force that forms, simplifies, shapes, invents" (1968: sec. 602). The original speaks of "die bildende, vereinfachende, gestaltende, erdichtende Kraft." He continues his argument in section 605 where he suggests that the "ascertaining of 'truth' and 'untruth,' the ascertaining of facts in general, is fundamentally different from creative positing, from forming, shaping, overcoming, willing, such as is of the essence of philosophy."

Nietzsche's desire to humanize the world and his stress on the subject's acts of creating, forming, and shaping that are central to his notions of de-deification and naturalization prepare the ground for the establishment of a genuinely postmetaphysical culture. His idea that only we have created the world that has value and that concerns humans would be central to Rorty's attempt to present his version of pragmatism as a humanism. This becomes obvious, for instance, when one considers how Rorty's antiessentialist suggestion "that there is nothing deep down inside us except what we have put there ourselves" (1982: xlii) goes back directly to the Nietzschean (and Kantian) proposal that "man finds in things nothing but what he himself has imported into them: the finding is called science, the importing—art, religion, love, pride" (1968: sec. 606). While both Nietzsche and Rorty radicalized Kant's Copernican Revolution, Nietzsche, as we will see in the next chapter (Section 2.2), accentuates his humanist position by also radicalizing the Romantics. Rorty learned the importance of this radicalization of Romanticism from his German fellow philosopher and anti-Platonist.

Nietzsche's suggestion that only we have created the world that concerns us as human beings and his emphasis on the subject's capacity to make knowledge are reflected in Edward Said's Vichian version of humanism. The humanism that connects Vico, Nietzsche, and Said no longer leaves room for the notion of passively absorbing knowledge. Moreover, it demonstrates how important the notion of *poiesis*, as the creative production of meaning and the world-shaping power of the imagination, is for the humanist intellectual. The subject's poetic agency, as I have termed it, is central to humanism from Vico to Said. Understanding knowing as making implies that the intellectual or critic can present themselves as a maker of meaning. The Vichian link between *poiesis*, humanism, and anti-authoritarianism is explained as follows in Said's *Reflections on Exile*:

> There is no center, no inertly given and accepted authority, no fixed barriers ordering human history, even though authority, order, and distinction exist. The secular intellectual works to show the absence of divine originality and, on

the other side, the complex presence of historical actuality. The conversion of the absence of religion into the presence of actuality is secular interpretation. (2000: 131)

In the last monograph that he completed before his death, *Humanism and Democratic Criticism* (2004), Said advances the idea that humanism is an ongoing practice, it is something we do, "a useable praxis" and "critique" (2004: 6, 22). When Said talks about humanism he talks about praxis, labor, creative energies, and the act of form-giving. At the beginning of this chapter, I have quoted one of the most far-reaching sentences of the later Said: "Humanism is the achievement of form by human will and agency" (2004: 15). Most presumably, this is his most Nietzschean moment. Humanism here is intimately linked to the individual act of form-giving, the idiosyncrasies of poetic agency, or the unpredictable praxis of the subject in its historical situation. Consequently, humanist praxis is the opposite of the dispassionate search for truth and disengagement, as they characterized Platonism and traditional humanism. Said's Vichian humanism, like Nietzsche's naturalism, always returns one to the world of practice, in which humans as natural creatures are situated at a particular time and place. Furthermore, Said's version of humanism radically questions metaphysical and transcendental entities, principles, and abstractions, together with their binary oppositions (e.g., Occident—Orient). Moreover, it warns against the endeavor, by Platonists and theologians, to reify words and concepts by turning sensuous particulars into ultimately real and transhistorical entities. This critique also concerns traditional forms of humanism, since "for them [traditional humanists] theology, not history, is the presiding authority over humanism" (2004: 46).

When Said underlines that he understands humanism as "a process of unending disclosure, discovery, self-criticism, and liberation" (2004: 21–2), it becomes obvious that he interprets the modern development from finding to making not as radically as most pragmatists. The notions of "disclosure" and "discovery" do not find their place in a naturalist or pragmatist framework. However, Said comes closer to a pragmatist position when he maintains that the purpose of humanism is "to make more things available to critical scrutiny as the product of human labor, human energies for emancipation and enlightenment" (2004: 22). The radical historicism that is central to the pragmatist story of progress and emancipation also characterizes Said's humanism. He not only claims that history should be regarded "as an agonistic process still being made, rather than finished and settled once and for all," he also argues "that the essence of humanism is to understand human history as a continuous process of self-understanding and self-realization" (2004: 25–6).

Humanism, to Said, is "an unsettling adventure in difference" (2004: 55). This adventure cannot be fully understood without considering the role of the aesthetic. The complexity of Said's position becomes obvious when one realizes that he, on the one hand, politicized literary studies in the 1970s and 1980s and hence also helped initiate the dominance of cultural studies that began in the 1980s. On the other hand, in contrast to most literary scholars and cultural theorists in those times he was never willing to consign the idea of the aesthetic to the dustbin of history. The older Said got the more obvious it became how much his thought had been influenced by Adorno's aesthetic theory.[10] The latter's conception of the radical autonomy of the avant-garde work of art is reflected in Said's suggestion that there is "a fundamental irreconcilability between the aesthetic and the nonaesthetic that we must sustain as a necessary condition of our work as humanists" (2004: 63). Art, according to the Adornian Said, "exists intensely in a state of unreconciled opposition to the depredations of daily life, the uncontrollable mystery of the bestial floor" (2004: 63). This notion of "unreconciled opposition" goes back to Adorno, who states that art is part of society but that its function is that of an antithesis: "Art is the social antithesis of society, not directly deducible from it" (1997: 3). In his *Ästhetische Theorie*, Adorno highlights the tension that arises from the fact that the modern work of art is both autonomous and a *fait social* (it is social and historical through and through). Aesthetic form is one of the central categories of Adorno's aesthetic theory. He contends that the avant-garde artwork refrains from commenting directly and explicitly on the state of society, and it is precisely this refusal that enables it to tell the truth about late-capitalist society.

Whereas Said does not concentrate as much on form as Adorno, he admits that he "cannot do without the category of the aesthetic as, in the final analysis, providing resistance not only to my own efforts to understand and clarify and elucidate as reader, but also as escaping the leveling pressures of everyday experience from which, however, art paradoxically derives" (2004: 63). In contrast to Rorty's brand of literary criticism, Said's approach underlines that the aesthetic is an integral part of humanist practice.[11] He argues that one must assume "that there is always the supervening reality of the aesthetic work without which the kind of humanism I am talking about here really has no essential meaning, only an instrumental one" (2004: 64).

If one endeavors to highlight the complexity of the connection between humanism and anti-authoritarianism, why should one become interested in the deplorably old-fashioned topic of Marxism and form? In particular, the question arises as to what a genuinely modern philosopher, or theorist, such as Adorno has to tell us in the twenty-first century. In 1990, Fredric Jameson proposed that Adorno's version of Hegelian Marxism was precisely what was needed in times often designated as postmodern. In *Late Marxism: Adorno, or, The Persistence of the Dialectic*, Jameson maintains that Adorno

> may turn out to have been the analyst of our own period, which he did not live to see, and in which late capitalism has all but succeeded in eliminating the final loopholes of nature and the Unconscious [sic], of subversion and the aesthetic, of individual and collective praxis alike, and, with a final fillip, in eliminating any memory trace of what thereby no longer existed in the henceforth postmodern landscape. It now seems to me possible, then, that Adorno's Marxism, which was no great help in the previous periods, may turn out to be just what we need today. (1990: 5)

Jameson's suggestion probably sounds less frivolous today than it did in the early 1990s. However, what is important for our purposes is that Adorno's conception of form played no role in postmodernism. And this was not only due to the fact that the field of aesthetics was neglected or completely marginalized in most cultural studies and postcolonial discourses. As I have pointed out, Adorno was a truly modern aesthetician. Espen Hammer correctly states that "with the rise of postconceptual art and postmodern theory, his modernist commitments grounded in complicated dialogues with Kant and Hegel began to seem less relevant" (2015: vii).[12] After the demise of postmodernism and the exhaustion of poststructuralist and deconstructionist thought, the aesthetic theory of Adorno might prove to be of great interest again. His *Ästhetische Theorie* is a highly complex text whose full potential still waits to be used. I will argue that Adorno's aesthetic thinking is useful for the attempt to show that the resurgence of humanism can be fruitfully connected with a renaissance of interest in form-giving as an anti-authoritarian act or gesture. This means that after the end of postmodernism (or late modernism), the link between humanism, anti-authoritarianism, and form can lead to a postmetaphysical thinking that avoids the mechanistic rigidity and predictability of too many versions of poststructuralism, the one-sidedness of a new formalism, and the retrospective and anti-aesthetic character of a version of humanism that only pretends to be new. From the perspective of his Vichian humanism, as we have seen, Said wants to demonstrate that humanism is "the achievement of form by human will and agency." I intend to do the same, only from the perspective of a pragmatist humanism.

2

"We Have No Duties to Anything Nonhuman": Richard Rorty's Anti-Authoritarianism

Does pragmatism continue the Enlightenment philosophical tradition that runs from Descartes to Kant? Does this American philosophy even urge one to contemplate the possibility of developing the idea of a Second Enlightenment? The idea of a pragmatist enlightenment should be of primary concern in any discussion that seeks to elucidate the significance of pragmatism in the twenty-first century. Anti-authoritarianism is central to the notion of a pragmatist enlightenment. No philosopher has introduced an understanding of anti-authoritarianism as radical as that of Richard Rorty.[1] For four decades, from the 1970s until his death in 2007, he demonstrated how his combination of anti-authoritarianism and Darwinism enabled him to tell his antifoundationalist and antirepresentationalist story of progress.[2] The later Rorty's anti-authoritarianism is central to his version of pragmatism as humanism.[3] In most of his texts, Rorty teaches the same lessons: there is no nonhuman authority whose commands human beings have to obey (neither the Will of God, the Intrinsic Nature of Reality, the notion of an Objective Reality, nor the Truth). There is no such thing as human answerability to something nonhuman. Furthermore, we should radically question the gesture of a convergence to the antecedently real, true, or pure. Instead of questing for the certainty, reliability, solidity, transhistoricity, immutability, or purity of something that would be more than another human creation or invention, humans should finally appreciate that they have no duties to anything nonhuman, that their norms for beliefs and actions are solely their doing and responsibility, that normative statuses thus are ultimately social statuses, and that they should strive to reach a point where they no longer experience the desire to humble themselves before a nonhuman authority. Rorty's anti-authoritarianism as part of his humanism teaches us that there is nothing to be responsible to except ourselves and that our self-understanding and self-description should no longer be intimately linked to the idea of human nature or essence, but should rather be constructed around a relation to a particular collection of human beings. In other words, Rorty's anti-authoritarian and humanist thought is directed against the picture of a common nature that is oriented toward correspondence to reality as it is in itself, and it insists that we have to start from where we are (without metaphysical crutches) and that we moreover must work by our own lights.[4]

Radically demetaphysicizing the world, Rorty's anti-authoritarianism suggests that instead of losing themselves in theoretical abstractions, philosophers should focus on the practices of real live humans who are engaged in causal interactions with the environment. Rorty's texts are governed by the endeavor to call attention to the significance of making, creating, inventing, poeticizing, dreaming up, or imagining; that is, his emphasis on *poiesis*, imagination, and creativity seeks to convince his readers that they ought to develop a new understanding of intellectual progress. According to Rorty, we ought to switch from the authoritarian Cartesian-Kantian picture of intellectual progress, which is dominated by the correspondence theory of truth and the notion of an increasingly better fit between mind and world, to a Darwinian picture. The latter would help us reject the alleged necessity of arriving at some goal nature has set for us, it would aid us in grasping that we no longer need the nonlocal and noncontingent rightness or the noncausal condition of possibility with which religion and traditional philosophy provided us, and, above all, it would let us see intellectual progress as an increasing ability to shape the tools that are needed for the species' survival and permanent transformation. Rortyan anti-authoritarianism constantly stresses humans' creativity and their desire for novelty: new vocabularies, new metaphors, new tools, new logical spaces, and new practices. As we will see, Rorty's anti-authoritarian and antirepresentationalist story of progress culminates in his idea of a literary or poeticized culture, whose members, as postmetaphysicians, concentrate on the contingent plurality of acts of *poiesis*, who understand Nietzsche's lesson that once God and his view go, there is just us and our idiosyncratic and ethnocentric view, and who have stopped to ask for noncausal, nonempirical, and nonhistorical conditions and thus for a human language that corresponds to some nonhuman, eternal entity.

By showing that the only possibility human beings have of getting beyond their current practices is dreaming up and creating better practices, a Rortyan poeticized culture makes clear that the notions of "answering" and "representing" are still governed by the image of the relation between humans and nonhuman entities that can be termed authoritarian; that is, an image of human beings as subject to a judgment of an authority that would trump the consensus and free exchange of justifications of other humans. In this new anti-authoritarian and postmetaphysical culture, we would finally be capable of realizing the full implications of the attempt to give up world-directedness and rational answerability to the world. Moreover, by grasping that the hope for a noncontingent, nonhistorical, and powerful ally is the common core of Platonism, most religions and their notion of divine omnipotence, as well as Kantian moral philosophy, Rortyan postmetaphysicians would be in a position to continue the secularism of the Enlightenment by underscoring that human beings are on their own and have no supernatural light that guides them to the Truth or the Real.[5] When pragmatists interpret the quest for certainty as an attempt to escape from the world of praxis, they simultaneously argue that there is no such thing as ultimate justification; that is, justification before God, Reason, or timeless moral imperatives, but only men and women's attempts to justify their beliefs and actions to a finite human audience in a historical world.

The following three sentences highlight the far-reaching implications of Rorty's anti-authoritarianism. They are among the most important sentences he ever wrote:

> The line of thought common to Blumenberg, Nietzsche, Freud, and Davidson suggests that we try to get to the point where we no longer worship *anything*, where we treat *nothing* as a quasi divinity, where we treat *everything*—our language, our conscience, our community—as a product of time and chance. (1989: 22)

> The process of de-divinization [...] would, ideally, culminate in our no longer being able to see any use for the notion that finite, mortal, contingently existing human beings might derive the meanings of their lives from anything except other finite, mortal, contingently existing human beings. (1989: 45)

> We have no duties to anything nonhuman. (1998b: 127)

Rorty's pragmatist humanism is an anti-authoritarian philosophy of human freedom and social justice that proposes that progress is possible without reliance on a nonhuman power and that moreover suggests that talk about humans' responsibility to Truth, Nature, or Reason must be replaced with talk about their responsibility to their fellow human beings. In Rorty's opinion, for humans, there is no duty that would supersede their duty to cooperate with one another in order to reach free consensus, to replace force with persuasion in the public sphere, and to make room for the Nietzschean and Proustian idea that the unpredictable contingency of self-creation can take the place once occupied by obedience in the private sphere.

Wilfrid Sellars's "Empiricism and the Philosophy of Mind" (1956) had a profound influence on Rorty's understanding of the connection between antirepresentationalism and anti-authoritarianism. In a central passage Sellars writes: "The essential point is that in characterizing an episode or a state as that of *knowing*, we are not giving an empirical description of that episode or state; we are placing it in the logical space of reasons, of justifying and being able to justify what one says" (1997: 76 [sec. 36]). This sentence is of the utmost importance if one seeks to understand the argument that Rorty develops in *Philosophy and the Mirror of Nature*, and it would shape his version of pragmatism for the next decades. According to him, Sellars helps one see knowledge as a matter of conversation and social practice. It must not be regarded as the attempt to faithfully and objectively represent or mirror nature. In chapter IV in *Mirror* ("Privileged Representations"), which Rorty considered to be the most important chapter, he points out that "the crucial premise" of his argument "is that we understand knowledge when we understand the social justification of belief, and thus have no need to view it as accuracy of representation" (1979: 170). He expands on this later in the same chapter when he explains that Sellars shows "that justification is a matter of social practice, and that everything which is not a matter of social practice is no help in understanding the *justification* of human knowledge, no matter how helpful it may be in understanding its *acquisition*" (1979: 186).

When one appreciates that an explanation of the nature of knowledge cannot rely on a theory of representations that stand in privileged relations to reality, and when one thus grasps that an elucidation of the nature of knowledge can only be a description of human behavior and the contingent and historical plurality of social practices, the necessity of obeying nonhuman forms of authority is no longer given. The social practice approach and the notion of conversational justification help us regard the community as the only source of epistemic authority. When representationalism goes, as Rorty proposes, humans will no longer experience the desire to transcend their practices by questing for the certainty of a nonhuman foundation or by striving to make sure that their assertions and actions correspond to something that is authoritative because it stands apart from what humans say and do. By bringing together his Sellarsian understanding of knowledge as conversational justification and social practice with his Darwinian and Deweyan notion of knowledge as a complex means of adjusting, Rorty in the 1970s sought to make his idea of a post-philosophical culture look attractive.

Rorty's pragmatism as anti-authoritarianism is incompatible with the idea of a fixed, ahistorical framework of human existence and with the suggestion that there is a permanent, ahistorical matrix for human thought. It is in his final volume of essays, *Philosophy as Cultural Politics* (2007), that he explicitly states that the humanistic claim that human beings have responsibility only to one another "entails giving up both representationalism and realism" (2007: 134). Rorty's anti-authoritarianism is supposed to prepare the ground for "a utopian human future in which the very idea of responsibility to anything except our fellow-humans has become unintelligible, resulting in the first truly humanistic culture" (2007: 135). However, Rorty not only paints this utopian scenario. Robert Brandom has repeatedly called attention to the idea that Rorty's brand of pragmatism continues, or even completes, the project of the Enlightenment.[6] Speaking of "the new pragmatist Enlightenment" (2011: 36), Brandom comments on the radical nature of his former academic teacher's pragmatism as follows:

> That undertaking is nothing less than to complete the project of the Enlightenment, as Kant codifies it in "Was ist Aufklärung?": to bring humanity out of its adolescence into full maturity, by taking *responsibility* for ourselves, where before we had been able only to acknowledge the dictates of an alien *authority*. Rorty's biggest idea is that the next progressive step in the development of our understanding of things and ourselves is to do for epistemology what the first phase of the Enlightenment did for religion. (2000a: xi)

In *Perspectives on Pragmatism*, Brandom expands on this crucial point thus:

> Rorty was finally led to call for a *second* Enlightenment: one that would extend to our *theoretical* conception of *knowledge* the same insight that animated the first Enlightenment's constructive criticism of traditional ways of construing the *practical* sphere. Here, too, Rorty thinks, we need to find ways to free ourselves from the picture of humans as responsible to something nonhuman. On the theoretical side the nonhuman putative authority to which we find ourselves in thrall is not God, but objective Reality. […] We need collectively to deliberate and decide what we should *say* in very much the same way the first Enlightenment taught us we need collectively to deliberate and decide what we should *do*. And the reason is the same in both cases: anything else is unworthy of our dignity as self-determining creatures. (2011: 108)[7]

In this chapter, I wish to add a new perspective to the discussion of Rorty's endeavor to continue the project of the Enlightenment. I will do this by asking two questions. First: What role does Rorty's anti-authoritarianism play for his antirepresentationalist and antifoundationalist story of progress? Second: To what degree does an analysis of his anti-authoritarianism help one understand his version of pragmatism as a form of humanism? I will argue that if one considers the answers to these questions together, they will contribute to the attempt to illuminate the contemporary significance of pragmatism. In my discussion of Rorty's anti-authoritarianism, I will explain why he highly values the Romantics, Nietzsche, Proust, and Dewey in this context. Furthermore, I shall discuss the importance of literature for his anti-authoritarian story of progress and social hope. Finally, I shall explain the meaning of Rorty's notion of a literary or poeticized culture; the establishment of this kind of postmetaphysical culture is the final chapter of his narrative.

2.1 The Romantics

It is impossible to understand Rorty's version of pragmatism without considering the impact that the Romantic poets had on him. On Rorty's account, at the end of the eighteenth century a profound change took place. The protagonists are the German idealists, the French revolutionaries, and the Romantic poets. These heroes of our story were the first to glimpse the enormous power of redescription; that is, they no longer sought to depict things as they really were and they no longer thought of the world and the human self as possessing an intrinsic nature, an essence which could be discovered and represented. Instead, they found out that anything could be made to look good or bad by being redescribed. A thing or person that had formerly been considered utterly unimportant and negligible could now be valued as central and useful simply by using a new way of speaking, by finding new words that had not been used in this context before. At the end of the eighteenth century European linguistic practices changed at an enormously fast rate, and redescriptions became ever more radical in nature. By telling this anti-authoritarian and antirepresentationalist story of progress, Rorty makes clear that the Romantics are very valuable for two reasons: they emphasized the significance of the imagination, and they replaced the notion of obedience to a nonhuman authority or standard with the plurality of contingent acts of self-creation. At the same time, however, one ought to see that Rorty advances the argument that pragmatism goes further than Romanticism as regards the desire for a postmetaphysical or poeticized culture. His attempt to demystify or deromanticize Romanticism has to be regarded as a crucial part of his pragmatist, and Nietzschean, endeavor to de-divinize the world and the self and thus of his attempt to complete the process of secularization. In other words, Rorty's elucidation of the significance of Romanticism and his critique of the Romantic poets are both central to his anti-authoritarian story of progress.

Rorty's discussion of Romanticism covers more than twenty-five years—from "Nineteenth-Century Idealism and Twentieth-Century Textualism" (1981) to "Grandeur, Profundity, and Finitude" and "Pragmatism and Romanticism" (both in *Philosophy as Cultural Politics*). The chapters "Universalist Grandeur and Analytic Philosophy" and especially "Romanticism, Narrative Philosophy, and Human Finitude" in his posthumously published *Philosophy as Poetry* (2016) mostly repeat arguments from the two chapters in *Philosophy as Cultural Politics*. "Pragmatism and Romanticism" is particularly important as far as Rorty's notion of imagination is concerned. He thinks that at the heart of Romanticism "is the thesis of the priority of imagination over reason—the claim that reason can only follow paths that the imagination has broken" (2007: 105). In the context of the quarrel between the two cultures he draws attention to "the fear of both philosophers and scientists that the imagination may indeed go all the way down. This fear is entirely justified, for the imagination is the source of language, and thought is impossible without language" (2007: 106–7). Later in his paper he formulates even more pointedly: "No imagination, no language. No linguistic change, no moral or intellectual progress. Rationality is a matter of making allowed moves within language games. Imagination creates the games that reason proceeds to play" (2007: 115). What this signifies is that imagination and imaginativeness go all the way back. It is in "Pragmatism and Romanticism" that Rorty makes particularly clear that his understanding of Romanticism profoundly differs from traditional ones. On his account, Romanticism "is a thesis about the nature of human progress" (2007: 108). Most presumably, this is Rorty's central idea as regards Romanticism's contemporary significance and the role it plays in his antifoundationalist story of progress. When he maintains that "the romantic movement marked the beginning of the attempt to replace the tale told by the Greek philosophers with a better tale" (2007: 117), it becomes obvious that the Romantics initiated a process of creative redescription and imaginative recontextualization that would eventually allow us to recognize the possibility of establishing a postmetaphysical culture characterized by anti-Platonism and antirepresentationalism.[8] Furthermore, the Romantics began the modern process of questioning the desire to stand in humble relation to a nonhuman reality, as well as the sense of dependence upon something antecedently present. One only has to think of Ralph Waldo Emerson and Walt Whitman's future orientation in order to grasp the radical nature of this change.[9]

Rorty's anti-authoritarianism repeatedly highlights the modern development from finding to making. The made-found distinction has been central to pragmatism from James and Dewey to contemporary New Pragmatists. It plays an important role in James's notorious conception of truth and in Dewey's critique of epistemological foundationalism in *The Quest for Certainty* (1929), as well as in Rorty's version of pragmatism. The realization that truth is made and not found is a crucial part of our antifoundationalist story of progress. For our purposes, it is important to note that Rorty terms the idea that truth is made and not found a "Romantic idea." In a central passage in *Contingency, Irony, and Solidarity* he writes:

> But if we could ever become reconciled to the idea that most of reality is indifferent to our descriptions of it, and that the human self is created by the use of a vocabulary rather than being adequately or inadequately expressed in a vocabulary, then we should at last have assimilated what was true in the Romantic idea that truth is made rather than found. What is true about this claim is just that *languages* are made rather than found, and that truth is a property of linguistic entities, of sentences. (1989: 7)

Again, it becomes clear that Rorty's modern antifoundationalist narrative of progress, centering on the development from finding to making as a story of increasing (Emersonian) self-reliance and imaginative redescription, begins with the Romantic poets. In this context, one should also see that Isaiah Berlin maintains that the Romantics for the first time in the history of human thought taught man "that ideals are not to be discovered at all, they are to be invented; not to be found but to be generated, generated as art is generated" (1999: 87).[10]

Rorty's critique of the Romantic poets in "Pragmatism and Romanticism" is less direct in comparison with "Grandeur, Profundity, and Finitude." In the former piece he writes: "Just as the Enlightenment had capitalized and deified Reason, so Shelley and other Romantics capitalized and deified Imagination" (2007: 109). As we have seen, Rorty, from his anti-authoritarian position, tries to convince us that we should no longer deify anything and that we should strive to continue the process of secularization that ought eventually to culminate in a postmetaphysical and poeticized culture. In "Grandeur, Profundity, and

Finitude," Rorty argues that the Romantic poets only took the first necessary steps in this direction. Concerning his attempt to demystify or deromanticize Romanticism, this essay is particularly suggestive. He concentrates his critique on two points: the Romantics' passionate commitment and their metaphors of depth and profundity. One might feel tempted to surmise that a poeticized culture, whose hero is the strong poet and whose virtues and advantages are praised by antirepresentationalists, nominalist historicists, and other anti-Platonists, is perfectly compatible with passionate gestures and commitments. However, as a Deweyan liberal, Rorty questions the necessity of the attempt to seek what Habermas has termed "an other to reason." Exalting passion at the expense of reason, as Rorty claims, can be seen as part of "the Platonist hope of speaking with an authority that is not merely that of a certain time and place" (2007: 83).

In contrast to the Romantics' passionate commitment, their search for new realms beyond the ordinary and for something deep within the subject, pragmatists want us to understand that we are "finite creatures, the children of specific times and specific places" (2007: 82). Furthermore, they call attention to the fact that this Romantic desire, the harmful Platonist search for what is more than another human creation or invention, threatens to end the conversation of mankind, while Rorty seeks to convince us that this conversation goes "its unpredictable way for as long as our species lasts—solving particular problems as they happen to arise, and, by working through the consequences of those solutions, generating new problems" (2007: 79).

Rorty always vehemently rejected traditional understandings of subjectivity. To him, there is no such thing as a core self whose real inner nature might be discovered and accurately represented. Influenced by Quine's epistemological holism, Rorty holds that we are best described as centerless webs of beliefs and desires or as sentential attitudes. Consequently, he rejects "the romantic metaphor of descent to the very bottom of the human soul" (2007: 80). Rorty wants to deromanticize Romanticism by critiquing these metaphors of depth and profundity, as well as the ideas of the infinite, the ineffable, and the attempt to save us from finitude. Trying to help us get away from Platonist representationalism with its appearance-reality distinction or from what Heidegger called the ontotheological tradition, of which Romanticism has proven to be still a part, Rorty puts a premium on the pragmatist idea (unbearably frivolous to many) of experimentalist tinkering. Universalist grandeur, the appeal to something permanent, transhistorical, and overarching, and Romantic depth, the appeal to something ineffable and poetically sublime, do not find their place in a pragmatist vocabulary:

> If one thinks that experimentalist tinkering is all we shall ever manage, then one will be suspicious of both universalist metaphors of grandeur and romantic metaphors of depth. For both suggest that a suggestion for further tinkering can gain strength by being tied in with something that is not, in Russell's words, merely of here and now—something like the intrinsic nature of reality or the uttermost depths of the human soul. (2007: 86)

What does Rorty mean when he advances the idea that pragmatism goes further than Romanticism in the establishment of a radically new kind of culture? In his account, Nietzsche and William James were enormously important concerning this replacement of Romanticism by pragmatism, since "instead of saying that the discovery of vocabularies could bring hidden secrets to light, they said that new ways of speaking could help us get what we want" (1982: 150). Furthermore, Rorty's contention is that "Romanticism was *aufgehoben* in pragmatism, the claim that the significance of new vocabularies was not their ability to decode but their mere utility" (1982: 153). The Romantic notions of depth, profundity, the ineffable, and the poetically sublime are almost diametrically opposed to this pragmatist utilitarian understanding of art. New and stimulating vocabularies are useful because they open another chapter in the modern story of progress, but they must not be seen as offering a sudden unmediated vision of what is deep down inside us and what defines who we really are.

It was left to the pragmatists to reject radically the correspondence theory of truth and, moreover, to make their fellow human beings understand that in a world of blind, contingent, and mechanical forces they must not expect, and do not need, any kind of metaphysical comfort. What Rorty's discussion of Romanticism boils down to, I suggest, is that he sees the Romantics "as toolmakers rather than discoverers" (1989: 55). Not yet fully escaped from Platonism and still governed by a metaphysical need or urge, the Romantics creatively, and passionately, contributed to the development of conceptual tools (e.g., imagination, redescription, vocabulary, plurality, metaphor, and self-creation) that would eventually offer the possibility of establishing a postmetaphysical poeticized culture. In other words, it was the Romantics' position between metaphysical need and imaginative conceptual innovation that initiated a process that would eventually lead to the realization that we no longer need the reliability, certainty, immutability, and purity of what would be more than another human creation. What this means is that Rorty's "story of poeticizing and progress" (1991b: 110), his anti-authoritarian narrative centering on the development from finding to making, begins with the Romantics.[11] It continues with Nietzsche.

2.2 Nietzsche

Whereas Heidegger, notoriously enough, thought of Nietzsche as the last metaphysician and an inverted Platonist, Rorty holds that Nietzsche's philosophy is radically postmetaphysical in nature. Rorty's interpretation is undoubtedly more convincing and stimulating. Nietzsche's philosophy, as a unique mixture of naturalism and aestheticism, critiques the idea that something supernatural or transcendental might shape one's thoughts and actions. Whereas Platonism and Christianity were governed by dichotomies such as appearance-reality, subject-object, and becoming-being, Nietzsche's antidualism urges one to develop a new way of thinking. His critique of metaphysics—that is, his attempt at a radical detranscendentalization and de-divinization—wants to put is in a position where we are no longer able to deify anything, or rather, where we no longer see the necessity of doing so.[12] As he makes clear in *Thus Spoke Zarathustra*, not only is God dead, but we have killed him, that is to say, we do not need him anymore since we have learned to speak and act differently.

Nietzsche's philosophy of becoming, with its emphasis on particularity, contingency, history, and man-made conventions and rules (or normativity), seeks to convince one that the imperatives and demands of metaphysics and ontotheology have been damaging to the progress of mankind. His new philosophy argues that the subject does not have to answer to the world; that is, it had better stop considering the idea of human answerability to something nonhuman. However, the new poet-philosophers will not only refuse to obey the commands of something nonhuman, they will also never imitate and will criticize any attempt to call attention to the significance of antecedently formulated criteria. Instead of claiming that our rational beliefs and sentences ought to be world-directed and ought to correspond to reality as it really is, we should understand the far-reaching implications of one of Nietzsche's most dangerous suggestions: "Wir erst haben die Welt, *die den Menschen etwas angeht*, geschaffen!" (1988: sec. 301); "Only we have created the world *that concerns man*!" (1974: sec. 301). For a pragmatist reading of Nietzsche, it is crucial to see how he combines an emphasis on human creativity, making, and *poiesis* with the suggestion that the dissolution of the traditional theologico-metaphysical world picture leads humans to drop the idea of the One True Account of How Things Really Are.[13] Striving to contribute to the "artistic refashioning of *mankind*" of which he speaks in *Beyond Good and Evil* (2003: sec. 62) and proposing that "it is only as an *aesthetic phenomenon* that existence and the world are eternally *justified*" in *The Birth of Tragedy* (1999: sec. 5), Nietzsche helps one appreciate the damaging consequences of the Platonist attempt to get free of society, of *nomos*, convention, and to turn to *physis*, nature.

Rejecting the ideal of knowledge as providing a God's-eye view on the world that would offer immutable and objective truth, and critiquing the attempt by Platonists and theologians to reify words and concepts by turning sensuous particulars into ultimately real and transhistorical entities, Nietzsche warns again and again that human beings must not try to get beyond their practices to a nonhuman authority. Furthermore, he maintains that in creatively articulating the aspirations of self-reliant human (discursive) practices, we might eventually find out that every form of nonhuman authority has never been anything but man-made in the first place. Nietzsche intends to convince his readers to stop telling themselves that their lives would be easier, truer, more moral, and more beautiful if something large and powerful were on their side; that is, his naturalism as humanism critiques the Platonist, Kantian, and positivist idea that one should seek to ground one's thought in the certainty, reliability, solidity, purity, and immutability of something that would be more than another human creation or invention. Continuing to think of epistemology and metaphysics as first philosophy would show that we are still enthralled by "the shadows of God" (1974: sec. 109).

Lighting your lantern in broad daylight always is a bad sign. In section 125 in *Die fröhliche Wissenschaft* Nietzsche tells his parable of the madman. Like sections 108 and 109, 125 focuses on the idea that God is dead and that humans still have to vanquish his shadows. Nietzsche's idea of the death of God is central to his anti-authoritarianism. His parable of the madman is crucial if one seeks to understand his version of anti-authoritarianism. One should see that the madman does not try to convince Christian believers that God is dead and that we are his murderers. In the market place, he is surrounded by those "who did not believe in God" (1974: sec. 125). Not even atheists are capable of appreciating the far-reaching consequences of the death of God: " 'Is not the greatness of this deed too great for us? Must we ourselves not become gods simply to appear worthy of it? There has never been a greater deed; and whoever is born after us—for the sake of this deed he will belong to a higher history than all history hitherto'" (1974: sec. 125). As Nietzsche strives to make clear, the death of God radically changes everything. In a de-deified and naturalized world, men and women will finally be capable of grasping that they have to invent and create their laws, norms, and morality (see Section 7.4). When there are no more prescriptions and commands from a higher being, and no more promise of salvation and redemption, humans have to create a completely new system of values and meanings.

In *Dawn*, Nietzsche contends that "up until now, however, the moral law was supposed to stand *above* inclination; one did not so much want *to give* oneself this law as *to take* it from somewhere or *to discover* it somewhere or *to let oneself be commanded* from somewhere" (2011: sec. 108). With God's death, the notion of discovery or finding is replaced with the activity of making. Humans' familiar habits of moral thought are no longer possible, since the notion of obeying the commands of a nonhuman authority has become increasingly problematic. In "The madman" in *The Gay Science*, Nietzsche shows that the prophet of a new postmetaphysical age is aware that he might be too early. As we have seen, not even atheists can understand the effects of the "tremendous event"; that is, the deed is done but its consequences—the revaluation of all values, the development from finding to making, and the transformation of the Christian believer into *homo poeta*—are not yet realized:

> "I have come too early," he said then; "my time is not yet. This tremendous event is still on its way, still wandering; it has not yet reached the ears of men. Lightning and thunder require time; the light of the stars requires time; deeds, though done, still require time to be seen and heard. This deed is still more distant from them than the most distant stars—*and yet they have done it themselves.*" (1974: sec. 125)

However, it has to be noted that Zarathustra, in his final speech at the end of the first part of *Thus Spoke Zarathustra* ("On the Gift-Giving Virtue"), explicitly advises his disciples that after God's death they have to think for themselves. He will not command them, he will not tell them what to do and think. There will be no more obedience to a nonhuman authority and no more desire to obey Zarathustra's words. The disciples will have to find themselves after Zarathustra has left and engage in contingent practices of self-creation. Moreover, they will have to fully grasp the implications of the idea that only they have created the world that concerns them as human beings:

> You say you believe in in Zarathustra? But what matters Zarathustra? You are my believers—but what matter all believers? You had not yet sought yourselves: and you found me. Thus do all believers; therefore all faith amounts to so little. / Now I bid you lose me and find yourselves; and only when you have all denied me will I return to you. (1982a: 190)

This is more than the radical anti-Kantian Nietzsche insisting upon the significance of Kant's *sapere aude*. We should destroy the old authoritarian frame of reference and radically reject the notion that something supernatural or transcendental will shape our thoughts and benevolently guide our actions, but we can do so only as creators. As he pointedly writes in *The Gay Science*: "We can destroy only as creators" (1974: sec. 58). Nietzsche's anti-authoritarianism does not focus on the vulgarity of simply destroying the old, but rather on creatively abolishing it by radically redescribing it and by "giv[ing] things a new color" (1974: sec. 152). According to him, "the illumination and the color of all things have changed" (1974: sec. 152), and humans have to learn how to creatively read and interpret those colors and, above all, to add their own new colors in an idiosyncratic manner.

In Rorty's opinion, Nietzsche radicalized the Romantic legacy, and his anti-Platonism ought to be regarded as a radical anti-authoritarianism. Not only did Nietzsche's romantic anti-Platonism prophesy the coming of a postmetaphysical age, he also urged us, in *The Gay Science*, to "become the poets of our own lives" (Rorty 2007: 110). Rorty reads Nietzsche as a poet-philosopher who is fascinated with the radical gestures of the Romantics, but who at the same time realizes their limitations. For writers like Coleridge and Emerson it had been possible "to run together romanticism with idealist metaphysics" (2007: 110). Rorty, like Nietzsche, wants a kind of Romanticism without idealist metaphysics. Nietzsche, on Rorty's reading, radicalized Romanticism by ridiculing the idealist metaphysicians' "cowardly unwillingness to acknowledge our finitude," and by vehemently criticizing the hope "to find something that would trump poetry" (2007: 110). As Rorty interprets Nietzsche, nothing will ever trump poetry, and humans should finally learn to refrain from hoping to find something unredescribable (from the Platonic notion of truth to the Romantic idea of the sublime).

Rorty's contention is that Nietzsche's radicalization of the Romantics illustrates how vehemently this German philosopher rejects the common-sense claims that there is a way that nature is in itself and that there is a way reality is independent of the way humans describe it. Nietzsche's "prophecy of a post-metaphysical age" (2007: 112) lets us imagine a future society where people will no longer be disoriented, shocked, or appalled in the confrontation with the ideas that our human lives are the results of contingent processes of poetic self-creation and that the world in which we live is a creation of the human imagination. That nothing will ever trump poetry also means that one will never find something that is not itself a human creation, but rather stands over and against all such creations. In *Philosophy as Poetry*, Rorty highlights the significance of

> the question of whether Nietzsche was right to think of the world as our poem rather than as something that somehow communicates information about itself to us. How we answer that question determines whether we think of the progress human beings have made in the last few millennia as a matter of expanding our imagination or as an increased ability to represent reality accurately. (2016: 18)

In Rorty's story of progress Nietzsche appears as a poet-philosopher, a romantic anti-Platonist or pragmatist, who values the Platonic notion of "the really real" as a poetic achievement, but who simultaneously contends that this notion, together with "the true world," belongs to a fable that has exhausted its utility. Rorty avers that in Nietzsche's opinion "the answer to a great poem is a still better poem, and that is what Nietzsche thought of himself as writing" (2016: 19).

In order to fully understand Rorty's argument that Nietzsche radicalizes the Romantic poets and hence continues the antirepresentationalist and anti-authoritarian story of progress, I would like to briefly come back to Nietzsche's aforementioned statement that only we have created the world that concerns us as human beings (in section 301 of *The Gay Science*). Rorty's most detailed discussion of this Nietzschean dictum can be found in the first chapter, "Getting Rid of the Appearance-Reality Distinction," in *Philosophy as Poetry*. Rorty differentiates between a conservative and a decidedly more radical interpretation of Nietzsche's suggestion. According to the conservative interpreter, there are two worlds. There is the natural world, which is not made by us and which is given to us through the senses. This world has no significance for us until we have invented a second world, and only in the latter can we lead a properly human life. This second world we have created, it is our poem, as it were; it is governed by our unpredictable desires and shaped by our idiosyncratic imagination. Moreover, this second world reflects our needs, affirmations, negations, and perspectives. At the same time, however, this conservative interpretation still works with the appearance-reality distinction insofar as it insists that only in the second world, the one that we have created, reason follows the imagination. The first world, by contrast, is still governed by the natural sciences, and reason has priority over the imagination. In this first world, in other words, there is still a way nature really is and it is still dominated by the act of penetrating to the really real. If one properly uses one's experimental procedures and conceptual tools, one will find out how nature is apart from human needs and interests.

Rorty makes the interesting suggestion that this conservative interpretation would have satisfied the Romantic poets. Since he intends to show to what degree Nietzsche goes further than the Romantics, he argues that this "interpretation is insufficiently radical. It does not take account of Nietzsche's frequent polemics against the appearance-reality distinction" (2016: 9). According to Nietzsche, there have never been two worlds, but only the world of human praxis. Consequently, we will never reach a stage where appearance is put behind us and true reality finally revealed (in the first world), since the notion of a true reality has been nonsensical from the start.

A radical reading of Nietzsche's suggestion that only we have created the world that concerns us as humans not only underlines that he urges one to stop asking what is really real, but it also directs attention to "the claim that nature itself is a poem that we humans have written and to the claim that the imagination is the principle vehicle of human progress" (2016: 11).[14] In the confrontation with Rorty's choice of words not only empiricist philosophers will most presumably become apoplectic or advance the idea that he has finally gone completely off the rails. However, I think that Rorty wants to use the formulation "that nature is a poem that we humans have written" to accentuate the far-reaching consequences of "Nietzsche's prophecy of a postmetaphysical age," and at the same time he tries to convince his readers that Nietzsche's romantic anti-Platonism "is a coherent philosophical position" (2016: 10).

As I hope to have demonstrated, Rorty reads Nietzsche's philosophical position as a form of anti-authoritarianism that is extremely useful for the endeavor to make the pragmatist story of poeticizing and progress look attractive. Whereas Nietzsche asks when we will finally get rid of God's shadows, Rorty poses the question of whether the change that led from worshiping Gods to worshiping sages to worshiping natural scientists might not eventually bring us to a position where we no longer worship anything. Rorty holds that Nietzsche helped us reach a position where we can no longer make sense of the idea that a great gulf separates the way the world is and the way we describe it. Moreover, Nietzsche repeatedly proposed that the notion of answerability to the world retained the figure of the world as a nonhuman authority to whom humans owed some sort of respect. Nietzsche detested the notion of (liberal) democracy, and he would have ridiculed the Rortyan ideas of social hope, solidarity, and conversation. Nonetheless, Rorty thinks that Nietzsche's anti-Platonism as anti-authoritarianism is highly valuable for the pragmatist attempt to emphasize continuity over duality and disjunction and production of the novel over contemplation of the eternal (or obedience to the transcendental). However, as Rorty stresses, Nietzsche is still a theorist. How can a novelist contribute to the anti-authoritarian story of progress, poeticizing, and making? Proust gives the answer.

2.3 Proust

In the final volume of Proust's *Recherche*, *Le Temps retrouvé*, the narrator, Marcel, is invited to a matinée at the Princesse de Guermantes. Marcel is now a middle-aged man. In the de Guermantes' library, this future writer's aesthetic theory appears full-blown. His thought repeatedly returns to the insufficiency of realism. Marcel speaks of "the falseness of so-called realist art" (2000: 235), and he inveighs against what he terms "the literature of description" (2000: 253). Ironically enough, if one follows Proust's narrator, realist art is "the furthest removed from reality" and utterly incapable of grasping and representing the essence of the past:

> And this is why the kind of literature which contents itself with "describing things," with giving of them merely a miserable abstract of lines and surfaces, is in fact, though it calls itself realist, the furthest removed from reality and has more than any other the effect of saddening and impoverishing us, since it abruptly severs all communication of our present self both with the past, the essence of which it preserved in things, and with the future, in which things incite us to enjoy the essence of the past a second time. Yet it is precisely this essence that an art worthy of the name must seek to express; then at least, if it fails, there is a lesson to be drawn from its impotence (whereas from the successes of realism, there is nothing to be learnt), the lesson that this essence is, in part, subjective and incommunicable. (2000: 241–2)

Neither a Balzacian kind of mimesis nor the Flaubertian ideal of "impassibilité" is a goal worth pursuing for Marcel (and the author of the *Recherche*).[15] In rare moments, the essence of the past can be grasped because of Marcel's involuntary memory ("la mémoire involontaire"), which the future writer will seek to recreate by means of his metaphorical transposition (the theory of which is central to his aesthetic musings in the library). It is interesting to note that Marcel not only directs attention to the insufficiency of realist art but also mentions that reality itself has repeatedly disappointed him. It seems that what is simply there, in its brutish thereness, stifles his imagination. In a quasi-Romantic moment, Proust's narrator emphasizes that only the work of the imagination makes the enjoyment of beauty possible: "So often, in the course of my life, reality had disappointed me because at the instant when my senses perceived it my imagination, which was the only organ that I possessed for the enjoyment of beauty, could not apply itself to it, in virtue of that ineluctable law which ordains that we can only imagine what is absent" (2000: 223).

As a novelist, who after so many years is about to confront his gigantic task, Marcel understands that his novel will never mirror reality as it really is.[16] He realizes that his task will be to establish links and relations between objects, experiences, situations, and people in different stages of their development (e.g., Palamède de Charlus as a hysterical dandy in a salon, in chains in a male brothel in wartime Paris, or as a white-haired dying man, who reminds Marcel of King Lear, at the very end). The writer will seek to solve the mysteries of time and remembrance by creating his idiosyncratic metaphors. Marcel goes very far by stating that the only life really lived is literature (think of Nehamas's interpretation of Nietzsche in this context): "Real life, life at last laid bare and illuminated—the only life in consequence which can be said to be really lived—is literature" (2000: 253).[17]

Proust's antirealist stance, his emphasis on the novelist's contingent sets of metaphors, and his suggestion that art creates a plurality of worlds (and thus of vocabularies, perspectives, and norms) very much appeal to Rorty.[18] He reads Proust as an ironist novelist. Rorty submits that this French writer does not strive to escape from contingency, but rather uses it in order to redescribe and rearrange all the people he has met and all those little things that have been a part of his former life. All the characters in his monumental work, for instance, Swann, Albertine, Gilberte, the grandmother, the Prince de Guermantes, Odette, and Baron de Charlus, appear as shaped by contingent circumstances and as webs of relations. The same can be said about Marcel. Striving for autonomy, Proust redescribes those people who have described him, and he does so from different perspectives and from different positions in time. None of these characters manages to escape from finitude and history. None occupies a privileged standpoint that would allow him or her to ignore the changes time brings. The jealousies, the humiliations, desires, anxieties, losses, rumors, sounds, colors, tastes, and memories—this is the all-too-human material from which Proust creates the world of his novel. The *Recherche* is an ironist and anti-authoritarian text insofar as its author elegantly combines perspectivism, panrelationalism, and antiessentialism in order to show that even former authority figures eventually appear as characters of contingent circumstances (think of, e.g., Swann and Charlus). As Rorty reads the *Recherche*, in this novel there is no privileged perspective from which any character could be described. This anti-Platonic novel illustrates the futility of the quest for the certainty, immutability, and purity of something that would be more than another human creation or perspective. It seems that Rorty reads the *Recherche* as depicting a de-deified and detranscendentalized world that is governed by acts or processes of temporalization and finitization. He writes:

> The result of all this finitization was to make Proust unashamed of his own finitude. He mastered contingency by recognizing it, and thus freed himself from the fear that the contingencies he had encountered were more than just contingencies. He turned other people from his judges into his fellow sufferers, and thus succeeded in creating the taste by which he judged himself. (1989: 103)

Chapter 5 of *Contingency, Irony, and Solidarity*, "Self-Creation and Affiliation: Proust, Nietzsche, and Heidegger," is one of the most stimulating texts Rorty ever wrote. Particularly his elucidation of the difference between Proust, as an ironist novelist, and Nietzsche, as an ironist theorist, has to be mentioned in this context. Both Proust and Nietzsche sought to get out from under inherited contingencies and make their own contingencies or invent their idiosyncratic vocabularies. Moreover, both were masters of redescription and self-redescription. Both did not try to escape from finitude, but they on the contrary tried to use time and chance for their idiosyncratic forms of private self-creation. On Rorty's account, Proust and Nietzsche are "paradigm nonmetaphysicians" (1989: 98). However, the main difference is that "whereas Proust took metaphysics as just one more form of life, it obsessed Nietzsche. Nietzsche was not only a nonmetaphysician, but an antimetaphysical theorist" (1989: 98). Nietzsche the antimetaphysical or ironist theorist wants more than a Proustian rearrangement of all those little things, more than a new beautiful pattern, and more than a plurality of perspectives that never pretends to be more than a plurality of temporary human perspectives. As an ironist theorist,

Nietzsche wants more than beauty, he wants sublimity. He forgets about his nominalism, and instead of rearranging and redescribing all those little things, he (sometimes) wants something big. In an important passage, Rorty even goes so far as to advance the idea that an ironist theorist like Nietzsche continually runs the risk of relapsing into metaphysics:

> Sublimity is neither transitory, relational, reactive, nor finite. The ironist theorist, unlike the ironic novelist, is continually tempted to try for sublimity, not just beauty. That is why he is continually tempted to relapse into metaphysics, to try for one big hidden reality rather than for a pattern among appearances—to hint at the existence of somebody larger than himself called "Europe" or "History" or "Being" whom he incarnates. (1989: 105)

Whereas Proust strives to achieve private autonomy and private perfection—his "mémoire involontaire" creates his own version of Combray that is meaningless for anybody else—Nietzsche desires to reach a position where he will be in touch with something large and ineffable. Furthermore, the ironist theorist, wanting the kind of power that comes from an intimate relation to something sublime and thus incommensurable, abhors the idea that a successor might redescribe him, that someone might just use his grand theory as material for a new redescription. According to Rorty, in contrast to an ironist novelist like Proust an ironist theorist such as Nietzsche does not want to be redescribed; that is, he wants to have the last word and explain to his readers why Western civilization will no longer be the same if they follow his advice.

Desiring a historical sublime, and thus betraying his own perspectivism and nominalism, Nietzsche sometimes leaves the impression that he has found a way to subsume all his important predecessors under a general idea. By achieving this, he has found more than another redescription of them and has gotten in touch with a power other than himself. It is, of course, primarily Nietzsche's hypostatization of the will to power that bothers Rorty. Heidegger's reading of Nietzsche as an "inverted Platonist" and as "the last metaphysician" has to be mentioned in this context. Rorty comments on the metaphysical aspect of Nietzsche's oeuvre as follows: "But Nietzsche the theorist of the will to power—the Nietzsche whom Heidegger attacked as 'the last metaphysician'—is as interested as Heidegger himself was in getting beyond all perspectives. He wants sublimity, not just beauty" (1989: 106). Later in *Contingency* Rorty asserts that " the same urge to affiliate with somebody bigger which has led Plato to reify 'Being' led Nietzsche to try to affiliate himself with 'Becoming' and 'Power'" (1989: 107).

How can a theorist avoid this relapse into metaphysics? Is it sufficient when he presents himself as an *ironist* theorist? When he acknowledges and creatively uses his contingency, or rather, the contingency of his final vocabulary? Rorty's discussion shows that even an ironist theorist and romantic anti-Platonist like Nietzsche can succumb to metaphysical temptations; that is, even this proponent of a postmetaphysical culture sometimes longs for the discovery of something larger than himself and a redescription that will prove useful for more than the purpose of private self-creation. At the end of his discussion of Proust and Nietzsche, Rorty poses the cardinal question of "how can we write a historical narrative about metaphysics—about successive attempts to find a redescription of the past which the future will not be able to redescribe—without ourselves becoming metaphysicians?" (1989: 108). On Rorty's account, ironist theorists like Nietzsche and Heidegger, writing a narrative that centers on ideas rather than people, demonstrate that the relapse into metaphysics is inevitable.

In contrast to ironist theorists, a novelist like Proust does not see the necessity of ascending from a perspectival and historically conditioned mode to a nonperspectival and abstract mode of description. This is one of the main reasons why Rorty prefers the novel as the ideal medium for an anti-authoritarian and poeticized culture. He points out: "So the lesson I draw from Proust's example is that novels are a safer medium than theory for expressing one's recognition of the relativity and contingency of authority figures. For novels are usually about people—things which are, unlike general ideas and final vocabularies, quite evidently time-bound, embedded in a web of contingencies" (1989: 107).

Rorty holds that the *Recherche* helps one understand how limiting the notion of a nonhuman authority is, and that it moreover demonstrates that the novelist's taste for narrative, perspective, detail, plurality, diversity, and contingency clearly is preferable to the theorist's taste for contemplation, abstraction, structure, and essence. Furthermore, Proust's combination of anti-authoritarianism, historicism, and panrelationalism strengthens one's ability to live with the thought that there is no convergence to the antecedently real or true and no human answerability to the world.

2.4 Dewey

In *Reconstruction in Philosophy* (1920) and *The Quest for Certainty* (1929), John Dewey, elegantly combining philosophy and intellectual history, tells antifoundationalist and anti-authoritarian stories of progress and emancipation. In the former book, he maintains that "philosophy originated not out of intellectual material, but out of social and emotional material" (1957: 25). Moreover, he argues that one should "study the history of philosophy not as an isolated thing but as a chapter in the development of civilization and culture"; that is, one ought to "connect the story of philosophy with a study of anthropology, primitive life, the history of religion, literature, and social institutions" (1957: 25). The history of philosophy must not be studied in isolation because philosophy must never be practiced in isolation from social practice; that is, from the problems men face at a particular time and under particular social conditions. The task of philosophy, as Dewey maintains, "is to clarify men's ideas as to the social and moral strifes of their own day"; it should strive to get involved with "the drama of the struggle of social beliefs and ideals" (1957: 26). What this boils down to is that the historicist Dewey holds that philosophical problems arise out of specific social conditions and that there is no such thing as a timeless or eternal philosophical problem. Dewey's worldly philosophy, like James's version of pragmatism, turns its attention to the contingent problems facing contemporary society. It becomes a kind of social criticism.[19]

Rorty learned much from his favorite philosopher. The idea that philosophy ought to be regarded as social or cultural criticism he always considered one of the primary Deweyan lessons. Another lesson is intimately connected with this one. It concerns the aforementioned notion of a Second Enlightenment. Dewey not only taught Rorty to see pragmatism as a form of anti-authoritarianism, he also convinced and stimulated him to extend Enlightenment anti-authoritarianism from ethics to epistemology. Extending anti-authoritarianism from politics and ethics to epistemology, or from the practical domain to the cognitive sphere, is one of the later Rorty's most radical and far-reaching ideas. I wish to put this even more pointedly: this extension of anti-authoritarianism should be regarded as the real core of his version of pragmatism as humanism. A pragmatist humanist cannot go further than propagating and contributing to this extension of anti-authoritarianism.

While Dewey stimulated Rorty to develop his own version of anti-authoritarianism, these two pragmatists approached the task of completing the project of the Enlightenment in a completely different manner. Whereas Rorty wants to do for epistemology what the philosophers of the Enlightenment did for religion and the practical sphere, Dewey intends to universalize the method and spirit of scientific inquiry. In *Reconstruction in Philosophy*, Dewey highlights the significance of the endeavor to apply the methods and conclusions of natural science to moral theory and practice. His contention is that the new philosophy that he describes in his book, aiming at a new self-definition and a modern understanding of human activities and interests, "must undertake to do for the development of inquiry into human affairs and hence into morals what the philosophers of the last few centuries did for promotion of scientific inquiry in physical and physiological conditions and aspects of human life" (1957: xxiii). Reconstruction, as Dewey asserts, "can be nothing less than the work of developing, of forming, of producing (in the literal sense of that word) the intellectual instrumentalities which will progressively direct inquiry into the deeply and inclusively human—that is to say, moral—facts of the present scene and situation" (1957: xxvii).

From the new science of early modernity to twentieth-century scientific inquiry, the question about the trustworthiness of its methods has accompanied the development of science. Advancing the idea that this has much to do with the question of authority, Dewey directs attention to the question of "whether we are to move forward in a direction made possible by these new resources or whether the latter are so inherently untrustworthy that we must bring them under control by subjection to an authority claiming to be extra-human and extra-natural" (1957: xxxv). Dewey's anti-authoritarianism proposes that the extension of the methods of scientific inquiry to moral inquiry will help humans to no longer see the necessity of appealing to an extra-human authority. What this boils down to is that Dewey needs a positive notion of the practice of scientific inquiry in order to develop his version of anti-authoritarianism, whereas Rorty does not.

In "Pragmatism as Romantic Polytheism," Rorty highlights Dewey's "lifelong distaste for the idea of authority—the idea that anything could have authority over the members of a democratic community save the free, collective decisions of that community" (2007: 38). Furthermore, Rorty claims that once Dewey rejected his mother's Calvinism, "he distrusted nothing more than the suggestion that there was a non-human authority to which human beings owed respect" (2007: 40). To Dewey, the idea that there is an authority that exists outside human experience is nonsensical. Rorty's most detailed discussion of Dewey's anti-authoritarianism can, of course, be found in "Pragmatism as Anti-authoritarianism." In this piece, Rorty draws attention to the analogy between anti-authoritarianism in ethics and in epistemology when he advances the argument that Dewey "viewed the theory that truth is correspondence to Reality, and the theory that moral goodness is correspondence to the Divine Will, as equally dispensable" (2009: 258). Rorty expands on this crucial point as follows:

> What Dewey most disliked about both traditional "realist" epistemology and about traditional religious beliefs is that they discourage us by telling us that somebody or something has authority over us. Both tell us that there is Something Inscrutable, something toward which we have duties, duties which have precedence over our cooperative attempts to avoid pain and obtain pleasure. (2009: 258)

Dewey's antirepresentationalist story of expanding human freedom is dominated by his historicism, naturalism, and utilitarianism and not by any form of authoritarianism.[20] His pragmatist philosophy as social criticism focuses on how to enable humans to appreciate that in order to develop and regulate their actions and beliefs they do not need to stand in a correct relation to something nonhuman and eternal. Rather, human beings should join other humans in cooperative projects without seeking transcendental help. If there is such a thing as spiritual significance, and Dewey unfortunately holds onto this idea, then it can only be found in cooperation between finite mortals in a democratic society. Rorty asserts in this context: "Dewey's stories are always stories of the progress from the need of human communities to rely on a non-human power to their realization that all they need is faith in themselves; they are stories about the substitution of fraternity for authority" (2009: 262). The focus always is on social cooperation, the contingent plurality of social practices, the idea that only the latter create our norms, as well as on the idea that genuinely free inquiry is only possible in a democratic society. Only in a democratic society, that is, is the consensus reached by free inquiry the only kind of authority one needs.

The first sentence of "Pragmatism as Anti-authoritarianism" summarizes the thought that Rorty develops in his posthumously published lecture series *Pragmatism as Anti-Authoritarianism* (2021): "There is a useful analogy to be drawn between the pragmatists' criticism of the idea that truth is a matter of correspondence to the intrinsic nature of reality and the Enlightenment's criticism of the idea that morality is a matter of correspondence to the will of a Divine Being" (2009: 257). As we have seen, Rorty's contention is that human beings must never humble themselves before anything nonhuman, anything that pretends to offer the certainty, solidity, reliability, immutability, or purity of what would be more than another human creation or invention. According to Rorty, Dewey thought that "the romance of democracy […] required a more thoroughgoing version of secularism than either Enlightenment rationalism or nineteenth-century positivism had achieved" (2009: 257). Rorty seeks to continue this Deweyan project, and partly radicalizes it, by arguing that the successor candidate for humans' subjection to a nonhuman authority is now proposed by science (or the natural sciences). In other words, objective reality has taken the place formerly occupied by God. In the Foreword to *Pragmatism as Anti-Authoritarianism*, Robert Brandom summarizes Rorty's central idea thus:

> At the center of the version of pragmatism Rorty announces in this book is the thought that just as we should be anti-authoritarian in ethics in rejecting the authority of God over the correctness of what we do, we should be anti-authoritarian in epistemology by rejecting the authority of objective reality over the correctness of what we believe. Construed as the non-human locus of this sort of authority, Reality no more exists than God does. (2021: xi)

What a discussion of Rorty's pragmatism as anti-authoritarianism once more confirms is that he is no irrationalist or relativist who radically rejects the Enlightenment. Rather, what he criticizes, as Brandom explains, "is only the *epistemology* of the Enlightenment, specifically its placing of its master-concept of *representation* at the center of our philosophical understanding of our discursive practice, reason, and mindedness in general" (2021: xxv). Brandom puts a premium on the idea that Rorty intends to *complete* the project of the Enlightenment. According to Brandom, for his academic teacher this

> requires correcting its epistemology, so as to repair the deformations wrought by its reliance on the representational model. For, properly understood, that model turns out to be incompatible with essential progressive insights and impulses of the Enlightenment: the distinctive fusion of freedom and responsibility it began to make visible, if at first only dimly. (2021: xxv)

Authority, as Dewey argues in many of his texts, often is synonymous with dogmas, rigid institutions, firm doctrines, stasis, order, and the otherworldliness of traditional philosophy. Radically rejecting any "subjection to an authority claiming to be extra-human and extra-natural" (Dewey 1957: xxxv), Dewey's thought, like that of F. C. S. Schiller, James and Rorty, shows how pragmatism, humanism, anti-authoritarianism, and postmetaphysics hang together. As far as epistemology is concerned, Dewey argues that the notion of authority implies the idea of an antecedently real, which the knower tries to discover and on which he can rely, as well as that of a superior because timeless truth. In *Reconstruction*, Dewey explains this point as follows:

The older conception worked out practically to identify truth with authoritative dogma. A society that chiefly esteems order, that finds growth painful and change disturbing, inevitably seeks for a fixed body of superior truths upon which it may depend. It looks backward, to something already in existence, for the source and sanction of truth. It falls back upon what is antecedent, prior, original, *a priori*, for assurance. (1957: 159)

Dewey's antifoundationalist and humanist story of progress depicts history as a story of increasing human freedom, of an increasing willingness to experiment, of humanity constantly reinventing itself, and of a heightened awareness that it might be fruitful to see cultural evolution as continuous with biological evolution. Rorty adds another important chapter to this Deweyan story of progress by elucidating the role literature, and particularly the novel, could play.

2.5 Literature, or, The Task of the Novel

In the famous last sentence of the preface to *The Liberal Imagination* (1950), Lionel Trilling avers that "literature is the human activity that takes the fullest and most precise account of variousness, possibility, complexity, and difficulty" (2000: 548). This is also Rorty's opinion. Both American liberals also agree that literature, particularly the novel, can shape our morality. Novels that offer detailed descriptions of forms of cruelty, pain, and humiliation might increase their readers' sensitivity and their responsiveness to the needs of others. Hence, they ought to be regarded as contributing to moral progress. Faithful to his anti-Kantianism, Rorty maintains that we do not need theoretical abstraction, formalist analysis, or firm and transhistorical moral principles, but as malleable human beings we need storytelling. By speaking of "sentimental education" (1998b: 181) in this context, he also proposes that a pragmatist literary criticism ought to refrain from becoming interested in aesthetic theory and the question of form. The abstraction of form, as he seems to hold, is incompatible with pragmatist anti-authoritarianism.[21]

In *Contingency, Irony, and Solidarity*, Rorty develops his notorious private-public distinction. According to him, it is one of the consequences of this dichotomy that one ought to distinguish books that help one become autonomous from books that help one become less cruel in one's behavior toward other people. There is, of course, no need to discuss this Rortyan idea once more.[22] However, for our purposes it ought to be noted that his differentiation between the poet and the novelist goes back to this private-public split. The Nietzschean strong poet serves as a model for the pursuit of private perfection; that is, he has created himself by creating a vocabulary that completely belongs to him. Furthermore, in an Emersonian manner he has demonstrated that he will never imitate, while in a Coleridgean manner he has created the taste by which he will be judged by posterity. The strong poet's self-creation and self-renewal should lead us to reweave our webs of beliefs and desires in a way that results in the same kind of originality. By contrast, the novelist serves as a moral exemplar. There are certain novelists, such as Proust, who are primarily useful for purposes of self-creation. However, novelists like, for instance, Stowe, Dickens, Zola, Wright, and Orwell are supposed to sensitize their readers to the pain, suffering, and humiliation of others. On Rorty's account, literature offers models of self-description that call attention to the suffering of others and seek to avoid humiliation. He claims that literature, particularly the novel, ought to be regarded as a principal medium of a liberal democratic culture, since it allows the reader to recognize that cruelty is the worst thing we do (think of Judith Shklar's influence on Rorty's understanding of what it means to be a liberal here). Literature, ethnography, and journalism are supposed to offer a "thick description of the private and the idiosyncratic" (1989: 94), and by doing so, they sensitize us to the pain and suffering of those who otherwise would be ignored since they do not speak our language. One of the central sentences of Rorty's *Contingency, Irony, and Solidarity* concerns the role of literature in a nominalist and historicist liberal culture: "The metaphysician's association of theory with social hope and of literature with private perfection is, in an ironist liberal culture, reversed" (1989: 94).[23]

The novel for Rorty is the ideal medium for what he terms sentimental education, since it draws attention to the possibility of developing an antiessentialist understanding of morality and moral progress. Offering a plurality of perspectives, viewpoints, descriptions, self-descriptions, characterizations, contingent belief systems, and moral outlooks, the novel prevents one from asking big questions about human nature or the meaning of life. Rather, it focuses on more practical questions. In "Heidegger, Kundera, and Dickens," Rorty expands on this aspect thus:

> A society which took its moral vocabulary from novels rather than from ontotheological or ontico-moral treatises would not ask itself questions about human nature, the point of human existence, or the meaning of human life.

Rather, it would ask itself what we can do so as to get along with each other, how we can arrange things so as to be comfortable with one another, how institutions can be changed so that everyone's right to be understood has a better chance of being gratified. (1991a: 78)

For an understanding of Rorty's interpretation of the task that the novel can fulfill in Western democratic societies, Milan Kundera's *The Art of the Novel* (2003) is particularly important. Kundera makes unequivocally clear that he opposes what he calls "the spirit of the novel" to the singularity of Truth, that is, the Platonist yearning for a transcultural and transhistorical Truth: "The world of one single Truth and the relative, ambiguous world of the novel are molded of entirely different substances. Totalitarian Truth excludes relativity, doubt, questioning; it can never accommodate what I would call the *spirit of the novel*" (2003: 14). Moreover, Kundera stresses that the novel, with its plurality of perspectives, its ambivalences and ironies, is incompatible with ideological and theoretical closure. He writes of the novel that it "does not by nature serve ideological certitudes, it contradicts them. Like Penelope, it undoes each night the tapestry that the theologians, philosophers, and learned men have woven the day before" (2003: 160). In *The Curtain*, Kundera characterizes the relationship between the novel and the idea of authority thus: "But putting a novel to the service of an authority, however noble, would be impossible for a true novelist" (2007: 60).

In his reading of Kundera's *The Art of the Novel*, Rorty pays particular attention to the notion of plurality. To Rorty, one may insinuate, Kundera's essay is of crucial importance since it is useful in the attempt to bring postmetaphysics, plurality, novelty, and morality together. Rorty describes Kundera's anti-Platonist emphasis on a plurality of perspectives, descriptions, and redescriptions as follows:

The novelist's substitute for the appearance-reality distinction is a display of diversity of viewpoints, a plurality of descriptions of the same events. What the novelist finds especially comic is the attempt to privilege one of these descriptions, to take it as an excuse for ignoring all the others. What he finds most heroic is not the ability sternly to reject all descriptions save one, but rather the ability to move back and forth between them. (1991a: 74)

Kundera, as Rorty understands him, makes the term "the novel" "roughly synonymous with 'the democratic utopia'—with an imaginary future society in which nobody dreams of thinking that God, or the Truth, or the Nature of

Things, is on their side" (1991a: 75). What this boils down to is that Rorty reads the Franco-Czech novelist as someone who also realizes the possibility, and the necessity, of developing a postmetaphysical culture. Rorty speaks of "Kundera's utopia" which "is carnevalesque, Dickensian, a crowd of eccentrics rejoicing in each other's idiosyncrasies" (1991a: 75).

"Philosophy as a Transitional Genre" is one of Rorty's last and most important essays. In this piece, the significance of literature and the idea of a literary culture for his pragmatist anti-authoritarianism becomes particularly obvious. Desiring a "new intellectual world" and "a new self-image for humanity" (2004: 4), Rorty tells a story that is full of replacements and transitions. Religion was replaced by philosophy, Kant's transcendental idealism and its ideal of philosophy-as-science was replaced by Hegel's historicism, Romanticism was replaced by pragmatism, and philosophy has finally been replaced by literature. Underscoring the humanistic character of a literary culture, Rorty contends that this sort of culture "drops a presupposition common to religion and philosophy—that redemption must come from one's relation to something that is not just one more human creation" (2004: 11). Moreover, he states a thesis that is central to many of his texts: "It is that the intellectuals of the West have, since the Renaissance, progressed through three stages: they have hoped for redemption first from God, then from philosophy, and now from literature" (2004: 8). In a genuinely antifoundationalist, nominalist, and de-divinized culture, a culture that is humanist and historicist, one must no longer strive to enter into a relation with a nonhuman entity or power; instead, one should try to get in touch with the present limits of one's imagination. The profoundly Romantic character of a Rortyan literary culture becomes clear when he points out that "it is a premise of this culture that though the imagination has present limits, these limits are capable of being extended forever. The imagination endlessly consumes its own artifacts. It is an ever-living, ever-expanding, fire" (2004: 12).

Rorty once more underscores the necessity of getting beyond representationalism and of imagining a world in which humans are responsible only to each other. In this new literary culture, as we will see in the next part of this chapter, its inhabitants will not hesitate to drop "a presupposition common to religion and philosophy—that redemption must come from one's relation to something that is not just one more human creation" (2004: 11). Furthermore, as Rorty suggests, in this utopian culture "the intellectuals will have given up the idea that there is a standard against which the products of the human imagination can be measured other than their social utility, as this utility is judged by a maximally free, leisured, and tolerant global community" (2004: 27).

In "Philosophy as a Transitional Genre," Rorty develops his notion of "redemptive truth." He highlights the fact that this idea of "redemptive truth" is incompatible with an anti-authoritarian and postmetaphysical culture. It is the kind of truth that philosophy has traditionally hoped to offer; a truth that provides one with a firm set of beliefs. Once one is in possession of those beliefs, one would no longer see the necessity of imaginatively reflecting on what to do with oneself; that is, one would no longer desire new kinds of self-description and redescription. "Redemptive truth," in other words, would fulfill the philosophical need "to fit everything—every thing, person, event, idea, and poem—into a single context, a context that will somehow reveal itself as natural, destined, and unique" (2004: 7). To believe in redemptive truth, if one follows Rorty, is to believe in "something that is the reality behind the appearance, the one true description of what is going on, the final secret" (2004: 7). Redemptive truth, governed by a "desire for completeness," would produce "maximal clarity and maximal coherence" (2010a: 391–2).

From what we have discussed thus far, it should be obvious that Rorty thinks that the novel does not offer redemptive truth. On the contrary, it critiques the notion that there is only one context that would matter for purposes of shaping humans' lives; only one context, that is, in which those lives appear as they really are. In Rorty's view, novels depict human attempts to meet human needs, they are about concrete cases of particular people being insensitive to or even ignoring the suffering of other particular people in specific historical circumstances. Hence, they (indirectly) contribute to the critique of the alleged necessity of acknowledging the power of a nonhuman being that is what it is apart from human needs and desires. The novel expands our sense of solidarity and of the diversity and variety of human life, and it strengthens the notions of historicity, particularity, and contingency. Novels can be useful when we seek to balance our needs against those who are unlike ourselves, whose values differ profoundly from ours, and whose actions we thought we would never understand or be able to justify. "To have a more educated, developed and sophisticated moral outlook," as Rorty maintains, "is to be able to grasp more of these needs, and to understand more of these self-descriptions" (2010a: 393). His contention is that the novel has contributed enormously to the attempt to replace religion and philosophy with literature, since it has helped young intellectuals grasp that one might enlarge one's self by becoming acquainted with other ways of being human and that this imaginative and creative enlargement of self is preferable to the idea that the subject should strive to be adequate to the demands and imperatives of a nonhuman, noncontingent authority. Rorty states that the "great virtue of the literary culture that is gradually coming into being is that it tells young intellectuals that the only source of redemption is the human imagination, and that this fact should occasion pride rather than despair" (2004: 13).

Whereas the novel contributes to an anti-authoritarian and antiessentialist understanding of moral progress in the public sphere, the effects of the texts of Jacques Derrida are strictly limited to the private sphere. One often gets the impression that Rorty reads Derrida as a writer who is only good for purposes of private self-creation. Derrida's texts are also governed by anti-authoritarian gestures, but Rorty asserts that their effects should not reach the public sphere. His discussion of Derrida goes back to the 1970s, and he published numerous essays on his French colleague. In his early texts on Derrida, Rorty already underlines that he enormously values the playful, funny, and creative side of this deconstructionist. To Rorty, Derrida is an ironist theorist as ironist writer. Hence, he plays an important role when one intends to illuminate Rorty's notion of literature.

In his seminal essay "Philosophy as a Kind of Writing," Rorty stresses that Derrida intends to make philosophy impure, "more unprofessional, funnier, more allusive, sexier, and above all, more 'written'" (1982: 93). Furthermore, the most shocking thing about Derrida's work, according to Rorty, "is his use of multilingual puns, joke etymologies, allusions from anywhere to anywhere, and phonic and typographical gimmicks" (1982: 96). Being against the notion of "first philosophy," Derrida protests against the idea that philosophy of language, pursued methodologically and with scientific rigor, could be considered *prima philosophia*. Rorty sees Derrida as a "philosopher of philosophy, where philosophy is just the self-consciousness of the play of a certain kind of writing" (1982: 103). Derrida simply wants to play with, for instance, Hegel's texts. He is not interested in the nature of language, in contrast to analytic philosophers, for instance, but he is fond of playing with texts that were written by people who thought that they were writing about language. In this early text on the French philosopher, Rorty already warns against the allegedly bad side of Derrida's work, his penchant for philosophical system-building: "For there is a side of Derrida which looks unfortunately constructive, a side which makes it look as if he in the end succumbs to nostalgia, to the lure of philosophical system-building, and specifically that of constructing yet another transcendental idealism" (1982: 99).

Against theorists such as Rodolphe Gasché, Paul de Man, Jonathan Culler, and Geoffrey Bennington, Rorty criticizes the suggestion that one needs a method of deconstruction, a system, a rigorous deconstructive argumentation that leads to philosophical conclusions. In other words, one should not see Derrida as a transcendental philosopher.

Rorty, the "longtime puzzled admirer of Derrida" (1998b: 348), does not modify his reading of Derridean deconstruction in the 1980s. Chapter 6 ("From ironist theory to private allusions: Derrida") of *Contingency* discusses the "Envois" section of *La Carte postale*. Emphasizing the importance of "private jokes" and the fact that the later Derrida apparently "simply drops theory" and "privatizes his philosophical thinking" (1989: 125), Rorty holds that Derrida encourages us to give up the attempt to unite the private and public. With the creative help of this French deconstructionist, we are finally capable of realizing that we had better stop trying to bring together a quest for private autonomy, self-perfection, and self-creation, on the one hand, and an attempt at public utility and effectiveness, on the other. Derrida's play with his predecessors in the "Envois" section, his fantasizing, and his associative style are the end product of ironist theorizing. According to Rorty, Derrida privatizes the sublime. Rorty explicitly states in *Contingency* that he considers Derrida as politically useless: "I agree with Habermas that as *public* philosophers they [Nietzsche, Heidegger, and Derrida] are at best useless and at worst dangerous, but I want to insist on the role they and others like them can play in accommodating the ironist's *private* sense of identity to her liberal hopes" (1989: 68).

On Rorty's account, the line of ironist thinking that runs from Hegel through Foucault and Derrida is "largely irrelevant to public life and to political questions. Ironist theorists like Hegel, Nietzsche, Derrida, and Foucault seem to me invaluable in our attempt to form a private self-image, but pretty much useless when it comes to politics" (1989: 83). Offering a quasi-religious form of spiritual pathos, these antimetaphysical, anti-Cartesian, and anti-Kantian nominalists and historicists should be relegated to private life and no longer taken as useful guides to political deliberation and action. Nobody needs concepts such as "différance," "trace," "supplement," "unrepresentability," "iterability," "unreachability," and "impossibility (of justice)" in the public realm. Effective political organization ought to center on the idea of necessary piecemeal reforms and on the protection and the improvement of the institutions of bourgeois liberal society. In Rorty's opinion, liberal politics is synonymous with the notion that "true" or "good" can be considered as the outcome of free discussion— "that if we take care of political freedom, truth and goodness will take care of themselves" (1989: 84). Philosophers such as Nietzsche, Heidegger, and Derrida have created new discourses and ways of speaking that have enlarged the realm of possibility. But these are new private possibilities that are, as Rorty puts it in "Habermas, Derrida, and the Functions of Philosophy," "only incidentally and contingently relevant to liberal social hope" (1998b: 311). Derrida is brilliant as far as placing books next to other books is concerned, but the Derridean dissolving of substances and essences into webs of relations and his blurring of genres do not contribute much to the political idea of a genuinely liberal society. Reading Derrida as a "romantic utopian" (1998b: 138) and a "romantic idealist" (1999: 212), Rorty calls his readers' attention to his private-public split and to his notorious idea of the incommensurability of these two vocabularies.

Rorty regards Derrida as an "écrivain" who produces strange and opaque texts (e.g., his book on Hegel and Genet, *Glas*). Derrida is an ironist theorist who has become an ironist writer, and as such he might be of help regarding one's project of private self-creation. Consequently, Rorty does not see the necessity of approaching the questions of deconstruction and ethics, deconstruction and justice, and, of course, deconstruction and Marxism that were at the center of discussions in the 1980s and 1990s (Derrida's *Spectres de Marx*, e.g., was published in 1993). Undoubtedly, Rorty's analysis of Derrida is reductionist and one-sided (especially when compared with that of his fellow pragmatist, Richard Bernstein).[24] However, for our purposes it is useful, since it once more confirms to what degree Rorty relies on his private-public distinction whether he discusses novelists, theorists, or philosophers who make it almost impossible to clearly differentiate between philosophy and literature.

Crucially, Rorty complicates this private-public dichotomy in his posthumously published essay, "Redemption from Egotism: James and Proust as Spiritual Exercises." He depicts the relation between James and Proust and their readers as very intimate. These novels, as he writes, "helped make us the people we are, and our gratitude remains intense. Insofar as we consider any books sacred, their novels count as such" (2010a: 396). Regarding the notion of redemption from egotism, he explains:

> For anybody who has been caught up in the work of either man is likely to be exceptionally sensitive to the dangers of egotism. Such people are more aware than most of how easy it is to describe other people in ways tailored to our

own needs rather than to theirs. Readers of James and Proust are not only more aware to the needs of others, but also more likely to aspire to the sort of experience which is vaguely and roughly called "a higher state of consciousness." (2010a: 396)

Rorty even goes so far as to compare the readers' "moments of understanding and revelation" (2010a: 396) to those described by William James in *The Varieties of Religious Experience*. Rorty uses this analogy with religious experience in order to further differentiate the texts by Proust and James from those of writers like Dickens, Balzac, Stowe, Dreiser, and Wright. His discussion of Proust and James in "Redemption from Egotism" complicates the categories that he introduced in *Contingency, Irony, and Solidarity*. In this book, as we have seen, he contended that works like the *Recherche* were important as far as our attempts at self-creation are concerned, they illuminate the meaning of self-overcoming, and they thus help us become autonomous. In "Redemption from Egotism," Rorty advances the argument that the novels of James and Proust, in contrast to those of Dickens, unsettle our intuitions and "force us to experience vivid doubts about ourselves" (2010a: 397). In other words, they arouse "doubts whether there is any health in us, whether our egotism may not go much deeper than we have realized" (2010a: 397). According to Rorty, those novels do not offer a firm truth, a system of beliefs, or a morality derived from principles. What counts is "the experience of reading the novel" and the readers' "relation to the novels themselves" (2010a: 397). The readers of James and Proust, if one follows Rorty, engage in a "secret converse" with these writers, and they "find themselves caught up in the sort of suddenly shared enlargement of the imagination and suddenly shared intensity of appreciation of the passing moment that occurs when two lovers find their loves reciprocated" (2010a: 397). His argument culminates in the suggestion that the novels of James and Proust do not offer redemptive truth but "redemption" (2010a: 397).[25]

The important aspect concerning Rorty's reading of James and Proust in this piece is neither the vagueness of his suggestions nor the religiously connoted vocabulary he uses. Rather, it is to be seen in his (implicit) contention that James and Proust are not only useful for private purposes of self-fashioning, but that they also indirectly contribute to moral reflection in a liberal democratic culture and that they moreover make their readers appreciate the implications of the notion of an antiessentialist moral community. By redeeming their readers from egotism and insensitivity and by bringing them to doubt their moral outlook, these two writers, in Rorty's opinion, contribute to the forging of a liberal moral community in which the appeal to a transcendent source of authority (God, Truth, Knowledge, or Reason) seems no longer necessary or desirable. As regards Rorty's understanding of moral progress, I think his discussion of James and Proust demonstrates that even in a genuinely postmetaphysical culture the strict separation between private irony and social hope cannot always be maintained and that the phrase "public irony" is not as unnecessary or oxymoronic as Rorty most of the time pretends it to be.[26]

In the "Redemption" essay, Rorty once more emphasizes how highly he values the novel as regards the endeavor to establish a new kind of culture: "I want to see the rise of the novel in the last two centuries as something new under the sun, something that may help initiate a new form of cultural life by helping to create a self-image for human beings as different from the one Aristotle proposed as his cosmology is from our own" (2010a: 404). Whereas devotional reading "emphasizes purification rather than enlargement, getting rid of distractions rather than incorporating them in a larger unity," novel reading, as he contends, "aims at encompassing multitudes rather than eliminating superfluities" (2010a: 406). While novel reading is of the utmost importance to Rorty, and functions as an anti-authoritarian practice, as it were, he does not really add anything new to the liberal version of literary criticism that runs from Trilling and Richard Chase to Wayne C. Booth and Martha Nussbaum. After decades of innovative work in literary studies and literary theory, Rorty feels free to go back to an almost premodern version of literary criticism (and partly even to a "critique biographique" à la Sainte-Beuve). His radical anti-Kantianism inevitably results in an instrumentalization of the novel for purposes of moral progress. Completely and wilfully neglecting the aspects of aesthetic form and narrative technique, Rorty's pragmatist version of literary criticism is incapable of grasping the multilayered complexity of modern artworks.[27] Form is more than the authority of abstraction, and more than something universal, static, or immutable that is opposed to the empirical world (for Rorty, the world of idiosyncratic experiences of particular people in specific historical circumstances). In other words, the form-content dialectics is more than an aesthetic version of the scheme-content distinction. I will expand on this in the following chapter. We will see that the question of pragmatism and aesthetic form, which has hitherto been neglected, is of the utmost importance for the revival of pragmatism.

2.6 A Literary or Poeticized Culture

As always, it was all Hegel's fault. In "Nineteenth-Century Idealism and Twentieth-Century Textualism," Rorty illuminates the significance of Hegel for the development of a literary culture. His judgment of Hegel as far as the narrative about the origin of the modern age is concerned would not change very much in his later texts. Interestingly enough, Rorty maintains that metaphysical idealism ought to be seen as only a brief interlude on the way to Romanticism and thus to a pragmatist literary culture. Rorty is not at all interested in Hegel's system-building, but he concentrates exclusively on the latter's historicism. Hence, it is the early Hegel's *Phenomenology of Spirit* (1807) that is of primary concern in this context. It was the idealist Hegel who contributed enormously to the establishment of a literary culture shaped by a Romanticism that replaced the pursuit of truth with the search for new vocabularies. According to Rorty, Hegel was of great importance for the development of a postmetaphysical literary culture, since he not only celebrated the invention of radically new vocabularies, but at the same time underscored their transitoriness and finality, the fact that any certainty a new vocabulary seems to offer lasts but a moment. Hegel prepared us, as Rorty seems to hold, for the recognition of the contingency of the vocabularies that constitute our beliefs and desires: "Hegel left Kant's ideal of philosophy-as-science a shambles, but he did, as I have said, create a new literary genre, a genre which exhibited the relativity of significance to choice of vocabulary, the bewildering variety of vocabularies from which we can choose, and the intrinsic instability of each" (1982: 148).

It becomes obvious in Rorty's essay that he took the term "the literary culture" from C. P. Snow's work on the "two cultures," and would later, in *Contingency*, introduce his own term, "poeticized culture" (1989: 53).[28] Rorty's contention is that Hegel exemplified, like no one before him had done, what such a radically new culture could offer; "namely, the historical sense of the relativity of principles and vocabularies to a place and time, the romantic sense that everything can be changed by talking in new terms" (1982: 149). Contrary to his own intentions, Hegel wrote the charter of our modern literary culture. In "Philosophy as a Transitional Genre," Rorty once more underlines the significance of Hegel for his narrative of emancipation and secularization. He explicitly contends that the transition from a philosophical to a literary culture began with this German philosopher. It was with Hegel that philosophy reached its most ambitious and presumptuous form which almost instantly turned into its dialectical opposite; that is, the Hegelian system eventually turned out to be a kind of utterly nonironical self-consuming artifact. Hegel's system was serious in its desire to depict things as they really were and it sought to fit everything into a single context. This also signifies, of course, that it pretended to represent the totality. Rorty writes: "Since Hegel's time, the intellectuals have been losing faith in philosophy. This amounts to losing faith in the idea that redemption can come in the form of true beliefs. In the literary culture that has been emerging during the last two hundred years, the question 'Is it true?' has yielded to the question 'What's new?'" (2004: 9).[29]

In today's literary culture, philosophy and religion have become marginal, they appear as only optional literary genres. A literary culture still offers the possibility of redemption, but the kind of redemption has changed. As Rorty points out:

> As I am using the terms "literature" and "literary culture," a culture that has substituted literature for both religion and philosophy finds redemption neither in a noncognitive relation to a nonhuman person nor in a cognitive relation to propositions, but in noncognitive relations to other human beings, relations mediated by human artifacts such as books and buildings, paintings and songs. These artifacts provide a sense of alternative ways of being human. (2004: 10)

What this also means is that the search for God was replaced by the striving for Truth, and that the latter has finally been replaced by the search for novelty and by the recognition that redemption can only be found in human creations and artifacts and not in the escape from the temporal to the eternal or transcendental.

At the beginning of *Contingency*, Rorty makes clear that his anti-authoritarian and humanist story of progress begins at the end of the eighteenth century. What the German idealists, the French revolutionaries, and the Romantic poets had in common was "a dim sense that human beings whose language changed so that they no longer spoke of themselves as responsible to nonhuman powers would thereby become a new kind of human beings" (1989: 7). At the end of the eighteenth century European linguistic practices changed at an increasingly fast rate, and more and more people seemed willing to accept the Romantic idea that truth is made rather than found. This suggestion has to be seen in connection with the idea that a human self is not adequately or inadequately expressed in a vocabulary, but that it is rather created by the use of a vocabulary. In *Contingency*, it becomes clear from Rorty's elaborations on his notion of a poeticized culture that he intends this kind of culture to be the final, and most exciting, stage of the process of secularization. His anti-authoritarian and antifoundationalist story of progress ends here. In other words, Rorty wants us to no longer deify anything and to continue the process of emancipation and secularization that ought to eventually culminate in a postmetaphysical poeticized culture. Combining anti-authoritarianism and humanism, his utopian literary or poeticized culture would be a culture whose inhabitants no longer saw the necessity of striving for the certainty, reliability, firmness, immutability, and purity of what would be more than another human creation and whose members, moreover, were capable of appreciating the full implications of Nietzsche's proposal that only we have created the world that concerns us as human beings. Rortyan postmetaphysicians as pragmatist humanists will treat nothing as a divinity, will reject any form of God-substitute, and will try to convince their fellow humans that in a world of contingent social practices the only authority is that of human consensus. Rorty's anti-authoritarian story of progress culminates in this notion of a postmetaphysical or poeticized culture, and the latter should be central to discussions seeking to elucidate the possibility—and the advantages—of a pragmatist enlightenment.[30]

In Rorty's poeticized culture, strong poets, creative redescribers, nominalist historicists, and other anti-Platonists would delight in the stimulating plurality of new ways of speaking that do not pretend to offer a single, firm, unequivocal, and transhistorical truth and that contribute to the critique of the idea that there is a permanent reality to be found behind the many temporary appearances. For the members of the literary culture, the literary intellectuals, "a life that is not lived close to the present limits of the human imagination is not worth living" (2004: 12). How does Rorty define those literary intellectuals? His understanding of the function of the literary intellectual combines a Bloomian interpretation of the autonomy of the self with Emersonian self-reliance. A literary intellectual has constant doubts about the (final) vocabulary she is currently using, she does not want to get stuck in it. She longs to become acquainted with other ways of speaking, other ways of interpreting the purpose of life. For that reason, she reads as many books as possible. By becoming acquainted with so many alternative vocabularies and ways of being human, the literary intellectual enlarges her self. Because of her reading she is introduced to a great number of alternative purposes, and ways of expressing those purposes, and she is thus given the possibility of radically questioning traditional vocabularies and explanations. To put it simply, the literary intellectual's reading leads to her self-creation; it offers her the possibility of creating an autonomous self. Rorty apparently agrees with

Harold Bloom that the more books you have read, the more descriptions and redescriptions you have come across, the more human and at the same time autonomous you become. A Rortyan and Bloomian autonomous self puts a premium on the attempt to creatively expand the present limits of the human imagination, and it also seeks to demonstrate that the development from religion (God) to philosophy (Truth) to literature (novelty, imagination, redescription) is a story of increasing self-reliance.

In *Contingency*, Rorty calls the ideal member of a postmetaphysical poeticized culture a "liberal ironist." He suggests that liberal ironists continually look for new possibilities of creatively and imaginatively redescribing and recontextualizing things and persons; that is, their desire for novelty, new sets of metaphors, and surprising gestalt switches lets them contribute to the establishment of a radically new kind of postmetaphysical culture in which the notion of correct representation no longer plays a role and in which final vocabularies are considered as "poetic achievements." According to Rorty, the ironist's search for a new and better final vocabulary "is dominated by metaphors of making rather than finding, of diversification and novelty rather than convergence to the antecedently present. She thinks of final vocabularies as poetic achievements rather than as fruits of diligent inquiry according to antecedently formulated criteria" (1989: 77). Instead of the metaphysician's reality, objectivity, and essence, the universalist's grandeur and transcendence, and the Romantic's depth, the ironist is happy to admit that all she has to offer is the idea of "continual redescription" (1989: 80). The ironist's realization of the contingency of her final vocabulary, her awareness of the power of redescription, and her search for the most elegant way of combining certain vocabularies are characteristics of an aestheticized culture in which books are continually placed in new combinations, in which exciting new vocabularies kill off old ways of speaking, and in which persons and cultures are seen as "incarnated vocabularies" (1989: 80). When discussing Rorty's pragmatism it is one of the ultimate ironies that someone who radically rejects aesthetic theory and refuses to show an interest in aesthetic form depicts such an aestheticized culture as his utopian goal.

2.7 Conclusion

In this chapter, I have shown that Rorty's anti-authoritarianism is central to his pragmatism as humanism. Furthermore, I have suggested that the antifoundationalist and antirepresentationalist story of progress and emancipation should also be understood as an anti-authoritarian story of progress that illuminates the possibility of a pragmatist enlightenment. As far as this notion of a Second Enlightenment is concerned, it is crucial to see that Rorty extends Enlightenment anti-authoritarianism from ethics to epistemology. I have argued that this extension of anti-authoritarianism is the real core of the later Rorty's pragmatism as humanism. As we have seen, in his utopian postmetaphysical and poeticized culture people would no longer see the necessity of looking for the certainty, firmness, reliability, transhistoricity, immutability, and purity of what would be more than another human creation. While Rorty explains how this search for certainty, the notion of a nonhuman authority, and the quest for sublimity are linked, he also highlights the connection between his idea of anti-authoritarianism, the ideal of complete secularization, and the idea of the beautiful. For Rorty, accepting the power of a nonhuman authority and questing for sublimity hang together. This is the bad side of Romanticism.[31] A pragmatist, as he maintains, ought to be satisfied with the merely beautiful. In the preface to *Pragmatism as Anti-Authoritarianism*, Rorty asserts:

> The idea of a non-human authority and the quest for sublimity are both products of self-abasement. Pragmatism says that the conditioned is all there is: that human beings have nothing to know save their relations to each other and to other finite beings. To be satisfied with the conditioned, to give up the quest for the infinite, would be to rest content with beauty. (2021: xxx)

Anti-authoritarianism in a Rortyan poeticized culture also means that its members substitute history and beauty for eternity and sublimity. They no longer have use for the dark forces of the sublime, whether it is understood as the unrepresentable, the opaque, the ineffable, or the dissonant. According to Rorty, "a merely beautiful object or state of affairs unifies a manifold in an especially satisfying way. The beautiful harmonizes finite things with other finite things" (2021: xxvii). This is a profoundly Deweyan understanding of beauty that once again demonstrates Rorty's unwillingness to fully appreciate the multilayered complexity of modern artworks and their formal qualities. By establishing a link between nonhuman authority and the sublime, he makes clear that his anti-authoritarian story of progress, culminating in his literary or poeticized culture, consigns the notions of a dissonant and fragmented beauty and a dissonant and fragmented aesthetic form to the private sphere. In Rorty's pragmatism, the public sphere will never be more than beautiful. Beauty here signifies harmony, unity, wholeness, symmetry, balance, and organicity. These are exactly the terms that are central to Dewey's aesthetics as he develops it in *Art as Experience* (1934); and these are also exactly the terms that are radically questioned and criticized in many modern and avant-garde artworks.

Rorty's anti-authoritarianism teaches that sublimity has much to do with depth and height, and thus with verticality. By contrast, beauty is linked to horizontality. Pragmatists as panrelationalists clearly prefer the idea of an endlessly expanding horizon, endlessly expanded by human creativity, to the foundational and transcendental ways of speaking that are associated with verticality. Rorty's contention is that pragmatists "shall see everything on, so to speak, a single horizontal plane. We shall not search for the sublime either high above, or deep beneath, this plane. We shall instead move things about, rearrange them so as to highlight their relations to other things, in the hope of finding ever more useful, and therefore ever more beautiful, patterns" (2021: xxxiv). In *Contingency*, he uses the phrase "aesthetically useful" (1989: 167). His rejection of the moral-aesthetic distinction, his instrumentalization of the aesthetic, and his utter neglect of formal questions too often let his pragmatism degenerate into an almost premodern version of literary criticism. In the confrontation with the phrase "aesthetically useful," most literary scholars will most presumably be tempted to present themselves as unreconstructed Kantian formalists or Adornian aestheticians. And they undoubtedly have good reason to do so.

In his preface to *Pragmatism as Anti-Authoritarianism*, Rorty emphasizes "that we should separate the quest for greatness and sublimity from the quest for justice and happiness. The former is optional, the latter is not" (2021: xxxii). Rorty is perfectly willing to admit that the sublime, for instance, in the form of radically new ways of speaking or new metaphors, eventually can have an impact on the public sphere. He proposes that the "utility of imaginative feats, bound by no social norms, for the public discourse of later ages is undeniable. [...] Our lives would be less varied, and the forms of happiness for which we are able to strive would be much poorer. But this does not mean that we should arrange our public institutions to suit the quest for greatness or for sublimity" (2021: xxxii).

It is of the utmost importance to understand that this does not only concern Rorty's endlessly debated private-public dichotomy. By advancing the argument that the notion of a nonhuman authority and the quest for sublimity are intimately linked, his pragmatism as anti-authoritarianism also shows that it does not need the idea of the avant-garde. In "Philosophy of the Future," Rorty characterizes Dewey's understanding of the task of the philosopher thus: "Dewey construed Hegel's insistence on historicity as the claim that philosophers should not try to be the avant-garde of society and culture, but should be content to mediate between the past and the future" (1995a: 199). The philosopher's job, as Rorty interprets Dewey, is to bring together old beliefs and new beliefs and to solve problems that arise in "situations in which the language of the past is in conflict with the needs of the future" (1995a: 199). Rorty thinks that, together with the later Wittgenstein's notion of therapy, this Deweyan understanding of the philosopher's task is perfectly sufficient. Problems arise when philosophers want more and present themselves as radical antifoundationalists. Rorty writes: "Philosophers who specialize in antifoundationalism, however, often see themselves as revolutionaries rather than as rubbish-sweepers or visionaries. Then, alas, they become avant-gardist" (1995a: 201).[32] In this chapter, I have tried to demonstrate that Rorty also reacts idiosyncratically to the avant-garde in aesthetic matters. A dissonant and fragmented beauty and the practice of radical form-giving are regarded as forms of the sublime that are consigned to the private sphere (although they may eventually have a contingent impact on the liberal public sphere). Hence, the question arises as to whether an anti-authoritarian and poeticized culture will not deprive itself of the possibility of fully using the potential of those radical practices of form-giving; that is, the question must be posed whether it is precisely the link that Rorty establishes between authoritarianism and the sublime that allows one to see the severe limitations of Dewey's aesthetics and Rorty's brand of literary criticism when it comes to modern and late-modern works of art.[33]

3

Pragmatism, Humanism, and Form

Pragmatism is a humanist philosophy. It is difficult to approach the contemporary significance of pragmatism without considering the role of humanism. At least since the 1970s, humanism, mostly in its liberal version, has been vehemently attacked and criticized. Poststructuralists, deconstructionists, posthumanists, postcolonial theorists, and proponents of race and gender studies have called attention to its shortcomings, insufficiencies, and totalizing gesture. Liberal humanism has been the *bête noire* of most post-1945 French intellectuals (whether Derrideans, Foucauldians, or Deleuzians). Furthermore, most (post-) Marxists, seeking to develop new conceptual tools in the fight against late capitalism and its archeo-teleological metaphysics, have questioned the humanist legacy.[1] In pragmatism, however, a particular understanding of humanism has persisted. This persistence of humanism is of the utmost importance, since one can only grasp the unique contemporary significance of pragmatism when one appreciates how pragmatism, humanism, anti-authoritarianism, and postmetaphysics are interlinked, and how this link has gained in importance after the exhaustion of antihumanist theories.[2]

The idea of a pragmatist humanism becomes clearer when one notes how one of Nietzsche's most far-reaching suggestions, "Only we have created the world *that concerns man!*" (1974: sec. 301), is linked to William James's famous dictum that "the trail of the human serpent is [...] over everything" (1907: 515), and how Nietzsche and James's proposals are connected with Rorty's scenario of a radically de-divinized, that is, poeticized and postmetaphysical culture: "The process of de-divinization [...] would, ideally, culminate in our no longer being able to see any use for the notion that finite, mortal, contingently existing human beings might derive the meanings of their lives from anything except other finite, mortal, contingently existing human beings" (Rorty 1989: 45).[3] Rorty's contention is, and Nietzsche would have agreed, that in a truly de-divinized culture there is no form of nonhuman authority that human beings have to obey. Seemingly *en passant*, Rorty, in *Contingency, Irony, and Solidarity*, speaks of the "sort of humanism and pragmatism advocated in this book" (1989: 116). The humanist, as he understands him or her, is a radical postmetaphysician. In other words, pragmatist humanists such as James, F. C. S. Schiller, John Dewey, Richard Bernstein, and Rorty replace the metaphysician's narrative with a more useful and stimulating narrative. They show how their antirepresentationalist and antifoundationalist story of progress and emancipation is connected with the modern development from finding to making. Furthermore, they explain to us the full implications of the Nietzschean suggestion that only we have created the world that concerns us as human beings. They do this by bringing together pragmatism, humanism, anti-authoritarianism, and postmetaphysics. Their position is directed against the notion of the human answerability to the world, to something nonhuman, as well as against the gesture of a convergence to the antecedently real or true. While their antirepresentationalism critiques the understanding of the world-word relation that is governed by the idea of correspondence or accurate representation, their Deweyan anti-authoritarianism proposes that human beings must not humble themselves before something nonhuman, whether the Will of God, the Really Real, or the Intrinsic Nature of Reality. In other words, the pragmatist humanists, in a Nietzschean manner, intend to demetaphysicize or detranscendentalize the world. By doing so, they want to help their fellow humans to reach a point where they no longer deify anything or look for God-substitutes and where they recognize the advantages of treating everything as a product of time and chance. At the end of this pragmatist process of de-divinization one will hopefully have reached a position that allows one to criticize the hypostatizations of the world and the self as entities that speak to us and that, moreover, want to be expressed and represented in a particular way.

This chapter is divided into three parts. In the first part, I will endeavor to illuminate why pragmatism is a humanist philosophy. The second part discusses why most pragmatists have been unwilling to consider the significance of aesthetic form. Central to my argument is the idea that Dewey's naturalist aesthetics does not offer a convincing conception of form. Insisting upon the unity of form and content and considering the distinction between form and matter a metaphysical gesture, Dewey's aesthetics is of only limited value in the confrontation with modern works of art. In the final part, I will argue that a pragmatist humanism that refuses to historicize the concept of form and ignores the radical formal and narratological innovations of modern art and literature (from aestheticism to the historical avant-garde's attack on the organic artwork) weakens its own position.

It is crucial to note that I will consider form-giving as a kind of poetic agency. The latter term directs attention to the interwovenness of intelligent action and poetic imagination. It denotes creative forms of making, of *poiesis*, or constellations of contingent creative acts. Form-giving as poetic agency, as I will contend, is an integral part of the antirepresentationalist, antifoundationalist, and anti-authoritarian story of progress and emancipation that characterizes pragmatism. What pragmatism scholars have mostly ignored so far is that aesthetic theory can help one appreciate the far-reaching implications of this story.

3.1 Pragmatism as Humanism

The modern antifoundationalist story of progress starts with the Romantics.[4] Ralph Waldo Emerson's suggestion, in "Experience," that "the universe wear[s] our color" (1981: 286) offers one the possibility of grasping that there is an intimate connection between his emphasis on the world-shaping power of the poet, the Nietzschean idea that only we have created the world that concerns us, and what James calls the "humanistic principle" (1907: 598).[5] One understands pragmatism and its antifoundationalist and antirepresentationalist, or Deweyan and anti-authoritarian, story of progress and emancipation better when one regards it as continuing the humanistic tradition that links Emerson, Nietzsche, and James's texts. In their different ways, Emerson, Nietzsche, James, and Rorty demonstrate that the modern antifoundationalist story of progress is a humanist story of poetic agency (see Chapter 7). The latter brings creative practice, intelligent action, and poetic imagination together and, emphasizing the act of making, seeks to convince us that instead of asking ourselves whether there are truths out there that we still have to find or discover we should ask whether it would not be more stimulating to invent new ways of speaking and acting.

James's version of pragmatism is central to the notion of pragmatist humanism. In his texts, he seeks to convince his readers that the world is unfinished, incomplete, malleable, and thus waiting for humans to add something to it. In the manner of an Emersonian and Nietzschean poet-philosopher he maintains that the subject's creativity is capable of shaping and enriching the world that it finds. James holds that humans' worldly interpretations must not center on concepts such as correspondence, imitation, mimesis, or copying. In *The Meaning of Truth*, he unequivocally states that "thought's mission [is] to increase and elevate, rather than simply to imitate and reduplicate, existence" (1909a: 870). Knowing does not describe a process where a rational knower, in a dehistoricized realm, grasps and faithfully mirrors a passive object; that is, it is not a relation between the subject's rational ideas and a nonhuman reality. Rather, knowing is a process that offers one the possibility of getting into fruitful relations with a historical and cultural reality (as Dewey would later also argue in *The Quest for Certainty* and *Experience and Nature*).

Like Nietzsche's naturalism, James's pragmatist humanism criticizes systematic thought, the idea of a *prima philosophia*, and theoretical abstractions.[6] Both Nietzsche and James contribute to the development of a postmetaphysical form of humanism that illuminates the significance of creativity, praxis, plurality, and perspective. They do this, among other things, by repeatedly underscoring that the incomplete and malleable world is waiting or asking for interpretation. Hence, it is our activity as interpreters that is of the utmost importance for these philosophers. This incomplete world is subject to further change, addition, or modification, and it constantly changes because of the impact of, for instance, new vocabularies, cultural practices, or perspectives. However, while human subjects will never be capable of unifying this contingent material, they can try to creatively interpret it and thereby to achieve consequences in the world of practice. Concerning the subjects' activity and creativity as interpreters, James points out: "In our cognitive as well as in our active life we are creative. *We add*, both to the subject and to the predicate part of reality. The world stands really malleable, waiting to receive its final touches at our hands. Like the kingdom of heaven, it suffers human violence willingly. Man *engenders* truths upon it" (1907: 599).

As a pragmatist humanist, James proposes that movement, change, transition, and novelty are more than forms of mere appearance that distract from the ideal of immutability or transhistoricity as propagated by rationalism and monism. As a pragmatist, his primary focus is on the "world of finite multifariousness" (James 1909b: 652), which is the world of praxis, the world of our biased beliefs and daily desires. In James, the idea of pluralism is closely linked to the notion of free will; that is, only in a pluralistic world does the subject appear as the author of genuine novelty. Only in this kind of world does the human subject appear as maker; that is, someone who is fascinated with the plurality of perspectives and vocabularies, who is capable of confronting contingency and unpredictability, who realizes the value of redescription (to use Rorty's term), and who understands that every vocabulary and perspective that has produced something new can only be man-made and hence temporary. James writes: "Towards this issue, of the reality or unreality of the novelty that appears, the pragmatic difference between monism and pluralism seems to converge. That we ourselves may be authors of genuine novelty is the thesis of the doctrine of free will" (1911: 1055). Monism's apriorism, with its emphasis on fixed principles, abstract principles as finalities, first things, firm doctrines, and its gesture of converging to the antecedently real and pure, inevitably has to deny the possibility of a pluralistic world where humans engage in contingent forms of making that might result in genuine novelty. The link that James illuminates between pluralism, free will, and novelty prepares the establishment of a postmetaphysical culture, since it helps his readers to understand that instead of claiming that their rational beliefs and sentences are world-directed and correspond to reality as it really is, they should grasp the full implications of the idea that they, as makers and poets in the broadest sense, have created the world that concerns them and that has value. It is James's contention that one comes naturally "to the humanistic principle: you can't weed out the human contribution. Our nouns and adjectives are all humanized heirlooms, and in the theories we build them into, the inner order and arrangement is wholly dictated by human considerations, intellectual consistency being one of them" (1907: 598).

The Jamesian "humanistic principle" was radicalized by Schiller, who developed his own brand of pragmatist humanism.[7] His idiosyncratic version of pragmatism, or what he also termed humanism, personalism, and voluntarism, sought to undermine the authority of the Anglo-Hegelianism of F. H. Bradley, T. H. Green, and others (this was also one of the targets of James's critique). However, on a more general level Schiller tried to expose the weaknesses, shortcomings, and inconsistencies of forms of absolutism, Platonism, intellectualism, and monism. His thought is radically anthropocentric.[8] In the preface to the first edition of *Humanism*, he underlines that pragmatism is "not the final term of philosophic innovation" since "there is yet a greater, a more sovereign principle" (1903: xv). The latter he terms "Humanism" (1903: xvi). Humanism, as he makes clear, is strictly opposed to forms of abstract, technical, intellectualist, and otherworldly philosophy. Being convinced that humanism is an attitude that he shares with James, Schiller contends that "the study of a humaner philosophy" is destined "to win the widest popularity" (1903: xvi). In his opinion, Protagoras's dictum that "man is the measure of all things" is "the truest and most important thing that any thinker ever has propounded" (1903: xvii). Later in his text Schiller expands on this:

> To remember that man is the measure of all things, i.e. of his whole experience-world, and that if our standard measure be proved false all our measurements are vitiated; to remember that Man is the maker of the sciences which subserve his human purposes; to remember that an ultimate philosophy which analyzes us away is thereby merely exhibiting its failure to achieve its purpose, that, and more that might be stated to the same effect, is the real root of Humanism, whence all its auxiliary doctrines spring. (1903: xx)

For James and Rorty pragmatism is the broader term, and humanism denotes a special pragmatist attitude. By contrast, for the British pragmatist humanism serves as the broader term that is capable of subsuming other doctrines. Pragmatism, for Schiller, is a method, and it "is in reality only the application of Humanism to the theory of knowledge" (1903: 24).

Schiller's pragmatism is a philosophy of creativity or poetic agency that highlights the significance of imagination and novelty, as well as the idiosyncratic and unpredictable creativity of individuals in their particular historical circumstances. Instead of abstract ideals, eternal forms, or the rigidity of traditional logic, he appreciates the creativity of humans who suggest new ways of thinking, new forms of thought, which might help and stimulate their fellow human beings in the attempt to cope with their environment and to solve their problems. In "The Definition of Pragmatism and Humanism," Schiller pointedly defines humanism as "really in itself the simplest of philosophic standpoints; it is merely the perception that the philosophic problem concerns human beings striving to comprehend a world of human experience by the resources of human minds" (1907: 12).

Like Schiller, Dewey establishes an intimate connection between knowing and doing. Differentiating between pure rational or theoretical activity on the one side and practical action or doing and making on the other, as the pragmatists argue, is central to metaphysics. Dewey repeatedly underscores how crucial it is to appreciate that knowledge is this-worldly, it is a process that takes place in the world in which we live. His critique of traditional epistemology and metaphysics primarily concentrates on two aspects. First, the idea that pure knowledge or pure intellect would offer the subject the possibility of escaping from the world of peril and uncertainty to a higher realm. Second, Dewey criticizes the conception that knowledge is knowledge only when it is capable of disclosing the properties of the antecedently real or the ultimate real. He rejects the correspondence theory of truth and the idea of mimetically reproducing the antecedently real and instead emphasizes that knowledge is this-worldly and a form of doing.

This mode of doing is a central part of humans' attempt to cope with their environment and to project the consequences of their actions and experiments into the future. Knowledge is problem-oriented, and at the same time one cannot grasp its function without paying attention to the power of the imagination. Radically questioning the idea that there is a complete correspondence between knowledge and what is real, and thus the suggestion that what is known is real in being, Dewey repeatedly underscores that inquiry and philosophical analysis will never be able to exclude the element of practical activity. Moreover, it is this element of practical activity that enters into the construction of the object known and that also reminds one that inquiry, experiment, and analysis are historical:

> In dealing with the proximate instead of with the ultimate, knowledge deals with the world in which we live, the world which is experienced, instead of attempting through the intellect to escape to a higher realm. Experimental knowledge is a mode of doing, and like all doing takes place at a time, in a place, and under specifiable conditions in connection with a definite problem. (Dewey 1988: 82)

As a naturalist humanist, Dewey's contention is that philosophy must radically alter its nature. This primarily signifies that knowledge must stop being contemplative and focused on the stasis of the antecedently real and instead become practical and experimental—a form of intelligently conducted doing. For our purposes it is important to note that there are passages in Dewey's texts that show that his stress on experimental doing sometimes ought to be interpreted as the endeavor to illuminate the significance of experimental creation. In "The Development of American Pragmatism," for instance, he states that the "individual mind is important because only the individual mind is the organ of modifications in traditions and institutions, the vehicle of experimental creation" (1925: 12). On the one hand, Dewey, as a pragmatist humanist, is satisfied with the notion of knowing as doing, and he holds that neither his ideal of social democracy nor his idea of experimental inquiry needs an understanding of knowing as creating. On the other hand, he writes in *Experience and Nature* in a Nietzschean manner: "Thinking is preeminently an art; knowledge and propositions which are the products of thinking, are works of art, as much so as statuary and symphonies" (2008b: 283). We will see in the next part of this chapter that this ambivalence also characterizes Dewey's conception of form.

The process of making the idea of a pragmatist humanism look attractive culminates in Rorty's notion of a postmetaphysical and poeticized culture.[9] His humanist ideal culture is radically anthropocentric in a Nietzschean and

Schillerian sense. Moreover, it illustrates the centrality of human creativity of action for the completion of the process of enlightenment. Having taken the final step from the idea of finding to that of making, the ideal member of a Rortyan literary or poeticized culture will understand "that there is nothing deep down inside us except what we have put there ourselves, no criterion that we have not created in the course of creating a practice, no standard of rationality that is not an appeal to such a criterion, no rigorous argumentation that is not obedience to our own conventions" (Rorty 1982: xlii). Rorty seems to hold that only in his ideal poeticized culture would one achieve full human maturity and dignity.[10] It becomes clear from Rorty's elaborations on his postmetaphysical culture that he intends it to be the final, and most stimulating, stage of the process of secularization. He seeks to help us reach a point where we no longer deify anything and where we see the necessity of continuing the process of emancipation and secularization that should eventually culminate in a postmetaphysical poeticized culture. He wants us to "try to get to the point where we no longer worship *anything*, where we treat *nothing* as a quasi divinity, where we treat *everything*—our language, our conscience, our community—as a product of time and chance" (Rorty 1989: 22).

As we saw in the previous chapter, the members of a Rortyan poeticized culture, as ironists and nominalist historicists, always look for new possibilities of creatively and imaginatively redescribing and recontextualizing things and people and of introducing new forms of self-creation and self-overcoming. By suggesting that interpreting something or knowing it is just a way of "describing some process of putting it to work," Rortyan ironists bring together their insistence upon the centrality of the imagination with their idea that "all anybody ever does with anything is use it" (Rorty 1999: 134). In Rorty's postmetaphysical culture, the notion of accurate representation no longer plays a role, the activity called knowing no longer has a nature to be discovered, there is no longer a connection between justification and truth, the idea of separating the object from what one says about it appears unnecessary, and the quest for certainty, in a Deweyan manner, is replaced with the demand for imagination. In this kind of culture, in which vocabularies are regarded as "poetic achievements" and in which people and cultures are seen as "incarnated vocabularies" (Rorty 1989: 77, 80), final vocabularies, as poetic achievements, are all we have, and there is thus no possibility of comparing our current way of speaking with things as they really are. In this kind of culture, critique can only have the form of an imaginative redescription that makes the old vocabulary look bad and rather useless.

It is noteworthy that in highlighting the novelty of a poeticized culture, which prefers metaphors of making to those of finding and which centers on the potential of a plurality of forms of poetic agency, Rorty does not see the necessity of talking about the significance of aesthetic form. Form neither plays a role for his scenario of a poeticized culture nor for his pragmatist understanding of the task of the novel.

3.2 Pragmatism and Form

While poststructuralists like the later Roland Barthes, deconstructionists like Jacques Derrida and Paul de Man, and Marxist theorists like Theodor W. Adorno and Fredric Jameson have shown a profound interest in form, the same cannot be said about most pragmatists. Why have pragmatists always been reluctant to highlight the significance of form? In their opinion, form is abstraction and it transforms problems that have their origin in experience, the problems of men and women in the Deweyan sense, into purely formal issues. Furthermore, form is ahistorical and acontextual, without connection to the particulars it seeks to govern. Refusing to reconcile the world of pure reason with the concrete order of experience, form transcends life and descends from without upon material. Form is the general and universal, it categorizes and, moreover, strives to separate purely intellectual studies from the pragmatic and from action. One should also see that most pragmatists and pragmatist aestheticians would advance the idea that form is static, immutable, and necessary and hence directly opposed to the empirical world that is governed by contingency and the unpredictability of humans' actions. What this boils down to is that form belongs to a world of thought that is completely removed from the world of experience and ordinary life.

The form-content dualism in aesthetics, as we will see, confirms the pernicious subject-object dichotomy and is diametrically opposed to the Deweyan notion of continuity. On a more general level it is important to note that form reinforces the distinction between knowing and doing and thus the prestige of the theoretical over the practical. Form is central to what Dewey termed the quest for certainty, since it helps one to grasp that only the systematic discipline of philosophy, employing reason and logical form, can apprehend the absolute, noumenal, transcendent, or ultimate reality. In other words, a concentration on form is of the utmost importance if one intends to demonstrate that only the realm governed by philosophy is marked by a superior dignity, since only philosophy is capable of going beyond the ordinary, empirical, and phenomenal world of everyday experience. As Dewey pointedly puts it in *The Quest for Certainty*: "In form, the quest for absolute certainty has reached its goal" (1988: 16). Form, as pure thought, offers a higher knowledge.

While most pragmatists think that form is a metaphysical concept that they can do without, it plays an important role in Dewey's *Art as Experience*. At the same time, however, one has to see that while his naturalist aesthetics has gained in importance in the past two or three decades, particularly after the aberrations of poststructuralism and postmodernism, his understanding of aesthetic form is highly problematic. *Art as Experience*, which was published in 1934, is not a theory of aesthetic modernism or the avant-garde. Dewey's text does not try to explain the multilayered complexity of artworks by, for instance, Flaubert, Proust, Joyce, Woolf, Kafka, Eliot, Picasso, Kandinsky, or Schönberg.[11] Instead of illuminating this often hermetic and formally complex modernism, Dewey intends to make clear why one can speak of a continuity between ordinary, everyday experience and "intensified forms of experience that are works of art." Right on the first page of *Art as Experience* he comments on the task of the contemporary aesthetician as follows: "A primary task is thus imposed upon one who undertakes to write upon the philosophy of the fine arts. This task is to restore continuity between the refined and intensified forms of experience that are works of art and the everyday events, doings, and sufferings that are universally recognized to constitute experience" (2008a: 9). Seeking to elucidate the continuity of aesthetic experience with everyday processes of living, Dewey's aesthetics clearly centers on the notion of experience.[12] On the one hand, even everyday experience can be "art in germ": "Because experience is the fulfillment of an organism in its struggles and achievements in a world of things, it is art in germ. Even in its rudimentary forms, it contains the promise of that delightful perception which is esthetic experience" (2008a: 25). On the other hand, aesthetic experience does not belong to an isolated realm, but it gets integrated into human beings' other activities. Aesthetic experience enhances and deepens those other activities, it energizes and inspires them.

Dewey's aesthetics of continuity argues for the necessity of the endeavor to connect art and life; that is, it critiques aesthetic theories that sharply distinguish art from everyday life and want to consign art to a special or separate realm (e.g., the museum or theater). In his opinion, the trouble with existing theories is that they start from a ready-made compartmentalization, or from a conception of art that "spiritualizes" it out of connection with the objects of concrete experience. [...] Were works of art placed in a directly human context in popular esteem, they would have a much wider appeal than they can have when pigeon-hole theories of art win general acceptance. (2008a: 17)

Dewey's naturalism also governs his aesthetic theory. He contends, for instance, that all art expresses the relation of the subject and its environment, it is the product of forms of interaction between the live creature and its environment. Naturalism, as Dewey argues, "is a necessity of all great art, even of the most religiously conventional and abstract painting, and of the drama that deals with human action in an urban setting" (2008a: 156). How does Dewey interpret the meaning of aesthetic form? The "formal conditions of artistic form [are] rooted deep in the world itself" (2008a: 152). He expands on the relation between naturalism and form as follows: "Interaction of environment with organism is the source, direct or indirect, of all experience and from the environment come those checks, resistances, furtherances, equilibria, which, when they meet with the energies of the organism in appropriate ways, constitute form" (2008a: 152). It already becomes obvious from these quotations from *Art as Experience* that Dewey argues against formalism and any metaphysical version of art criticism and aesthetics. Forms are rooted in the world since they indicate a reorganization of energies, actions, desires, perspectives, and materials. They are part of the continuum subject-nature, since they are rooted in the subject's biological rhythms and the larger rhythms of nature. Dewey writes: "Underneath the rhythm of every art and of every work of art there lies, as a substratum in the depths of the subconsciousness, the basic pattern of the relations of the live creature to his environment" (2008a: 155).

Tracing the development of art out of normal, everyday experience, for Dewey, signifies that one will be in a position to illuminate the real roots of the aesthetic. Everything goes back to the organism that strives to cope with an indifferent and partly even hostile environment. The organism will eventually be capable of overcoming those factors of opposition and conflict; that is, after having dealt with tensions and resistances, it achieves temporary balance and harmony. Tension results in equilibrium. When forces and materials have been brought together in a meaningful whole and existing conditions examined for unrealized possibilities, the subject will have the feeling of living in a fuller and wider world. On Dewey's account, ordinary experience teaches us that (temporary) equilibrium is form: "There is in nature, even below the level of life, something more than mere flux and change. Form is arrived at whenever a stable, though moving, equilibrium is reached" (2008a: 20). However, at the same time one has to see that this equilibrium is not the final stage, since it "brings with it potency of new adjustments to be made through struggle" (2008a: 23). Although Dewey calls attention to this necessity of new adjustments, new techniques, and new forms of problem-solving, he also maintains that "through the phases of perturbation and conflict, there abides the deep-seated memory of an underlying harmony, the sense of which haunts life like the sense of being founded on a rock" (2008a: 23). Contending that the roots of the aesthetic can be found in everyday experience, Dewey always returns to this notion of "underlying harmony" and to the idea that equilibrium is form (or vice versa). As we will see, this would have a strong impact on his understanding of the work of art, and, above all, it would deprive him of the possibility of grasping the radical nature of modern art and literature. Modern artworks, whether in painting, music, or literature, show the limitations and insufficiencies of the Deweyan suggestions that equilibrium is form and that forms, like everything else, go back to the rhythms of the interactions between the live creature and its environment.

Regarding the form-content dialectics of the work of art, Dewey clearly reduces the significance of form (which should also be regarded as a gesture directed against the formalism of the New Critics and some analytic philosophers). This becomes obvious, for instance, in the chapter "The Common Substance of the Arts" in *Art as Experience*. Dewey goes very far when he avers: "Apart from some special interest, every product of art is matter and matter only, so that the contrast is not between matter and form but between matter relatively unformed and matter adequately formed" (2008a: 195). Further on he formulates even more pointedly: "'Stuff' is everything, and form a name for certain aspects of the matter when attention goes primarily to these aspects" (2008a: 195). Throughout *Art as Experience*, Dewey places a stress on the notions of wholeness, organicity, union, coherence, balance, and harmony. In a manner that reminds one of idealist aesthetics, he maintains: "The *form* of the whole is therefore present in every member" (2008a: 62). Moreover, he advances the idea that "mutual adaptation of parts to one another in constituting a whole is the relation which, formally speaking, characterizes a work of art" (2008a: 140). It is of the utmost importance to understand that Dewey does not see the necessity of historicizing his concept of aesthetic form. Rather, it is one of his primary concerns to make clear that one should not regard aesthetic form as a transcendent term, that is, as something that descends "from without": "Is 'beauty' another name for form descending from without, as a transcendent essence, upon material, or is it a name for the esthetic quality that appears whenever *material is formed* in a way that renders it adequately expressive?" (2008a: 112).

A discussion of the Deweyan conception of form offers one the possibility of bringing together his critique of traditional epistemology in *The Quest for Certainty* with his analysis of the function of art in *Art as Experience*. Dewey's antidualism calls attention to how problematic it is to identify form with the rational and intelligible and matter with the irrational, unpredictable, and contingent. His anti-Platonism, and anti-Kantianism, radically critiques this metaphysical understanding of the form-content dialectics. There is no room in Dewey's thought for the notion that form has a dignity and necessity that matter or content lacks. In the chapter "Substance and Form," he contends:

> Moreover, since things are rendered knowable by these forms, it was concluded that form is the rational, the intelligible, element in the objects and events of the world. Then it was set over against "matter," the latter being the irrational, the inherently chaotic and fluctuating, stuff upon which form was impressed. It was as eternal as the latter was shifting. This metaphysical distinction of matter and form was embodied in the philosophy that ruled European thought for centuries. Because of this fact it still affects the esthetic philosophy of form in relation to matter. It is the source of the bias in favor of their separation, especially when that takes the shape of assuming that form has a dignity and stability lacking to matter. (2008a: 120–1)

Dewey's reconstruction of aesthetic theory rethinks aesthetic experience as a special kind of consummatory experience and art as the enrichment of immediate experience. This endeavor highlights the aesthetic aspects of one's daily life and, as we have seen, proposes that our thinking about aesthetics inevitably reflects continuities connecting the live creature and its environment. According to Dewey, the interactions of the live creature with its world ought to play a central role if one intends fully to grasp the meaning of the union of form and matter: "Since the ultimate cause of the union of form and matter in experience is the intimate relation of undergoing and doing in interaction of a live creature with the world of nature and man, the theories, which separate matter and form, have their ultimate source in neglect of this relation" (2008a: 137). For our purposes, it should be noted that after Romanticism and the radical formal and narratological experiments of modernism Dewey's conception of form seems problematic (to say the least).[13] I do not claim that he is a traditionalist as regards aesthetic questions. Dewey is very fond of the idea of artistic experiment (and thus of formal innovations leading to new experiences): "Only because the artist operates experimentally does he open new fields of experience and disclose new aspects and qualities in familiar scenes and objects" (2008a: 149). Furthermore, he repeatedly underscores the significance of tension and resistance for the work of art; without these there would be no development and no genuine fulfillment: "Without internal tension there would be a fluid rush to a straightaway mark; there would be nothing that could be called development and fulfillment. The existence of resistance defines the place of intelligence in the production of an object of fine art" (2008a: 143).

From today's perspective, Dewey's aesthetics appears decidedly more thought-provoking than two texts that dominated discussions at the beginning of the twentieth century: Clive Bell's manifesto *Art* (1914) and Roger Fry's collection of essays, *Vision and Design* (1920). According to Bell, there is a distinctive emotion or affect that artworks evoke. The recipients' emotions, as he maintains, are provoked by "one quality without which a work of art cannot exist," and this he terms "significant form" (1958: 17). In contrast to Dewey's pragmatist aesthetics, Bell's aestheticism establishes a strict separation between the sphere of (significant) form and the content of artworks since the latter might establish a connection between the work and ordinary existence. As Paul Guyer points out: "Corresponding to his separation of aesthetic emotion from all ordinary human emotions, Bell separates the object of aesthetic emotion, significant form, from all of the content of works of art that might suggest or arouse ordinary human emotions" (2014b: 117). Distinguishing between aesthetic emotion and ordinary emotions, Bell is willing to concede that there is one kind of extraordinary human emotions that is comparable to aesthetic emotions, namely, religious emotions. Hence, his aestheticism establishes an intimate connection between aesthetic emotion and religious emotion, and this parallel in turn demonstrates that his desire for form is metaphysical insofar as it is linked to the desire to discover the ultimate nature of reality or the really real.[14]

Dewey's aesthetic thought indirectly warns against this metaphysical attempt to establish a link between form and the really real. At the same time, however, one has to see that his insistence upon the unity of form and content and his suggestion that aesthetic experience must attain unity and integration do not leave room for the idea that the modern hypostatization of form urges one to rethink the notions of unity, wholeness, harmony, and organicity.[15] Even if Dewey considers the distinction between form and matter a metaphysical gesture, it is problematic that he, in full modernism, criticizes art that is radically autonomous, cut off from the world of social practices and physical objects; that is, art that "has an occult source and esoteric character" (Dewey 2008b: 291). One of the most important passages concerning Dewey's understanding of form can be found near the end of *Experience and Nature*, where he avers: "'Forms' are not the peculiar property or creation of the esthetic and artistic; they are characters in virtue of which anything meets the requirements of an enjoyable perception. 'Art' does not create the forms; it is their selection and organization in such ways as to enhance, prolong and purify the perceptual experience" (2008b: 292).

Do Dewey's suggestions that forms "are not the peculiar property or creation of the esthetic and artistic" and that art "does not create the forms" offer the possibility of approaching the complexity of modernism from Flaubert to Joyce and Picasso or from aestheticism to the historical avant-garde (surrealism, dadaism, futurism, and constructivism)? Or is modern art and literature the limit, as it were, of Dewey's naturalist aesthetics? In what is still the most thought-provoking discussion of the Deweyan conception of form, Thomas M. Alexander directs attention to its complexity. According to Alexander, form in Dewey is historical and dynamic. Individualizing rather than universalizing experience, form can be regarded as the dynamic process of shaping experience with the ultimate goal of creating a consummatory whole. Aesthetic form in Dewey, if one follows Alexander, "by its nature is tensive, developmental, temporal, and includes within it the elements of activity, involvement, and growth" (1987: 193). Moreover, form "is the energetic process of organizing the material of experience into a funded, meaningful, consummatory event which does not transcend life but fully actualizes it" (1987: 234).[16] Both Alexander and Richard Shusterman argue that it would be too reductionist to claim that Dewey's aesthetics, in an almost idealist manner, concentrates on the notions of wholeness, organic unity, coherence, and harmony. In Shusterman's opinion, Dewey "repeatedly insists that the unity of aesthetic experience is not a closed and permanent haven in which we can rest at length in satisfied contemplation. It is rather a moving, fragile, and vanishing event, briefly savored in an experiential flux rife with energies of tension and disorder which it momentarily masters" (2000: 32).[17]

From what I have said so far it should be clear that I think that Alexander and Shusterman tend to ignore the limitations of Dewey's aesthetic theory in the confrontation with modern art and literature. When one considers Dewey's idea that form characterizes every experience that is *an* experience together with Alexander's suggestion that form "doesn't illuminate itself" (1987: 235), then the problematic nature of Dewey's aesthetics becomes obvious. For it is precisely in modern art and literature that aesthetic form does illuminate itself. Creative form-giving is a kind of poetic agency that is central to modernism. From Flaubert's obsession with style and desire to write "un livre sur rien" to Joyce's experiments with form in *Ulysses* (1921) and Faulkner's formal and narratological experiments in *The Sound and the Fury* (1929), *As I Lay Dying* (1930*), and Absalom, Absalom!* (1936), the significance of form makes it difficult to analyze and understand these texts within a Deweyan aesthetic framework. When Dewey maintains that the "general conditions of esthetic form [...] are objective in the sense of belonging to the world of physical materials and energies" (2008a: 151), he ignores that in aesthetic modernism the conditions of form are neither general nor objective. Rather, form is radically subjective and idiosyncratic; that is, forms do not have their origin in the physical world or reflect the rhythmic pattern in experience that grows out of the interaction of the live creature and its environment, but they increasingly appear as the last possibility of refuge, as it were, for the modern subject threatened by standardization, alienation, and reification. One certainly does not have to be a Marxist to appreciate how valuable Adorno's elucidation of form in the modern artwork is. In his posthumously published *Ästhetische Theorie* (1970), he pointedly formulates: "The concept of form marks out art's sharp antithesis to an empirical world in which art's right to exist is uncertain. Art has precisely the same chance of survival as does form, no better" (1997: 141).[18]

In this context, one ought to see that Dewey's aesthetics also does not offer the possibility of fully appreciating the iconoclastic gesture of the historical avant-garde. Both Dewey and, for instance, the surrealists around André Breton strive to abolish the strict separation between art and everyday life ("pratiquer la poésie!"). However, while Dewey, although he also calls attention to the meaning of tension and resistance, holds on to the notion of the organic work of art, the members of the historical avant-garde radically reject the last remnants of idealist aesthetics and hence clearly favor the fragmented and nonorganic artwork. The surrealist montage, a novel or "récit" like Breton's *Nadja* (1928), or the iconoclastic gesture dominating dadaist performances—all these urge one to rethink the significance of form for a naturalist aesthetics. In *Theorie der Avantgarde* (1974), Peter Bürger convincingly argues for the critical role the nonorganic artwork plays for the historical avant-garde. He expands on the difference between the organic and the nonorganic artwork thus (his understanding of this difference is strongly influenced by Walter Benjamin's concept of allegory):

> The organic work intends the impression of wholeness. To the extent its individual elements have significance only as they relate to the whole, they always point to the work as a whole as they are perceived individually. In the avant-gardiste work, on the other hand, the individual elements have a much higher degree of autonomy and can therefore also be read and interpreted individually or in groups without its [sic] being necessary to grasp the work as a whole. In the case of the avant-gardiste work, it is possible only to a limited extent to speak of the work as a whole as the perfect embodiment of the totality of possible meaning. (1984: 72–3)[19]

Presumably, my critique of Dewey's notion of art as experience will seem problematic, or pointless, to most pragmatist or naturalist aestheticians, since this critique can only be developed from a production-aesthetic point of view. However, I wish to submit that the shortcomings and inadequacies of a Deweyan aesthetic theory in the confrontation with aestheticism, the radical formal and narratological innovations of, for instance, Flaubert, Woolf, Gide, Joyce, and Faulkner, and the attack on the organic artwork by the historical avant-garde can only be dealt with if one is willing to consider the potential usefulness of this production-aesthetic position within a pragmatist framework. I will further expand on this in the next part of this chapter.

While Dewey saw the necessity of discussing the question of form within his pragmatist framework, and while Adorno demonstrated how especially a materialist aesthetics might profit from the attempt to examine the meaning of form, Richard Rorty has no use for the notion of aesthetic form. The latter's contention is that pragmatist literary critics should concentrate on highlighting the moral task of the novel and that this does not necessitate an analysis of aesthetic form. Rorty proposes that one must not regard the aesthetic as a "matter of form and language," but rather as being governed by "content and life." In *Contingency, Irony, and Solidarity*, he puts this as follows:

> This idea that somehow language can be separated from authors, that literary technique is a godlike power operating independently of mortal contingencies, and in particular from the author's contingent notion of what goodness is, is the root of "aestheticism" in the bad sense of the term, the sense in which the aesthetic is a matter of form and language rather than of content and life. (1989: 166–7)

Why does Rorty speak of "the disastrous Kantian distinction between form and content" (1989: 168n)? In his opinion, most literary and cultural critics refuse to ignore the question of form. He holds that this refusal confirms that professional literary critics and scholars, using abstract categories such as form and narrative technique, too often assume that their task has something to do with knowledge. By contrast, Rorty's notion of a literary or poeticized culture stands for the pragmatist move against theory and toward narrative. Literary and aesthetic theory that insists that literary criticism and aesthetics are forms of knowledge that can elucidate the real structure and meaning of a text or an artwork belongs to an old way of speaking. Theorists claim that one has to step back from the literary text and analyze it by means of conceptual tools, and this would eventually allow one to penetrate the text's depth. The direction of this process is vertical (like that of the metaphysician's perspective).

Novels, offering detailed descriptions of forms of cruelty, pain, and humiliation and thereby increasing our sensitivity and responsiveness to the needs of others, ought to be regarded as important contributions to moral progress. This cannot be the place to offer a detailed discussion of Rorty's understanding of the moral task of the novel, but for our purposes it is crucial to see that his discussions of, for instance, Orwell, Nabokov, Proust, and Dickens, show that his pragmatist version of literary criticism has no use for the traditional moral-aesthetic distinction.[20] An insistence upon this distinction, as Rorty emphasizes, blurs the contrast he seeks to accentuate between the desire for private perfection and autonomy on the one hand and the relevance to cruelty on the other. One of the primary consequences of his critique of the moral-aesthetic dichotomy is his suggestion that we do not need theoretical abstraction, formalist analysis, or firm and transhistorical moral principles, but as malleable human beings we need storytelling. Rorty speaks of "sentimental education" (1998b: 181) in this context. Telling a "long, sad, sentimental story" (1998b: 185), according to him, is more useful than the search for the certainty, reliability, immutability, and purity of what would be more than another human creation or invention.

What our discussion so far has shown is that both Dewey and Rorty tell their antifoundationalist and antirepresentationalist stories of progress and emancipation without considering the modern notion of aesthetic form. Can pragmatism as humanism and anti-authoritarianism really afford to ignore the work of aesthetic form?

3.3 Pragmatist Humanism, Form, and Poetic Agency

The primary task of a pragmatist humanism is to elucidate the significance of poetic agency. The latter term urges one to see how intimately connected intelligent action and poetic imagination are. Poetic agency brings together the notion of embodied, interested, and purposeful human agency with the Romantic stress on the power of the imagination. It refers to humans' creativity of action, imaginative redescriptions, inventions of new vocabularies and metaphors, and unpredictable forms of self-creation. This term thus denotes creative forms of making, of human practice, or constellations of contingent creative acts, which confirm humanity's permanent desire for creative action and linguistic novelty. Form-giving is poetic agency; it is an integral part of the antirepresentationalist and antifoundationalist story of progress and emancipation. For pragmatists, poetic agency draws attention to the idea that humans' only responsibility is to their fellow human beings in the world of practice. Furthermore, the term illustrates the implications of the idea that humans, realizing that there is no outside authority (God, Truth, or Reality) to which they can appeal, come to regard the world of experience, in which they creatively and imaginatively act to solve problems and achieve purposes, as the only one they have. In other words, poetic agency stresses human finitude; that is, it is directed against the idea that there is something that is not itself a human creation but judges those human creations from an elevated and timeless standpoint. Poetic agency continues Nietzsche's revolt against Platonism, against the appearance-reality distinction, and against the notion of truth as neither a product of imaginative redescription nor of contingent circumstance.

Form-giving ought to be seen as central to the combination of creative action and poetic imagination that connects Romanticism and aesthetic modernism, and at the same time aesthetic form-giving is of primary importance as far as the pragmatist and anti-authoritarian story of progress is concerned.[21] What this boils down to is that poetic agency adds an important new aspect to pragmatism's story of progress by showing that the contingency of social practices has to include the contingency of form-giving. In this context the following question is of the utmost importance: Is it sufficient for a pragmatist aesthetics to state that forms ought to be seen as the creation of finite human creatures in response to finite human needs?

As a pragmatist, Dewey refuses to consign the act of form-giving to the aesthetic realm. Form-giving, in his opinion, dominates human subjects' daily attempts to cope with their environment. As we have seen, Dewey's thought is clearly directed against the artificiality of aesthetic form. Moreover, for him form too often is linked to the traditional aesthetic-practical dichotomy that defines art by its contemplative noninstrumentality. Within the framework of Dewey's anti-Kantianism, this notion of contemplative noninstrumentality of course appears as his *bête noire*. The problem with his naturalist aesthetics is that its usefulness is severely limited when it comes to modern art and literature. There are two reasons for this. First, Dewey offers a version of pragmatist humanism that illuminates the meaning of poetic agency, but ignores the production-aesthetic point of view. Second, he is so focused on warning against the attempt to turn form into a transcendental term that he does not see the necessity of historicizing the concept of form. In modernism, form can no longer be regarded as the rational, eternal, and necessary, but it has to be seen as the contingent, idiosyncratic, and fragmented. Dewey's aesthetics does not offer the possibility of analyzing these idiosyncratic contingencies of form.

In the chapter "Experience, Nature, and Art" in *Experience and Nature*, Dewey summarizes his aesthetic position as follows: "There are substantially but two alternatives. Either art is a continuation, by means of intelligent selection and arrangement, of natural tendencies of natural events; or art is a peculiar addition to nature springing from something dwelling exclusively within the breast of man, whatever name be given the latter" (2008b: 291). This is a stark dichotomy for an antidualist. When art appears as "a peculiar addition to nature" and when it "has nothing to do with other activities and products," as Dewey argues, it has "an esoteric character" (2008b: 291). Modernism, from Mallarmé's hermetic symbolism to Kafka's angst-ridden allegories and Picasso's cubist paintings, indeed often seems esoteric. However, simply stating this esoteric character is insufficient. The idea of art as experience here has to be supplemented by a production-aesthetic perspective, which would analyze how form, history, and the artist's subjectivity hang together and which would thus explain how the form-giving process reflects social developments. One can only approach these artworks if one seeks to explain why the artist has chosen such an idiosyncratic form for their text, painting, or musical composition. How does an artist work with the artistic material that is available to them? Why do they privilege one material over all others? Do they advance the idea that in their society there can be only one artistic material that is historically most advanced and that the material's transformation coincides with that of society? In what way does the artist condemn art that uses regressive materials? Do they hold on to the category of the work, or do they challenge the modern principle of aesthetic purity? It is also interesting to ask how the artist establishes a link between their chosen form and society (or refuses to do so). A production-aesthetic perspective will offer the possibility of answering these questions. These questions, admittedly, sound Adornian. This is due to the fact that I think that Adorno has theorized the social nature of aesthetic form as radically as no one else in the twentieth century (see Chapter 5).

Without using the production-aesthetic perspective, one most presumably will never get further than calling those radically innovative works of art esoteric, abstract, or occult. It is crucial to grasp that I do not claim that Dewey's naturalist aesthetics centering on the idea of art as experience was hopelessly obsolete in the 1930s and is of only nostalgic value from today's perspective. *Art as Experience* served an important function as a critique of versions of formalism when it was published in 1934, and it is still thought-provoking today (particularly in view of the discussions surrounding the notion of a new formalism or new aestheticism).[22] However, I wish to submit that when Dewey critiques the artificiality and abstraction of form, his naturalist framework does not allow him to understand that it is precisely this artificiality and nonorganicity of form that became increasingly prominent in modernism and that his aesthetics would therefore profit from adding a production-aesthetic perspective.

In her discussion of the Coleridgean notion of "forma efformans," Angela Leighton underlines the agency of form: "The idea of '*forma efformans*' (forming form) is a curious investment of activity in the thing. Form by itself has to be modified by a verb, as if to stop it hardening into a mere object. Form is not a body but an agent. It forms" (2007: 7). Moreover, as she contends, form in Coleridge, like the imagination, "is a shaping activity rather than a visual shape, and this leads to the curious self-involvement of what it does. It acts on itself, sees itself, is its own 'agency'" (2007: 7). According to the Marxist philosopher Georg Lukács, it is precisely this Romantic emphasis on form's agency that had a disastrous impact on modern literature and art. Throughout his long career as an aesthetician, from *Die Seele und die Formen* (1911, *Soul and Form*) and *Die Theorie des Romans* (1920, *Theory of the Novel*) to his late *Die Eigenart des Ästhetischen* (1963), Lukács was preoccupied with the idea of aesthetic form. Notoriously enough, as a materialist theorist, he condemned the naturalists and modernists and praised the virtues of critical realists like Balzac and Tolstoy and of contemporary social realists. From a pragmatist perspective, Lukács's texts, particularly in his middle period, are governed by the appearance-reality distinction and by the desire to discover the real essence of reality and of the subject. Moreover, they are dominated by the assumption of an immanent meaning to human existence and by the idea that a truthful reflection of reality is possible. While realist literature "had always assumed the unity of the world it described and seen it as a living whole inseparable from man himself," in modernism, as Lukács contends, "the artist's world disintegrates into a multiplicity of partial worlds" (2006: 39). It becomes obvious that he radically rejects a theoretical framework, and a way of speaking, which puts an emphasis on contingency, fragmentation, particularity, plurality, and irony or ironic juxtapositions.[23]

In Lukács's account, aesthetic form must never achieve autonomy. He holds that realism is incompatible with the idea that form would be more than a specific mode of the reflection of reality. Form that is divorced from any connection with life only leads to the worst extremes of modernist subjectivism. A reduced significance of form, an emphasis on the organic wholeness of the artwork, and the attempt to explain that the unity of the world that is depicted in the work of art ought to be regarded as a living whole that is inseparable from the human subject—these are important parallels between Lukács's materialist aesthetics and Dewey's pragmatist aesthetics. These parallels ought to make us think. The ultimate irony would be that a pragmatist aesthetics, when discussing modern art and literature, repeats some of the misjudgments of a materialist aesthetics governed by the idea of a "Widerspiegelungstheorie" (reflection theory).

3.4 Conclusion

Who needs aesthetic theory? Rorty obviously does not. Underscoring his "scepticism about 'aesthetics' as a field of inquiry," he makes clear that he is "not sure that we need an aesthetic theory, or an aesthetic programme, at all. I doubt that there is much to be said about what unites painting, literature, music, sex and birdwatching while distinguishing all these from science, morals, politics, philosophy and religion" (2001: 156). Faithful to his anti-Kantianism, Rorty, like Dewey, warns against the attempt to split culture up into three isolated spheres. This is problematic insofar as Rorty's version of pragmatist humanism particularly relies on the notion of poetic agency. Aesthetic theory, as I have suggested, can explain the significance of poetic agency and the role of form-giving for a pragmatist humanism. This also signifies that aesthetic theory adds to the pragmatist's understanding of the development from finding to making and to his or her endeavor to grasp the role of poetic agency and form-giving for the anti-authoritarian story of progress and emancipation.

Theory here should not be understood as a definition of necessary and sufficient conditions, or as defining rules and universal, necessary, and eternal principles in an abstract manner.[24] I think that pragmatist humanists could use aesthetic theory pragmatically; that is, by recognizing that pragmatist aesthetics has certain limitations, they could become interested in attempts at mediation with other approaches. An interest in aesthetics could show them that their toolbox needs additional tools. A more complex notion of aesthetic form, as I have argued, would offer them new possibilities of approaching modern and avant-garde art and of grasping the significance of poetic agency. As we will see in Chapter 5, Adorno's *Ästhetische Theorie*, a fragmented, dissonant, unfinished, and highly idiosyncratic text, is extremely useful and stimulating for pragmatist aestheticians who are willing to accentuate that their position between analytic aesthetics and continental aesthetics offers them fascinating possibilities of shaping twenty-first-century aesthetics. In my opinion, establishing a dialogue with Adorno's aesthetic theory is a decidedly more promising endeavor that striving to make Rorty's old-fashioned ethical literary criticism look attractive.

By presenting themselves as unwilling to consign aesthetic theory, or the practice of aesthetic theory, to the dustbin of history, pragmatist aestheticians would show that they appreciate that the new developments in late-twentieth- and twenty-first-century art necessitate a constant reorganizing and refunctioning of their tools. One of the most stimulating ways of confronting this task is by establishing dialogues with other versions of aesthetics. Pragmatist aesthetics is insufficient, but it is insufficient in a thought-provoking manner. Consequently, pragmatist humanists should no longer associate the term aesthetic theory with necessity, sufficiency, certainty, abstraction, and structure, but should rather understand it as a stimulus to constantly redefine their tasks and rethink their approaches and criteria by learning from other ways of speaking about art and literature.

By criticizing a priori philosophies and their ideal of timeless pure thought, as well as their theory-practice dichotomy, pragmatists argue that there are no nonhuman truths and forms of authority, no eternal moral principles, and no need for the subject's answerability to the world. In a detranscendentalized and postmetaphysical culture the world would no longer be a conversation partner, and the subject, by creatively and imaginatively acting to solve problems and achieve purposes, would appear as a maker. Faithful to the Nietzschean suggestion that only we have created the world that concerns us as human beings, pragmatist humanists contend that once we have set God and the various God-substitutes aside, we can present ourselves as the makers of our truths, principles, laws, and forms. Moreover, the immanence of pragmatist humanism also means that the subject as maker, refusing to lose himself or herself in theoretical abstraction, not only calls attention to the richness of the real world and its concrete facts, he or she also shows that this real world is incomplete, malleable, and hence waiting or asking for interpretation or other forms of human creativity and imagination (such as cooperating with each other for the common good). What this boils down to is that pragmatist humanism offers one the possibility of regarding form-giving as a central human activity, as creative action that radically questions the necessity of obeying a nonhuman authority. Developing a pragmatist aesthetics that offers a more nuanced and multilayered understanding of form than Dewey and Rorty is still a desideratum. The relation between pragmatism and aesthetic form is undoubtedly a topic that will preoccupy us in the future.

4

"... and the Practice Has to Speak for Itself": Wittgenstein, Pragmatism, and Anti-Authoritarianism

Was Wittgenstein a pragmatist? There are many interesting parallels between the later Wittgenstein and the American pragmatists. Both argue against the construction of philosophical theories; that is, both emphasize social practice and action. Both are antiessentialists and historicist nominalists. Moreover, both critique the idea that language mirrors the world and maintain that language's relation to reality is not one of correspondence. This also signifies that Wittgenstein and the pragmatists help one grasp the far-reaching implications of the suggestion that our conceptualization of the world is made and not found and that the only system or structure in reality is that which we impose on it. By arguing that our attitudes and beliefs are not grounded in or justified by how the world is, the later Wittgenstein's critique of traditional forms of foundationalism goes as far as that of William James and John Dewey. It is crucial to appreciate that Wittgenstein and the pragmatists also offer a critique of the gesture of a convergence to the antecedently real or true and clearly prefer the notion of proliferation (of new language games, forms of life, vocabularies, or perspectives).

For our purposes, it is important to see that the thought of the later Wittgenstein and the pragmatists is directed against the human answerability to something nonhuman. It criticizes the idea that there is a nonhuman authority whose commands human beings have to obey and whose constraints they have to confront. When Wittgenstein contends that our language games and grammatical classifications are not accountable or answerable to the world, as he does in *Philosophical Investigations* (1953) and *On Certainty* (1969), he prepares the ground for Richard Rorty's radical anti-authoritarianism. As two critics of metaphysics, Wittgenstein and Rorty illuminate the consequences of the modern development from finding to making and contribute important chapters to the humanist and antirepresentationalist story of praxis and emancipation. According to Robert Brandom, "we should learn to understand cognitive assessments in terms of relations among humans, without needing to appeal to any sort of authority apart from that manifested in social practices" (2000a: xii). Wittgenstein and the pragmatists teach the lesson that the only authority we should appeal to is that manifested in social practices and, moreover, that philosophy's task is to make human practices explicit (or describe them) instead of legitimizing them by reference to something beyond them. On Rorty's account, there "is no way for human beings to get beyond their own practices except by dreaming up better practices, and no way to judge these new practices better except by reference to their various advantages for various human purposes" (1998b: 127–8). In "Representation, Social Practice, and Truth," Rorty underscores that the "question of whether there is anything for philosophers to appeal to save the way *we* live now, what *we* do now, how *we* talk now—anything beyond *our* own little moment of world-history—is the decisive issue between representationalist and social-practise philosophers of language" (1991b: 158).

In this chapter, I will seek to answer the question of how a discussion of the relation between the later Wittgenstein and the pragmatists can illuminate the meaning of humanism as anti-authoritarianism. In other words, how does the refusal to obey a nonhuman authority, common to Wittgenstein and the pragmatists, help one grasp the significance of humanism? As we have seen in this study, humanists maintain that humans are engaged in causal interaction with nature and that the relation world-language is one of causality, not justification. Justification is a matter of our interactions with our fellow human beings. Wittgenstein and the pragmatists, I submit, help one reject the image of humans as being subject to a judgment other than that of a consensus of other human beings. Proponents of the new image are perfectly satisfied with the idea that the reference to the practices of humans in particular historical circumstances is the only justification one ever needs, and they propose that references to our essential humanity or the demands of rationality are only hindrances to the establishment of a humanist culture. While we will concentrate on the similarities between Wittgenstein and the pragmatists, one ought to note that there are also important differences.[1] I will focus on two crucial differences. First, Wittgenstein, although he is critical of traditional foundationalism, offers a particular form of foundationalism. Second, he does not reject the notion of certainty. Like the pragmatists, Wittgenstein critiques any form of transcendent certainty. However, in contrast to the pragmatists, he elucidates the significance of the quest for what could be termed human certainty.

4.1 Wittgenstein's *On Certainty*

The austerity and purity of Wittgenstein's *Tractatus Logico-Philosophicus* (1922) are notorious. This early text concentrated on the nature of logic and logical form and advanced the idea that language had an underlying structure.[2] While the early Wittgenstein conceived of language as logic, as a system of ideal rules or calculi, and submitted a text that was abstract, dogmatic, and technical (and partly mystical), the later Wittgenstein rejected the idea that language had a unitary nature or single essence that one could specify by illuminating its logical structure. His posthumously published *Philosophical Investigations* made its readers understand that it might be interesting to regard language as a set of social practices; that is, as a collection of different practices and vocabularies (as tools), each with its own logic. In the *Investigations*, the author stresses that he does not want to develop a new theory or replace one philosophical account with a better one. His aim is neither theory construction nor explanation. Wittgenstein underscores that "we may not advance any kind of theory" and that "all *explanation* must disappear, and description alone must take its place" (2009: sec. 109). Philosophy, as he maintains, "neither explains nor deduces anything" (2009: sec. 126). What exactly does Wittgenstein's new sort of investigation seek to achieve? It offers an examination of our life with language, an analysis of our employment of concepts and expressions, and a detailed study of humans' actual use of words in the context of their everyday lives and historical situations.[3] While one can say that the early Wittgenstein, together with Frege and Russell, invented analytic philosophy, the later Wittgenstein prepared the ground for what would later be termed ordinary language philosophy.

In the *Investigations*, the later Wittgenstein offers a grammatical investigation. For him, grammar does not refer to an abstract system of signs that governs the construction of sentences or to the classification of words according to their form. Rather, it relates to the actual use of words in practical situations. It illuminates the actual workings of language, and this also implies the endeavor to explain how language can mislead us through false analogies and surface similarities. Marie McGinn writes about Wittgenstein's method:

> Our problems are, Wittgenstein believes, conceptual ones, and the method we need is the method of grammatical investigation: a careful attention to our actual uses of words. It is by attending to the application of expressions—to what lies open to view in our use of language—that we will overcome our sense of philosophical perplexity concerning the phenomena that puzzle us, and achieve the understanding we seek. (2013: 22)

In the *Investigations*, Wittgenstein detranscendentalizes philosophy by focusing on how humans operate with words, how they use them in certain particular situations, and by describing what "lies open to view" (2009: sec. 126). He makes unequivocally clear that nothing is hidden, that there is no need for discovery, and that theory construction will only lead to further puzzlement. What we need, instead, is simply "an overview of the use of our words" (2009: sec. 122).

Wittgenstein wants us to radically change the way we see and approach philosophical questions and our way of investigating these questions. He tries to release us from a style of thought that is associated with theoretical contemplation, the idea of the mind apart, the act of finding immutable foundations, and the action of discovery. Wittgenstein continues this radical project in his final work, *Über Gewißheit* (*On Certainty*), written shortly before this death. This book takes as its starting point G. E. Moore's defense of common-sense realism in "A Defence of Common Sense" (1925) and "Proof of an External World" (1939).[4] In his discussion of Moore's ideas, Wittgenstein constantly returns to the idea of practice. In one section he makes clear that he is not willing to present himself as a pragmatist (1972: sec. 422), in spite of his interest in William James's pragmatist psychology and understanding of religion, but his last book is nonetheless useful for the attempt to highlight the parallels between his later thought and pragmatism. Furthermore, a discussion of *On Certainty* helps one grasp the meaning of humanism as anti-authoritarianism.

The later Wittgenstein's detranscendentalized and naturalized conception of philosophy, as a form of therapy, description, and recontextualization, puts an emphasis on social and institutional practices, cultural and historical contexts, and the contingent rules of a linguistic community. Furthermore, his critique of metaphysics and theoretical abstraction—and this also means his critique of his former Tractarian self and the crystalline purity of his first book—eventually leads to a combination of antirepresentationalism, antiessentialism, nominalism, and practice-orientation that comes close to the notion of a pragmatist humanism as I developed it in *Pragmatism and Poetic Agency: The Persistence of*

Humanism.⁵ Undoubtedly, Wittgenstein's critique of metaphysics does not seek to contribute to the artistic refashioning of mankind of which Nietzsche speaks in *Beyond Good and Evil* or to the development of what Rorty would later term a postmetaphysical or poeticized culture in *Contingency, Irony, and Solidarity*, but his detranscendentalized conception of philosophy can be seen as a refusal to accept the notion that there might be a theoretical barrier to an endless sequence of recontextualizations, redescriptions, vocabulary changes, and inventions of new linguistic tools.⁶ When the later Wittgenstein focuses on what human beings do with language and when he develops a social perspective that sees the language-using subject as part of a linguistic and cultural community, one might be inclined to state that this form of anthropocentrism (and ethnocentrism) too easily degenerates into cognitive relativism, or one might instead interpret his approach as a form of humanism as anti-authoritarianism.

In *On Certainty*, Wittgenstein questions a traditional understanding of the foundations of knowledge and critiques the traditional picture of basic beliefs. He holds that the foundations of our ordinary knowledge and daily life are only relatively foundational, and he moreover argues that our basic beliefs are not indubitable or self-justified propositions but that they rather start in the nonintellectual and nonconceptual realms of instinct and action. In other words, at the origin of knowledge is not thought or theoretical contemplation but the deed. According to Wittgenstein, what one finds at the basis of knowledge is not knowledge but nonintellectual, pragmatic certainties and nonpropositional and nonepistemic beliefs. As Danièle Moyal-Sharrock points out in this context:

> Here, at the origin of our knowledge, there are no such preliminaries as proposition, judgment and inference, but spontaneity, automatism, rule, reflex and instinct. Here, we do not go from the proposition to the deed, but vice versa: from a natural, nonreflective grasp to a sophisticated, reflective and hesitating pondering. From doing to thinking. (2004: 10)⁷

According to Wittgenstein, one should refrain from looking for an external justification or grounding for our practices. The only justification is in the plurality of our practices themselves: "Not only rules, but also examples are needed for establishing a practice. Our rules leave loop-holes open, and the practice has to speak for itself" (1972: sec. 139). This idea that "the practice has to speak for itself" is central to the thought of the later Wittgenstein, and the development of Wittgenstein's thought becomes clearer when one considers that the first sentence in his *Tagebücher 1914–16* is "Die Logik muß für sich selber sorgen [Logic must take care of itself]" (1979: 89). The philosophical notion of foundation becomes a background of certainties that are indubitable in practice and action, but at the same time potentially revisable or temporary, historical and cultural, since they are part of our form of life (and thus our world-picture ["Weltbild"]). By radically rejecting the quest for transcendental certainty, Wittgenstein proposes the notion of a human or life certainty. Combining anti-Cartesianism and anti-Platonism, he asserts that these certainties cannot be doubted since we do not begin with doubt (*pace* Descartes), and at the same time they are not transhistorical and immutable, a form of nonhuman authority. These certainties do not form a theoretical but a practical background; that is, our foundational certainty is a practical certainty. Wittgenstein is fully aware that for most people, particularly most philosophers, it is difficult to accept "the groundlessness of our believing" (1972: sec. 166) and the idea that the language-game "is not based on grounds. [...]/ It is there—like our life" (1972: sec. 559). But he thinks that if one appreciates that "justification comes to an end" (1972: sec. 192)—and that this end is our contingent and historical plurality of practices, our social and institutional practices creating meaning—then this will be a decisive step forward. In section 204 in *On Certainty*, Wittgenstein summarizes his argument as follows: "Giving grounds, however, justifying the evidence, comes to an end; —but the end is not certain propositions' striking us immediately as true, i.e. it is not a kind of *seeing* on our part; it is our *acting*, which lies at the bottom of the language-game."

4.2 Wittgenstein and Pragmatism

Wittgenstein's stress on practice, acting, and the contingency of our practices can be regarded as an important parallel with pragmatism. Moreover, like pragmatism, Wittgenstein's later philosophy sees knowledge and understanding as social phenomena. When he regards knowledge as an aspect of agency, a kind of doing, he helps one to fully appreciate the implications of the modern development from finding to making. To put it differently, Wittgenstein's insistence that knowledge is not at the base of knowledge, that we go from doing to thinking, adds an important aspect to the anti-authoritarian story of progress and emancipation. Furthermore, by arguing that normativity is instituted by social practices and that normative statuses are ultimately social statuses, he paved the way for pragmatists as different as Brandom and Rorty.[8] The later

Wittgenstein's critique of metaphysics resulted in a philosophy of practice that made it decidedly more difficult to accord certain representations a distinctive sort of epistemic privilege since they allegedly followed the imperatives of a nonhuman authority. In this context, it is interesting to see how Brandom comments on how Sellars and Quine's critique of representationalism and the idea of epistemic privilege and authority ought to be seen in connection with the later Wittgenstein's position:

> The Sellarsian and Quinean critiques belong in a box with the later Wittgenstein's investigations of the kind of social practical background against which alone items such as sentences, mental images, and consciously framed intentions can be understood as normatively binding on our activity, in the sense of determining what according to them it would be *correct* to go on to do. (2000b: 159)

For Wittgenstein and the pragmatists, the only authority is in our social practices, the constantly renewed and refined endeavor to exchange justifications of knowledge and to create forms of normativity most of us can live with. This is not a job for theorists, but for pragmatist humanists and Wittgensteinian postmetaphysicians who strive to "bring words back from their metaphysical to their everyday use" (2009: sec. 116), and who, moreover, want to leave the theoretical sphere since "there is no friction" and get back "to the rough ground": "We have got on to slippery ice where there is no friction, and so, in a certain sense, the conditions are ideal; but also, just because of that, we are unable to walk. We want to walk: so we need *friction*. Back to the rough ground!" (2009: sec. 107).

In *Cambridge Pragmatism* (2016), Cheryl Misak offers a stimulating discussion of the relation between Wittgenstein and pragmatism.[9] While there is an important parallel between Wittgenstein and the pragmatists since they place knowledge, mind, and meaning in their relation to human activity, Wittgenstein, as Misak contends, refuses to believe that pragmatism is a method only. Wittgenstein is unwilling to follow James's suggestion in *Pragmatism* since he holds that pragmatism is rather a philosophical theory or an "-ism." Misak proposes that "Wittgenstein himself had much to say that, while not amounting to anything like a grand theoretical system, certainly can be described as a low-profile, pragmatist sort of theory" (2016: 253). At the same time, however, she states that the later Wittgenstein "became, if you like, too extreme a pragmatist" (2016: 254). In spite of her often repeated critique of Rorty, Misak thinks that the latter might have been on the right track when he suggested that the position of the later Wittgenstein was truly radical insofar as he tried to bring philosophy to a close and replace it with therapy. Misak advances the idea that Wittgenstein's view that philosophy does not explain anything, simply puts everything before us, and leaves everything as it is (see Wittgenstein 2009: secs. 124, 126), connects the early Wittgenstein of the *Tractatus* with the later Wittgenstein. At the same time, however, one should see that the later Wittgenstein's idiosyncratic reaction to theory was to a great extent due to the overly ambitious project of the *Tractatus*. After having realized that the rigidity, severity, and purity of his early foundational theory led to an undesired otherworldliness, he reacted in a radical manner by not accepting any kind of theory at all. On the one hand, as Misak contends, the later Wittgenstein does offer a "pragmatist theory." In her opinion,

> the way of looking at things put forward in Wittgenstein's later work might as well be called a world-view. It is not, however, a high metaphysical theory that offers pure definitions, abstracted from what James called the concrete universe surrounding the knower and the known. It is a kind of pragmatist theory that tells us to look at our practices if we want to understand our philosophical concepts. (2016: 279)

On the other hand, Wittgenstein not only critiques metaphysical theory but also does not intend "to adopt pragmatism as a *theory of truth*." Misak writes:

> What Wittgenstein meant in claiming that a world-view was getting in the way of his embracing pragmatism is that he did not want to adopt pragmatism as a *theory of truth* (or, indeed, as a theory of anything else), but only as a method. The *Weltanschaulicher* [sic] character of pragmatism—that is, its being an "-ism" or a positive theory or explanation—disturbed him. (2016: 279)[10]

As a "kind of radical pragmatist," if one follows Misak, Wittgenstein "thought pragmatism too epistemological in orientation" (2016: 285, 279). When one considers Wittgenstein's critique of traditional epistemology together with his refusal to adopt pragmatism as a theory of truth or as a positive theory or explanation, the parallels with Rorty's version of pragmatism are obvious.[11] From *Philosophy and the Mirror of Nature* (1979) and "Keeping Philosophy Pure: An Essay on Wittgenstein" (1976) to "Wittgenstein, Heidegger, and the Reification of Language" (1991) and "Wittgenstein and the Linguistic Turn" (2007), Rorty repeatedly emphasized that he saw the later Wittgenstein, together with Dewey, as one of the masters of debunking traditional philosophical problems. Like Dewey, Wittgenstein was good at helping his fellow philosophers to get rid of traditional dualisms and break down distinctions that only hinder the progress of mankind. For Rorty, who never discussed *On Certainty*, Wittgenstein was clearly a therapist or someone who "sticks to pure satire" (1982: 34). In "Keeping Philosophy Pure," Rorty argues

> that the later Wittgenstein belongs with Dewey as much as the earlier Wittgenstein belongs with Kant—that Dewey's debunking of traditional notions of philosophy, and his attempt to break down the distinctions between art and science, philosophy and science, art and religion, morality and science, are a natural outcome of Wittgenstein's critique of the Cartesian tradition. (1982: 28)[12]

Since Rorty thinks that Wittgenstein belongs to the antifoundationalist and antirepresentationalist tradition, he does not see the necessity of clarifying whether the later Wittgenstein offers a special kind of foundationalism. For many pragmatists and adherents of Rorty's approach, to advance the argument that there is a foundationalist starting point in Wittgenstein would go too far in the direction of turning him into a transcendentalist philosopher. These people do not fully grasp the radically new character of Wittgenstein's understanding of humans' basic beliefs or what has come to be termed "hinge beliefs." I do not intend to discuss those hinges, which are nonpropositional and nonepistemic beliefs and do not reflect how the world really is, in detail. This has already been done. For Wittgenstein, our system of basic beliefs ought to be seen as an enacted know-how; our basic certainties are intuitive, animal, and practical. We do not know those basic beliefs but they enable us to act. Moreover, we do not reflect on them, we do not doubt or seek to verify them, we do not justify them, and we do not derive them (e.g., from our senses)—they are our foundational or primitive certainty. The important point is that those basic or hinge beliefs differ from the rest of our beliefs. Moyal-Sharrock is correct in pointing out how "revolutionary" Wittgenstein's gesture of drawing attention to this difference is. In the following passage, she uses the metaphors that Wittgenstein offers in *On Certainty* (bedrock, scaffolding, and hinges):

> Our certainty is not a flowing river, but the bedrock which allows the river to flow; not a construction, but the scaffolding which makes construction possible; the hinges on which a door can turn. The basis differs from what it supports. The revolutionary nature of Wittgenstein's depiction of our basic beliefs is their *differing* from the rest of our beliefs, and they do so in being nonpropositional and nonepistemic. We do not *know* the primitive beliefs that underpin our knowledge; they are not falsifiable propositions. (2004: 78)

What Moyal-Sharrock proposes is that Wittgenstein does not claim that foundationalism is all wrong.[13] Instead, he corrects the traditional foundationalist picture by maintaining "that its depiction of basic beliefs is wrong. He therefore retains the traditional structural metaphors (foundation and coherence), and replaces the basic structural components with nonpropositional items" (2004: 78).

Together with Avrum Stroll's, Moyal-Sharrock's interpretation of the later Wittgenstein's particular version of foundationalism is the most convincing. To her mind, Wittgenstein is a pragmatist who, interestingly enough, offers a pragmatism with foundations. He is "a pragmatist in the broad sense" (2004: 172) because of his idea that meaning is use, because he insists on the primacy of the deed over the word, and because he reevaluates some of our words *as* deeds. As I have mentioned before, for Wittgenstein our system of basic beliefs should be regarded as an enacted know-how. Moyal-Sharrock comments as follows: "The know-how *is* the ground. Wittgenstein's pragmatism is then a pragmatism with *foundations*, but the enacted nature of these foundations makes them congenial to the spirit of pragmatism. Moreover, part of the foundation is mutable, which allows for a *pluralism* that pragmatism cannot do without" (2004: 172). Wittgenstein's version of foundationalism indeed combines immutable and mutable beliefs, and he highlights "the enacted nature of these foundations." It is possible to see him as a foundationalist, but at the same time it is crucial to appreciate that he is not a Platonist or empirical foundationalist. Wittgenstein thinks that our basic beliefs, as nonpropositional, nonepistemic, and ungrounded certainties, condition and shape our acts and thoughts. Thus, he does not claim that the foundations are fixed, universal, timeless, and immutable, and therefore help humans achieve metaphysical certainty and absolute truth. Rather, he directs attention to the link between those foundations and the contingent plurality of forms of practice they make possible. What this boils down to is that Wittgenstein introduces a kind of foundationalism that is not ahistorical, decontextualized, or isolated from the sphere of practice and action. In this context, Moyal-Sharrock's contention is "that with *On Certainty* foundationalism sheds its old skin. To say that some of our bounds of sense (or rules of grammar) are universal or immutable is not *ipso facto* to say that they express metaphysical truths, truths independent of the human condition, or known in advance of use" (2004: 173).

In order to characterize Wittgenstein's version of foundationalism, Moyal-Sharrock speaks of his "*human-bound* foundationalism" (2004: 173). Her analysis of Wittgenstein's foundationalism is of particular value for the argument developed in this study.¹⁴ Her idea helps one grasp that humanism as anti-authoritarianism is not necessarily synonymous with radical antifoundationalism but that it might be characterized by a *"human-bound foundationalism."* Whereas Rorty's radical critique of foundationalism and metaphysics indicates the power of what he so vehemently rejects, Wittgenstein demonstrates that a *"human-bound* foundationalism" will eventually strengthen the notion of anti-authoritarianism.¹⁵ Our foundations are important not because they are foundations, but because they manifest themselves in what human beings say and do. By insisting that our basic certainties are grammatical (or logical), Wittgenstein does not establish a link between grammar and metaphysics, but on the contrary between grammar and the unpredictable plurality of language-games in the practical sphere. If the position of the later Wittgenstein can be called pragmatist, then it is a pragmatism that is perhaps even more humanist than Rorty's.

When Wittgenstein holds that our basic beliefs are ungrounded certainties, his position must not be confused with the metaphysical desire for the certainty, immutability, reliability, transhistoricity, and purity of what would be more than another human creation or invention. He does not strive for transcendent certainty, but for what might be termed human certainty. Dewey elucidates the severely damaging consequences of the search for transcendent certainty in *The Quest for Certainty* (1929) and *Reconstruction in Philosophy* (1948). In the former book, he argues that traditional epistemology introduced the idea that thought as purely inner activity, which is complete and self-sufficient in itself and is therefore utterly independent of the world of practice, would enable the subject to grasp universal, fixed, and immutable Being. By contrast, the lower realm of action and practice, of change and contingency, is the realm of nonbeing. In other words, only philosophy in the form of pure knowledge, strictly separated from the messy and contingent world of everyday life, can lead the subject to the realm of higher Being. As in *Reconstruction*, Dewey argues that this dichotomy of a higher realm of fixed reality or a world of ideal and abstract forms connected by eternal relations, on the one hand, and a constantly changing world of experience and practical matters, on the other, has governed philosophy since Plato and Aristotle. Furthermore, he advances the argument that this development "bequeathed the notion, which has ruled philosophy ever since the time of the Greeks, that the office of knowledge is to uncover the antecedently real, rather than, as is the case with our practical judgments, to gain the kind of understanding which is necessary to deal with problems as they arise"

(1988: 14). It is the subject's quest for certainty that led to the establishment of the dichotomy of theory and practice, and the latter in turn was responsible for the development of the idea of the correspondence theory of truth and of what Dewey famously termed "the spectator theory of knowledge" (1988: 19).[16]

How important a radical critique of the quest for certainty is for Dewey becomes obvious when one considers his suggestion that "the quest for certainty has determined our basic metaphysics" (1988: 18). He summarizes his main thesis as follows:

> All of these notions about certainty and the fixed, about the nature of the real world, about the nature of the mind and its organs of knowing, are completely bound up with one another, and their consequences ramify into practically all important ideas entertained upon any philosophic question. They all flow—such is my basic thesis—from the separation (set up in the interest of the quest for absolute certainty) between theory and practice, knowledge and action. (1988: 20)

According to Dewey, knowledge is this-worldly. It is a process that has effects on the world in which humans live. As we have seen in the previous chapter, his critique of traditional epistemology and metaphysics is focused on two aspects. First, Dewey questions the notion that pure knowledge or pure intellect offers the subject the possibility of escaping from the world of peril and uncertainty to a higher realm. Second, he seeks to convince us that we ought to reject the idea that knowledge is knowledge only when it is capable of disclosing the properties of the antecedently real or the ultimate real. Knowledge as a form of doing, as Dewey stresses, is an important part of humans' attempts to cope with their environment and to project the consequences of their actions into the future. His contention is that inquiry and philosophical analysis will never be able to exclude the element of practical activity.

In his critique of metaphysics and epistemology, Dewey only focuses on transcendent certainty and does not reflect on the notion of human certainty. He does not contemplate the possibility that there might be a background of certainties that are revisable or temporary, indubitable in practice but nonetheless historical and cultural. In *On Certainty*, Wittgenstein avers: "Forget this transcendent certainty, which is connected with your concept of spirit" (sec. 47). Wittgenstein's basic insight is that "'knowledge' and 'certainty' belong to different *categories*" (1972: sec. 308). This offers him the possibility of drawing attention to the notion of a human or life certainty. Giving or searching for grounds, as he repeatedly stresses in *On Certainty*, does come to an end: "But the end is not an ungrounded presupposition: it is an ungrounded way of acting" (1972: sec. 110). Our human certainty as a nonintellectual taking hold of the world is intimately linked to action, instinct, reflex, and spontaneous behavior. This human certainty, in other words, constitutes the pragmatic basis of our knowledge. It enables humans to simply act: "Why do I not satisfy myself that I have two feet when I want to get up from a chair? There is no why. I simply don't. This is how I act" (1972: sec. 148). When one understands that at "the foundation of well-founded belief lies belief that is not founded," one is in a position to appreciate that because of one's ungrounded system of beliefs or certainties "it is our *acting*, which lies at the bottom of the language-game" (1972: secs. 253, 204). In contrast to traditional forms of foundationalism, the later Wittgenstein does not search for certain, immutable, and transhistorical foundations of knowledge; that is, foundations that can ground and simultaneously justify the entire construction. Rather, he looks for nonepistemic foundations of our linguistic practices.[17] As I have mentioned at the beginning of this chapter, linguistic practices as social practices are the point to which the later Wittgenstein always returns.

4.3 Conclusion

With his "*human-bound* foundationalism" and his notion of human or life certainty, the later Wittgenstein contributes to the endeavor to illuminate the contours of humanism as anti-authoritarianism. Our discussion of the relation between Wittgenstein and the pragmatists has shown that the former constantly returns to the idea that practice has to speak for itself. I have suggested that if the later Wittgenstein's position can be termed pragmatist, it is a pragmatism that is perhaps even more radically humanist than Rorty's. The latter comments on Dewey's anti-authoritarianism thus:

> What Dewey most disliked about both traditional "realist" epistemology and about traditional religious beliefs is that they discourage us by telling us that somebody or something has authority over us. Both tell us that there is Something Inscrutable, something toward which we have duties, duties which have precedence over our cooperative attempts to avoid pain and obtain pleasure. (2009: 258)

In contrast to Dewey, Wittgenstein was neither a lover of democracy nor a utilitarian. However, his postmetaphysical approach, like Dewey's, teaches us that nothing nonhuman has authority over us and that there is nothing nonhuman toward which we have duties. Moreover, we cannot appeal to a nonhuman standard to determine whether our propositions are correct or our actions successful. The later Wittgenstein's antirepresentationalism can be regarded as a version of anti-authoritarianism, which adds an important chapter to the humanist story of progress and emancipation.

5

Marxism, Form, and the Negation of Aesthetic Synthesis

There is no love lost between Fredric Jameson and Richard Rorty. The former has always been highly critical of the latter's *"philosophie informelle"* (Jameson 1990: 246). Jameson holds that Rorty's version of pragmatism "destroys philosophy itself as a history and as a discipline (and leaves its Samson-like destroyer in the self-trivialized role as an aesthete and a belletrist, when not a merely liberal political and cultural critic and commentator" (2009: 136). Pragmatism as Rorty propagates it, in Jameson's view, signals "political resignation, the definitive renunciation of the 1960s, and the return to the two-party system and its limits" (2008: 292). Rorty in turn criticizes that Jameson's *Postmodernism, or, The Cultural Logic of Late Capitalism* (1991) is a "profoundly unromantic book" that "operates on a level of abstraction too high to encourage any particular political initiative" (1998a: 125, 78). Furthermore, Rorty argues that theorists like Jameson "substitute knowing theorization for awe, and resentment over the failures of the past for visions of a better future" (1998a: 126–7). In view of these severe critiques, it seems rather unlikely that a dialogue between pragmatism and Marxism will be possible or productive.[1] Moreover, for pragmatist humanism as anti-authoritarianism, as I have characterized it in Chapter 2, Marxism appears as still metaphysical and governed by authoritarian tendencies; that is, its foundationalism, essentialism, teleology, absolutism, and monolithic nature can be interpreted as the desire to strive for the certainty, reliability, firmness, immutability, transhistoricity, and purity of what would be more than another human creation or invention.

When Marxism too often appears as a caricature in a pragmatist framework, and vice versa, then the vehemence of these idiosyncratic reactions first of all indicates that much is at stake. Maybe it is a lovers' quarrel after all. In this chapter, I hope to offer a new perspective by focusing on aesthetic and literary theory. I will advance the argument that pragmatist humanists can learn and profit from materialist aesthetic theories.[2] As we saw in Chapter 3, pragmatist aesthetics has never developed a profound interest in aesthetic form. By contrast, Marxist aestheticians like Georg Lukács, Theodor W. Adorno, and Jameson have offered truly stimulating analyses of form. One might even be tempted to assert that these Marxists have offered the most convincing discussions of the social function of aesthetic form in the twentieth century. Consequently, they might teach pragmatist humanists and aestheticians a more complex understanding of form.

In the first part, I argue that, despite his metaphysical inclinations, Lukács can be useful for pragmatist aestheticians. The link that he establishes between narrative, form, wholeness, and totality can show pragmatist humanists that form is not necessarily synonymous with Kantian abstraction, stasis, necessity, and immutability. In the second part, I suggest that pragmatist aestheticians can learn even more from Adorno, who theorized the idea of form as radically as no other twentieth-century aesthetician. In my discussion of Adorno I concentrate on what he calls the negation of aesthetic synthesis. He introduces this term in his critique of the historical avant-garde movements and their practice of montage. I propose that pragmatist aesthetics can profit from his conception of form by developing a post-Adornian understanding of the negation of aesthetic synthesis. Finally, I argue that while the link between cognition, form, and totality governed Jameson's texts on postmodernism and postmodernity, the endeavor to establish another relation has been even more important for him. Throughout his career, from the 1970s to the present, his texts have highlighted the significance of the relation between narrative, form, and totality. Hence, Jameson's work as a literary and cultural theorist is clearly Lukácsian in nature. One might be tempted to state that Jameson urges one even more vehemently than his fellow Hegelian Marxist to grasp to what degree narrative is intimately connected with aesthetic form. The question is whether pragmatist humanists and aestheticians will profit from contemplating and analyzing the implications and consequences of this link.

5.1 Georg Lukács

Can aesthetic form be immoral and "unsittlich?" At the beginning of Thomas Mann's "Death in Venice" (1912), the narrator states that the protagonist, the writer Gustav von Aschenbach, strives to establish a new classicism and contribute to a new notion of morality. Developing this new understanding of morality, as the narrator contends, entails that Aschenbach's texts are characterized by an "adelige Reinheit, Einfachheit und Ebenmäßigkeit der Formgebung" (1992: 27–8; "his style took on the noble purity, simplicity and symmetry" [2006: 230]). At the same time, however, the narrator advances the idea that form is dominated by a profound ambivalence:

> Und hat Form nicht zweierlei Gesicht? Ist sie nicht sittlich und unsittlich zugleich, sittlich als Ergebnis und Ausdruck der Zucht, unsittlich aber und selbst widersittlich, sofern sie von Natur aus eine moralische Gleichgültigkeit in sich schließt, ja, wesentlich bestrebt ist, das Moralische unter ihr stolzes und unumschränktes Szepter zu beugen? (1992: 28)
>
> And is form not two-faced? Is it not at one and the same time moral and immoral—moral as the product and expression of discipline, but immoral and even anti-moral inasmuch as it harbours within itself an innate moral indifference, and indeed essentially strives for nothing less than to bend morality under its proud and absolute sceptre? (2006: 230–1)

It is undoubtedly one of the most fascinating aspects of Mann's novella that this ambivalence has completely disappeared at the end. Shortly before his death, Aschenbach, this former ascetic fighter for a new "Klassizität" and defender of a clear and sober style, realizes that aesthetic form ought to be regarded as a Dionysian force that inevitably leads to "Rausch und Begierde." In this novella, which is, together with *Doktor Faustus* (1947), one of Mann's most Nietzschean texts, even the master of a new classicism has to understand that form cannot function as a means to keep the dark Dionysian forces and the chaos at bay, but that it, on the contrary, leads to the "Abgrund." The poet, as Aschenbach comments on and plays with Plato's *Phaedrus* in a fever dream, rejects knowledge ("denn wir vermögen nicht, uns aufzuschwingen") and deliriously loses himself in the realm of form and beauty:

> Aber Form und Unbefangenheit, Phaidros, führen zum Rausch und zur Begierde, führen den Edlen vielleicht zu grauenhaftem Gefühlsfrevel, den seine eigene schöne Strenge als infam verwirft, führen zum Abgrund, zum Abgrund auch sie. Uns Dichter, sage ich, führen sie dahin, denn wir vermögen nicht, uns aufzuschwingen, wir vermögen nur auszuschweifen. (1992: 136)
>
> But form and naivety, Phaedrus, lead to intoxication and lust; they may lead a noble mind into terrible criminal emotions, which his own fine rigour condemns as infamous; they lead, they too lead, to the abyss. I tell you, that is where they

lead us writers; for we are not capable of self-exaltation, we are merely capable of self-debauchery. (2006: 296)³

For the early Mann, the endeavor to elucidate the relationship between "Kunst" (art), "Geist" (intellect, mind), and "Leben" (life) always included the attempt to clarify the relation between life or soul and form. Lukács's early text *Die Seele und die Formen* (1911, *Soul and Form*) had a certain influence on the young Thomas Mann; and this Hungarian philosopher would always count Mann among the most important twentieth-century critical realists.⁴ At the same time, however, one has to see that Lukács, throughout his career, concentrated on form with an intensity that seems even stronger than the one that characterizes Mann's literary texts and letters. This profound interest in questions of aesthetic form already governs *Soul and Form* and *Die Theorie des Romans* (1920, *The Theory of the Novel*). A discussion of Lukács's interest in form, as I will argue, shows that he never fully escaped from his metaphysical inclinations. However, this is not the complete picture. From his early to his late texts, he was preoccupied with the aesthetic and with form. For the early Lukács, literary and aesthetic form held a redemptive promise and it was connected to the idea of the absolute, and this metaphysical notion of form still governed his pieces on realism that he published in the 1930s, 1940s, and 1950s. Form in Lukács is tied to the notions of unity, organic wholeness, universality, the absolute, and totality.⁵

One of the most important passages in *Soul and Form* demonstrates the significance of form for the early Lukács. It is worth quoting in full:

> A real solution can only come from form. In form alone ("the only possible thing" is the shortest definition of form known to me) does every antithesis, every trend, become music and necessity. The road of every problematic human being leads to form because it is that unity which can combine within itself the largest number of divergent forces, and therefore at the end of that road there stands the man who can create form: the artist, in whose created form poet and Platonist become equal. (2010: 38–9)

As the famous "anarchy of light and dark" (2010: 176) passage also shows, what Lukács at this stage in his career desires is necessity, purity, continuity, unity, and wholeness. How can an authentic life be achieved when life is seemingly synonymous with contingency, disorder, impurity, and a protean plurality of contradictory feelings and experiences? Furthermore, when real life "is always unreal, always impossible, in the midst of empirical life" (2010: 176), the question arises as to whether there is a means of transcending this empirical life and, by doing so, of turning the accidental into necessity. As we have seen, Lukács holds that in form everything becomes necessity, and the unity of form alone can combine and contain contradictions, antitheses, and seemingly unruly forces. Moreover, Lukács thinks that form "is the highest judge of life. Form-giving is a judging force, an ethic" (2010: 197). In many of the essays in *Soul and Form*, Lukács seems to follow the Nietzschean imperative, in *The Gay Science*, that we should strive to "become the poets of our life [die Dichter unseres Lebens]" (1974: 240). However, he goes further by linking his conception of aesthetic form with the absolute. Simply confronting the formlessness and vulgarity of modern society by stressing the significance of artworks is not sufficient. The Lukácsian "quest for certainty" (to use John Dewey's term), by separating from the world of man's biased beliefs and daily desires, strives to achieve the purity, reliability, profundity, and immutability of what would be more than another human creation. Form is man-made, but in the early Lukács one often gets the impression that it is also more. In form, as he avers, "there is no more longing and no more loneliness; to achieve form is to achieve the greatest possible fulfilment" (2010: 123).

On the one hand, Lukács wants to find out how and why the authors he discusses in *Soul and Form* make the literary forms that they use in their texts, and he also underlines that he thinks that every author creates their own form. Hence, he pluralizes the notion of form. The early Lukács suggests that aesthetic form is a mediation between soul and life, forever vacillating between these two poles. Consequently, a return to Platonism seems no longer possible for modern man. On the other hand, one is tempted to surmise that he needs more than a plurality of artistic forms; namely, a formal redemption of life's contingency. Form cannot separate itself from life, as Lukács is painfully aware (and as even Mallarmé eventually had to acknowledge), but its power of redemption can be strengthened by linking it with the idea of a firm and unequivocal truth, as well as with the notion of essence. In her discussion of *Soul and Form*, Judith Butler speaks of "the redemptive promise of literary form," and of "a certain faith in a 'form' at once aesthetic and metaphysical" (2010: 13, 14). Form prepares the ground for truth-telling and for discovering the subject's essence.

In *Soul and Form*, Lukács's position is governed, to varying degrees, by Kantianism, a Nietzschean insistence on the poet's self-creation and world-shaping power, romantic anticapitalism, and a metaphysical quest for certainty and formal redemption. By contrast, his *The Theory of the Novel* is dominated by his attempt to apply Hegel's philosophy to aesthetics and literary theory. For our purposes it is crucial to see that the category of form still plays an important role, but that the concept of totality can be found at the center of Lukács's argument. As in *Soul and Form*, he is preoccupied with a profoundly disturbed subject-object dialectics in the modern world; that is, with the subject's alienation from a meaningless and incoherent world. Also, one can detect a feeling of nostalgia for a lost world in both texts. Comparing twentieth-century culture with that of the ancient Greeks, Lukács contends that "our world has become infinitely large and each of its corners is richer in gifts and dangers than the world of the Greeks, but such wealth cancels out the positive meaning—the totality—upon which their life was based" (1971: 34). While contemporary capitalist society is plagued by bourgeois antinomies, ancient Greek society and culture were characterized by homogeneity, wholeness, and a particular dialectics of totality and form:

> Totality of being is possible only where everything is already homogeneous before it has been contained by forms; where forms are not a constraint but only the becoming conscious, the coming to the surface of everything that had been lying dormant as a vague longing in the innermost depths of that which had to be given form; where knowledge is virtue and virtue is happiness, where beauty is the meaning of the world made visible. (1971: 34)[6]

In the modern world, as Lukács stresses, this unity or wholeness no longer exists, there is no more totality of being, and therefore the task form has to fulfill is much more demanding. He suggests that the forms "have to produce out of themselves all that was once simply accepted as given" (1971: 38). The modern forms of art have to face the problem that a totality that can simply be accepted no longer exists. Consequently, the novel "seeks, by giving form, to uncover and construct the concealed totality of life" (1971: 60). Lukács's metaphors of depth and finding once again confirm his metaphysical inclinations, but one should also realize that his elaborations imply the idea of a possible plurality of forms. The creativity of the form-giving process, in an increasingly complex and fragmented world in which the totality of being has disintegrated, cannot be dominated by immutable aesthetic rules. Each form-giving process confronts the missing totality of being, the missing extensive totality of life, the lack of an immanent meaning, as well as the "transcendental homelessness" (1971: 41) of the modern subject differently. Each modern novel necessarily fails in its endeavor to represent the totality, but it nonetheless holds on to the category of totality. In an important passage, Lukács writes:

> The epic and the novel, these two major forms of great epic literature, differ from one another not by their authors' fundamental intentions but by the given historico-philosophical realities with which the authors were confronted. The novel is the epic of an age in which the extensive totality of life is no longer directly given, in which the immanence of meaning in life has become a problem, yet which still thinks in terms of totality. (1971: 56)

Concerning the last sentence, it is important to note that the original says that the novel is the epic of an age, "das dennoch die Gesinnung zur Totalität hat" (1994: 47). It is precisely this notion of an "aspiration towards totality" that would never leave Lukács.

The modern novel, from Flaubert's *L'Éducation sentimentale* (1869) to Kafka's allegories, shows that in a world abandoned by God the form-giving process and the idea of narration are problematized. But while the novel undoubtedly mirrors the fragmentation and dissonance of the modern world, it also goes further by seeking a reconciliation between certain basic dichotomies. As Jameson correctly points out, *The Theory of the Novel* argues that "the novel as a form is the attempt in modern times to recapture something of the quality of epic narration as a reconciliation between matter and spirit, between life and essence" (1971: 171–2). In Lukács's account, the novel longs for the lost unity of subject and object. It nostalgically seeks totality, but can no longer achieve it. Moreover, it has to face the lack of an immanent meaning, as well as the increasingly opaque character of modern capitalist society. While Lukács's analyses of bourgeois society and culture in *Soul and Form* and *Theory of the Novel* are equally bleak, he continues to be preoccupied with the category of totality. In other words, the Hegelian theorist wonders what to do when the aforementioned aspiration towards totality is incompatible with bourgeois society and culture. His turn to Marxism-Leninism in 1917 helped him answer this question.

Emphasizing "the aspiration towards society in its totality" (2011: 174) in *History and Class Consciousness*, and seeking to demonstrate that middle-class philosophy is incapable of fully appreciating the significance of the category of totality, Lukács argues that totalizing knowledge is only possible from a proletarian standpoint.[7] However, as a Marxist, he not only continues to be preoccupied with the idea of totality but also with the category of aesthetic form. The question that interests me in this context is whether the materialist theorist Lukács, when theorizing his version of realism, manages to escape from the grasp of metaphysics or whether he continues his quest for certainty. In order to approach this question, I will try to clarify what he means when he talks about "true form" and "the genuine creation of form" (1978: 20). My intention is to show what a pragmatist humanist can learn from Lukács's understanding of form and what she ought to reject. A decisive parallel with Adorno's aesthetic theory is that Lukács maintains that literary forms are more than literary. Historicizing the concept of form, the latter's contention is that forms tell the recipient something about society, about political alternatives, and about the potentiality of reactionary and progressive forces shaping those alternatives. Hence, literary forms are "forms of life": "That is why the genuine categories of literary forms are not simply literary in essence. They are forms of life especially adapted to the articulation of great alternatives in a practical and effective manner and to the exposition of the maximal inner potentialities of forces and counterforces" (1978: 21).

Lukács's materialist reflection theory also governs his aesthetics and literary theory. At the beginning of his programmatic piece "Art and Objective Truth," he characterizes the significance of the notion of reflection ("Widerspiegelung") for a materialist epistemology thus:

> The basis for any correct cognition of reality, whether of nature or society, is the recognition of the objectivity of the external world, that is, its existence independent of human consciousness. Any apprehension of the external world is nothing more than a reflection in consciousness of the world that exists independently of consciousness. This basic fact of the relationship of consciousness to being also serves, of course, for the artistic reflection of reality. (1978: 25)

Neither philosophical idealism nor mechanistic materialism, if one follows Lukács, will ever be capable of approaching the insights of a materialist-dialectical theory of reflection, which does not lose itself in theoretical contemplation but brings together theory and practice. Materialist dialectics, in Marxism-Leninism, is intimately linked to practice.[8] One only has to think of Marx's early *Economic and Philosophical Manuscripts* (1844) in this context. In the *Manuscripts*, economic and aesthetic categories are interwoven, and the emphasis on human creativity indirectly warns against the development of a crude reflection theory.[9] Lukács writes: "The union of materialist dialectics with *practice*, its derivation from practice, its control through practice, its directive role in practice, rest on this profound conception of the dialectical nature of objective reality and of the dialectic of its reflection in consciousness" (1978: 28–9).

According to Lukács, all knowledge rests on direct reflections of the external world; the latter thus are the foundation for all knowledge. For the materialist theoretician Lukács, reality is objective and a correct and faithful cognition can bring our thought closer to this reality (which is always a historical reality). However, this notion of the possibility of a faithful representation must not lead one to surmise that the objectivity of the external world is inert, static, or rigid. In many of his texts, particularly those of his so-called middle period, Lukács underscores "that reality is always richer and more varied than the best and most comprehensive theory that can be developed to apprehend it" (1978: 29). Faithful to his Leninism, he explains that the objectivity of the external world always implies the idea of historical change, the contingency and unpredictability of human practice, and the stimulating potential of human creativity. A crude or vulgar reflection theory will not be able to penetrate deeply; that is, it will necessarily remain on the level of appearances, deprived of the possibility of reaching and depicting the really real. As we will see, the appearance-reality distinction is central to Lukács's aesthetics and literary theory.

To Lukács in the 1930s, 1940s, and 1950s, contemporary aesthetics suffered from two extremes; namely, a false objectivism and a highly problematic subjectivism. The false objectivism of naturalism, primarily in Zola, satisfies itself with a mechanical or photographic reproduction of a contingent scrap or slice of reality. It isolates objectivity from practice and historical change, eliminates all motion and process, and ignores the questions of typicality and potentiality. By contrast, the subjectivism of expressionism and most avant-garde texts, for instance, in Joyce, Woolf, Faulkner, and Beckett, results in an increasing alienation of art and literature from virulent social problems, an obsession with empty formal questions, and thus an elimination of all content from art and literature. In other words, the modern theory of abstraction leads to a worldless or "weltabgewandte" art.[10] In "Kunst und objektive Wahrheit," Lukács argues that in "the later art for art's sake of the imperialist period such subjectivism evolves into a theory of a contemptuous, parasitic divorce of art from life, into a denial of any objectivity in art, a glorification of the 'sovereignty' of the creative individual and a theory of indifference to content and arbitrariness in form" (1978: 42).[11]

Lukács claims that every significant work of art creates its own world, it reflects the process of life in motion and in a concrete dynamic context. Rejecting false objectivism and false subjectivism, the realist work of art strives to accurately and faithfully reflect the total process of objective reality. Moreover, it directs attention to the dialectical relationship between reality, form, content, and technique. Historicizing his aesthetic categories, Lukács underlines that the dialectic of form is a historical dialectic. In *The Meaning of Contemporary Realism*, he maintains that the "development of new forms is intimately related to [the] active, unceasing exploration of reality" (2006: 97–8). Nonetheless, there are severe limits to this development of new forms exploring new realities. Aesthetic form must never achieve autonomy, and it must never threaten to destroy the organic wholeness of the work of art (as it does in the surrealist or expressionist montage, e.g.). Realism, according to Lukács, is incompatible with the idea that form would be more than a specific mode of the reflection of reality.[12]

In "Art and Objective Truth," Lukács grounds his reflections on the dialectical unity of form and content on Hegel's suggestion, in *Enzyklopädie der philosophischen Wissenschaften im Grundrisse*, that "content is nothing but the conversion of form into content, and form is nothing but the conversion of content into form" (quoted in Lukács 1978: 45). However, at the center of Lukács's argumentation is the idea of "the objectivity of form" (1978: 44). To put it simply, in this piece Lukács underlines that content is more important than form. The latter arises out of historical and social content, that is, the total process of objective reality, and it is thus supposed to raise this worldly content to the level of objectivity in literary and artistic representation. What Lukács warns against is "an artificial independence of form" or "the subjectivizing of form" (1978: 53). When the reader becomes conscious of form as form, then this incomplete conversion of form into content indicates that the writer failed in their attempt to faithfully and comprehensively mirror reality. Lukács's contention is that while the only function of form "is the expression of this objectivity, this reflection of life in the greatest concreteness and clarity and with all its motivating contradictions," modern subjectivism and aestheticism "lead to the separation of form from content, to the blunt opposition of one to the other and thus to the destruction of the dialectical basis for the objectivity of form" (1978: 52, 58). In this context it is important to note that Lukács, as in *Soul and Form*, argues that aesthetic form cannot be adequately appreciated without considering the notions of wholeness and unity, but in his pieces on realism he adds the idea of objectivity.

Based on the objectivity of form, only realism can offer a faithful reflection of society in its totality. Furthermore, only realism can penetrate into the deeper concrete reality of the subject-object dialectics and can thus provide a dynamic and impelling wholeness to life. It becomes obvious how intimately related the concepts of form, totality, and wholeness are in Lukács's theory of realism. Depicting "man as a whole in the whole of society" (2002: 5), as he states in the preface to *Studies in European Realism*, is a part of the heritage of classical aesthetics that Marxist aestheticians have to accept as still important. Great realism depicts man and society "as complete entities" (2002: 6). In his piece on Balzac's *Illusions perdues* (1843), Lukács argues that this French realist shows "the total sum of [the characters'] own natures and the mutual interaction of this their nature with the total sum of objective circumstances" (2002: 53).

Whether in *History and Class Consciousness*, "Art and Objective Truth," or his essays on realism, Lukács always made clear that in his opinion Marxist theory and especially materialist aesthetics were capable of productively and creatively confronting the antinomies of bourgeois thought. Great art, according to him, resolves contradictions, it uses its self-contained context, which is always historical, to form those contradictions and antinomies so that they lead to new kinds of integrity and wholeness, it illustrates that its self-containment is the reflection of the process of life in motion, and it simultaneously demonstrates that it is able to offer a truer, more complete and dynamic, reflection of reality than its recipients otherwise can use. "The goal for all great art," as Lukács suggests,

> is to provide a picture of reality in which the contradiction between appearance and reality, the particular and the general, the immediate and the conceptual, etc., is so resolved that the two converge into a spontaneous integrity in the direct impression of the work of art and provide a sense of an inseparable integrity. The universal appears as a quality of the individual and the particular, reality becomes manifest and can be experienced within appearance, the general principle is exposed as the specific impelling cause for the individual case being specially depicted. (1978: 34–5)

As we have seen, the appearance-reality dichotomy is of the utmost importance when one seeks to appreciate the complexity of Lukács's thinking. One of the most illuminating discussions of this distinction can be found in his "Marx and Engels on Aesthetics." For pragmatists, it is certainly tempting to interpret the early Lukács's Kantianism as a version of Platonism and to state that the latter still governs his thought in his Marxist period. On Lukács's account, the dialectic of reality and appearance is not limited to consciousness, but it is primarily a central aspect of "Wirklichkeit." Furthermore, the idea of the appearance-reality distinction implies that reality has various levels and that the theorist, and the artist, has to go deep in order to find out about the really real and the laws shaping this really real:

> The true dialectic of reality (Wesen) and appearance rests on their being equal aspects of objective reality (Wirklichkeit), products of reality and not just of consciousness. Yet—and this is an important axiom of dialectical apprehension— reality has various levels; there is the ephemeral reality of the superfice, never recurring, momentary, and there are the more profound elements and tendencies of reality which recur in accordance with definite laws and change according to changing circumstances. (1978: 76–7)

In contrast to the still lifes or lifeless tableaux of naturalism and the form-obsessed, esoteric, and perversely idiosyncratic texts of modernism, "true" realistic art is capable of combining truth, profundity, depth, and totality in its successful endeavor to discover the reality behind the various layers of appearances. Refraining from representing the reality it has discovered abstractly, only realism can grasp and reproduce reality as it is objectively and essentially.[13] By applying the theory of reflection to aesthetics, only the Marxist conception of realism is able to artistically and perceptually expose the essence of reality. Lukács formulates thus: "True art thus aspires to maximum profundity and comprehensiveness, at grasping life in its all-embracing totality. That is, it examines in as much depth as possible the reality behind appearance and does not represent it abstractly, divorced from phenomena and in opposition to phenomena" (1978: 77). In the confrontation with the notion of "hidden reality," "the recognition and extrapolation of the reality from the network of contradictory phenomena" (1978: 80) becomes the main task of the creative artist. Marxist aesthetics, as Lukács argues, "views as the greatest achievement of the creative effort the artist's making us aware of the social process and making it meaningful and experientially accessible" (1978: 80).

Undoubtedly, Lukács's way of speaking is profoundly metaphysical. His use of the appearance-reality distinction and thus of the idea of the really real; his gesture of a convergence to the antecedently real or true; his gesture of looking deep and listening closely; his proposal that the Marxist theorist is capable of penetrating into the depth since he has special conceptual tools and philosophical methods (e.g., his materialist reflection theory); his talk of essences; his endeavor to see everything steadily and to see it whole, to discover unity and wholeness; his suggestion that only the Marxist theorist can rise above the plurality of appearances and then conceptually analyze what stands behind these contingent appearances and produces them; his belief in the promise of a formal redemption of life's contingency (which, at least to a certain degree, unites the early and the later Lukács); and his talk of the objectivity of form and his proposal that only Marxism can offer radical objectivity in aesthetic cognition and representation—it is indeed difficult to dismiss the idea that Lukács too often demonstrates that the phrase "materialist metaphysician" must not necessarily be considered oxymoronic. However, at the same time I wish to argue that the link that Lukács establishes between form, narrative, wholeness, and totality should also be of interest to a pragmatist humanist.[14] An analysis of this relation not only prevents pragmatist literary criticism from degenerating into ethical criticism, as in Rorty's case (see Chapter 3), but it also teaches pragmatist humanists that form is not necessarily synonymous with (Kantian) abstraction, acontextuality, and a process of dehistoricization. Form, as Lukács shows, is never static, immutable, necessary, universal, and therefore directly opposed to the empirical and historical world dominated by contingency and the creativity and unpredictability of humans' actions. Like Adorno, Lukács, despite his metaphysical tendencies, is in a position to teach pragmatist humanists a more complex notion of form in comparison with the one offered by pragmatist or naturalist aesthetics. Furthermore, it is crucial to see that the Lukácsian link between form, narrative, wholeness, and totality offers one of the most stimulating possibilities of confronting the stasis of the dualism formalism versus antiformalism. By elucidating the significance of relations between aspects that have hitherto been analyzed in isolation, Lukács might be useful for the endeavor to show that the idea of a new formalism is as unattractive as the proposal that it might be time for a revival of (Hegelian) content aesthetics.[15]

From a pragmatist perspective, Lukács's Marxist theory is a form of authoritarianism because of his belief in objective reality and the really real, the radical objectivity in aesthetic cognition and representation, and the theory of reflection. Moreover, he weakens his thought-provoking argument concerning the relations between hitherto isolated aspects by establishing an intimate interwovenness between those relations and the appearance-reality distinction. To Lukács, those relations are not useful because they offer new and stimulating perspectives or new ways of coping with phenomena, but because they inevitably lead to the discovery of the really real and hence the notion that it is possible to render reality comprehensively and realistically. Whereas a pragmatist humanism as nominalist historicism is a form of anti-authoritarianism, Lukács's Marxism is a humanism that is still authoritarian in the sense developed in this study. He makes unequivocally clear that socialist humanism is central to the materialist conception of history and is the core of Marxist aesthetics. In his view, humanism is supposed to focus on the questions of "how to defend man's integrity effectively, in actual life, in relation to actual men; how to change the material bases which cause the crippling and deformation of men; and how to awaken men to consciousness and to action as agents of this social and political consciousness" (1978: 87). As we have seen, the fact that a pragmatist humanism and a socialist humanism offer profoundly different definitions of the meaning of humanism must not prevent the former from learning from the latter. What can a pragmatist humanism learn from Adorno's conception of form?

5.2 Theodor W. Adorno

In the twentieth century, no one theorized the conception of aesthetic form as radically as Adorno. He holds that form ought to be at the center of aesthetic theory, and he uses this idea for his critique of traditional aesthetics.[16] Adorno follows Hegel in establishing an intimate relation between art and truth, but in contrast to Hegel he maintains that it is form that tells the truth about society. Adorno's contention is that the avant-garde artwork refrains from commenting directly and explicitly on the state of society, and it is precisely this refusal that enables it to tell the truth about late-capitalist society. The problems of reified and antagonistic reality are reflected in the aesthetic form of the authentic work of art. This is the only kind of reflection that he allows. Form, the radically composed form of the genuine avant-garde artwork, is the last possibility of refuge, as it were, for the subject threatened by late-capitalist reification, alienation, and standardization. In contrast to Lukács, Adorno asserts that the form-content dialectics of the artwork is clearly dominated by the category of form.[17]

According to Adorno, art is part of society, but its function is that of an antithesis: "Kunst ist die gesellschaftliche Antithesis zur Gesellschaft, nicht unmittelbar aus dieser zu deduzieren" (1973: 19); "Art is the social antithesis of society, not directly deducible from it" (1997: 8). This is one of the central sentences in his posthumously published *Ästhetische Theorie* (1970), and it directly leads one to the question of form.[18] "Not directly deducible" has to be understood as a critique of vulgar materialism and its simplistic notion of a reflection theory, but the question arises as to what Adorno means when he calls art "the social antithesis of society." This can be explained by what might be termed the social nature of form or the "Gesellschaftlichkeit der Form." Historicizing art's radical formal autonomy, Adorno thinks that form, on the one hand, separates art from society and lets it become a realm of freedom and, on the other, form in its dissonance and fragmentation enables the recipients to gain a profounder understanding of society and to develop a new perspective. Art becomes social precisely because of its radical practice of form-giving. It is aesthetic form, in its radical nature and newness, which separates the authentic and hermetic work of art from society, and at the same time, permanently facing the threat of heteronomy and having to deal with attempts to weaken the severity of its law, form tells the truth about historical reality. The fact that aesthetic form is central to Adorno's aesthetic theory also becomes clear from the following two sentences. They belong, together with the one I have just discussed, to the most important statements in *Ästhetische Theorie*: "Der Formbegriff markiert die schroffe Antithese der Kunst zum empirischen Leben, in welchem ihr Daseinsrecht ungewiß ward. Kunst hat soviel Chance wie die Form, und nicht mehr" (1973: 213); "The concept of form marks out art's sharp antithesis to an empirical world in which art's right to exist is uncertain. Art has precisely the same chance of survival as does form, no better" (1997: 141). These two sentences nicely characterize the complexity of Adorno's materialist aesthetics of form.

In Adorno's opinion, a content aesthetics is no longer possible under late-capitalist conditions. Against Hegel, and implicitly against Lukács, he argues: "In the dialectics of form and content, the scale also tips toward form—against Hegel—because content, which his aesthetics wanted to salvage, degenerated to a positivistic given, a mold for the reification against which, according to Hegel's theory, art protests" (1997: 145).[19] It is of the utmost importance to see how Adorno, in the passages discussing form, brings together two seemingly incompatible aspects: "Stimmigkeit" (coherence) and "Dissonanz."[20] This will play a crucial role for the argument developed in this chapter. He advances the idea that "the quintessence of all elements of logicality, or, more broadly, coherence in artworks, is form" (1997: 140). At the same time, however, he states that "every other element can be negated in the concept of form, even aesthetic unity, the idea of form that first made the wholeness and autonomy of the artwork possible. In highly developed modern works, form tends to dissociate unity, either in the interest of expression or to criticize art's affirmative character" (1997: 140–1). Later in his book, Adorno calls form "the nonviolent synthesis of the diffuse" and once more underscores the relation between form and truth: "Aesthetic form is the objective organization within each artwork of what appears as bindingly eloquent. It is the nonviolent synthesis of the diffuse that nevertheless preserves it as what it is in its divergences and contradictions, and for this reason form is actually an unfolding of truth" (1997: 143). Particularly by including dissonant elements and the idea of fragmentation, the hermetic work of art might eventually find itself in a position to unfold the truth.

Before expanding on dissonance and the question of the nonorganicity or organicity of the avant-garde artwork, I would like to briefly come back to the aspect of autonomy. Right on the first page of *Aesthetic Theory*, Adorno famously declares: "Yet art's autonomy remains irrevocable. All efforts to restore art by giving it a social function—of which art is itself uncertain and by which it expresses its own uncertainty—are doomed" (1997: 1). Lukácsian realism, Sartre's notion of a "littérature engagée," and the surrealist desire to "pratiquer la poésie" (as Breton put it in the first surrealist manifesto)—Adorno criticizes and rejects all three and vehemently insists upon art's autonomy.[21] Calling works of art "windowless monads" (1997: 5), he unequivocally rejects the idea of a reflection theory: "Art does not come to know reality by depicting it photographically or 'perspectivally' but by expressing, through its autonomous constitution, what is concealed by the empirical form reality takes" (1991: 227). Throughout his *Ästhetische Theorie*, Adorno stresses the tension that arises from the fact that the authentic work of art is both autonomous and a *fait social* (it is social and historical through and through):

> What is social in art is its immanent movement against society, not its manifest opinions. Its historical gesture repels empirical reality, of which artworks are nevertheless part in that they are things. Insofar as a social function can be predicated for artworks, it is their functionlessness. Through their difference from a bewitched reality, they embody negatively a position in which what is would find its rightful place, its own. Their enchantment is disenchantment. (1997: 227)

Its status as a *fait social* is reflected in the aesthetic form of the avant-garde work of art, but it must not be misused for the defense of a political position: "Social struggles and the relations of classes are imprinted in the structure of artworks; by contrast, the political positions deliberately adopted by artworks are epiphenomena and usually impinge on the elaboration of works and thus, ultimately, on their social truth content" (1997: 232). In Adorno's account, the authentic work of art opposes the idea of heteronomy; it critiques the notion of an idealist, or Hegelian, subject-object identity as it is typical of the organic and harmonious work of art; and it refuses to be turned into a commodity that is offered on the art market and thus succumbs to late-capitalist reification and commodification (think of Jameson's claim that postmodernity is characterized, among other things, by a universal commodification). One of the central dichotomies of Adorno's aesthetic thinking is undoubtedly that between the hermetic avant-garde work of art and the products of the culture industry. His time in the United States, as one can see from *Dialectic of Enlightenment* (1947), only intensified many of his positions in the field of aesthetic theory. This cannot be the place to comment on Adorno's many misjudgments and inadequacies as far as his texts on the culture industry are concerned, but I wish to underline that one of the things that resulted from his contact with American mass culture was that this German philosopher theorized the autonomy of art even more vehemently than before.

Highlighting the nondiscursive quality of the work of art, its enigmatic character and cryptic polysemy, Adorno contends that originality "withdrew into the artworks themselves, into the relentlessness of their internal organization" (1997: 172). In case this "relentlessness of their internal organization" is missing, the artwork can no longer claim to be genuine and unique, its cryptic character and above all its Kantian nonconceptuality will disappear, and the difference between it and the standardized commodities of the culture industry can hardly be made out any longer. In his discussion of the new, Adorno characterizes modern art thus: "Scars of damage and disruption are the modern's seal of authenticity; by their means, art desperately negates the closed confines of the ever-same; explosion is one of its invariants. Antitraditional energy becomes a voracious vortex" (1997: 23). In the confrontation with this talk about "disruption," "antitraditional energy," and "explosion," one might be tempted to surmise that Adorno sees the necessity of consigning the notions of harmony and organicity to the dustbin of (idealist) history and clearly favors the nonorganic and dissonant work of art. However, this would be a highly problematic misinterpretation of his aesthetic position. Undoubtedly, Adorno maintains that art "that makes the highest claim compels itself beyond form as totality and into the fragmentary" (1997: 147). Moreover, he calls attention to the fact that in many modern artworks, for instance, by Beckett and Schönberg, the "unity of form" was replaced by a decidedly more "open" form: "In many modern works that have attracted a large audience, the form was artfully held open because they wanted to demonstrate that the unity of form was no longer bestowed on them. Spurious infinity, the inability to close, becomes a freely chosen principle of method and expression" (1997: 147). In spite of this insistence upon the significance of fragmentation and openness for the modern artwork, Adorno does not simply reject the notions of harmony and coherence. This rejection would be incompatible with his desire to hold on to the concept of semblance ("Schein"). Adorno is willing to admit that "harmony was false from the beginning" ("weil das Stimmen von einst falsch war," 1973: 236), and he moreover argues that the notion of the closed artwork appears problematic and "dubious" in a closed, that is, totally administered society with its mechanisms of standardization and control:

> On no account does an artwork require an a priori order in which it is received, protected, and accepted. If today nothing is harmonious, this is because harmony was false from the beginning. The closure of the aesthetic, ultimately of the extra-aesthetic, system of reference does not necessarily correspond to the dignity of the artwork. The dubiousness of the ideal of a closed society applies equally to that of the closed artwork. It is incontestable that artworks have, as die-hard reactionaries never cease to repeat, lost their social embeddedness. (1997: 158)

Traditional idealist aesthetics, and Lukács's materialist aesthetic theory, too dramatically exalts the relationship of the whole to the parts and regards the eventual priority of wholeness as a confirmation of the indispensability of the category of totality. Wholeness eventually triumphs over the heterogeneous parts, and the link between unity, meaning, and totality is established and affirmed. There is no place for this maneuver in Adorno's aesthetics. At the same time, however, he asserts that harmony, unity, and coherence still play a critical role as regards the analysis of the modern artwork. In this context, one has to take into consideration Adorno's aforementioned idea that art functions as the antithesis of late-capitalist society. He opposes the coherence of the radically formed work to the cubist, surrealist, or expressionist montage; that is, he claims that only by presenting itself as formally coherent will the avant-garde artwork be capable of functioning as the antithesis of society:

> Categories such as unity, or even harmony, have not tracelessly vanished as a result of the critique of meaning. The determinate antithesis of individual artworks toward empirical reality furthers the coherence of those artworks. Otherwise the gaps in the work's structure would be invaded, as occurs in montage, by the unwieldy material against which it protects itself. This is what is true in the traditional concept of harmony. (1997: 157)

He further expands on the dialectics of dissonance and unity as follows: "Although art revolts against its neutralization as an object of contemplation, insisting on the most extreme incoherence and dissonance, these elements are those of unity; without this unity they would not even be dissonant" (1997: 157).[22]

Adorno's critique of montage offers an interesting perspective on his aesthetic thought and its dialectical relationship with idealist aesthetics. For our purposes, it is crucial to appreciate that he establishes a relation between montage and nonorganicity. Speaking of "the antiorganic praxis of montage" (1997: 156), Adorno criticizes montage for breaking the illusion of semblance by letting "ruins of empirical reality" ("Trümmer der Empirie," 1973: 232) become part of the artwork. By contrast, he wants everything to be touched by the artist's subjectivity, as it were; that is, everything has to be formed by him or her. Only by subjectively forming every aspect of the artwork can the artist hope to produce something that might function as an antithesis of society and that at the same time is in multiple ways mediated with it. Cubism first introduced the notion and technique of montage. Picasso and Braque produced their first "papiers collés" before the First World War. Adorno not only considers montage a counterproductive attack on semblance and the idea of formal coherence, he also calls it "the inner-aesthetic capitulation of art" to the notion of heteronomy. In other words, he reacts idiosyncratically and vehemently to anything that undermines art's autonomy:

> The semblance provided by art, that through the fashioning of the heterogeneously empirical it was reconciled with it, was to be broken by the work admitting into itself literal, illusionless ruins of empirical reality, thereby acknowledging the fissure and transforming it for purposes of aesthetic effect. Art wants to admit its powerlessness vis-à-vis late-capitalist totality and to initiate its abrogation. Montage is the inner-aesthetic capitulation of art to what stands heterogeneously opposed to it. (1997: 155)

While the assembled work and the radically formed avant-garde artwork once were identical, as Adorno proposes, the former can no longer claim to be part of the avant-garde. Designed to attack the idea of organic unity and wholeness, its potential to shock its recipients now seems neutralized. As even the disciples of Duchamp had to learn, one can only shock a limited number of times. Art as an institution has the capability, and the desire, of quickly incorporating even the most outrageous shocks and transgressive gestures.[23] Adorno writes:

> The idea of montage and that of technological construction, which is inseparable from it, becomes irreconcilable with the idea of the radical, fully formed artwork with which it was once recognized as being identical. The principle of montage was conceived as an act against a surreptitiously achieved organic unity; it was meant to shock. Once this shock is neutralized, the assemblage once more becomes merely indifferent material; the technique no longer suffices to trigger communication between the aesthetic and the extra-aesthetic, and its interest dwindles to a cultural-historical curiosity. (1997: 155–6)

Central to Adorno's critique of the assembled work and its attack on formal coherence is the following sentence: "Negation der Synthesis wird zum Gestaltungsprinzip" (1973: 232); "The negation of synthesis becomes a principle of form" (1997: 155). In order to approach the multilayered complexity of Adorno's modernist aesthetics it is critical to fully understand the meaning of this sentence. Espen Hammer writes in this context: "Yet the most forceful factor in accounting for the fragmentation of the work is the negation of aesthetic synthesis, which according to Adorno has become the central preoccupation of all modern art" (2015: 200). Hammer does not realize that the Adornian notion of a negation of aesthetic synthesis is a negative comment on the cubist, surrealist, and expressionist montage and does not refer to "all modern art." In other words, Adorno's critique of the assembled work is part of what Peter Bürger termed his "anti-avant-gardism" (1991: 50). Like Adorno, Hammer does not strictly differentiate between the modernist avant-garde artwork and the products of the historical avant-garde movements (surrealism, dadaism, futurism, and constructivism). As we have seen, the modernist work, as Adorno characterizes it, is not the radically fragmented work, it includes the moments of dissonance, fragmentation, and fissure, as well as the tension between whole and parts, but it simultaneously does not radically reject the notions of harmony, unity, and formal coherence since doing so would prevent it from appearing as a semblant entity. By contrast, the products of the historical avant-garde movements rebel against "Schein," the ideal of a unified, well-rounded whole, and formal coherence. They vehemently attack art's autonomy and thus the strict separation between art and life.[24] According to Bürger,

> Adorno frantically attempts to insure that the border separating art from the rest is not violated, against the tendencies of collapsing art into action (dadaism), expression (expressionism), and the revolution of everyday life (surrealism). Since he cannot conceive of the attempt to return art to praxis as a necessary step in the development of art in bourgeois society, but can only proclaim a

regression into barbarism, his critique of idealist aesthetic categories ends in their recovery. (1991: 56)[25]

In contrast to the historical avant-garde movements, Adorno holds on to an almost classical concept of the work of art. Criticizing the hypostatization of the work as harmonic totality and simultaneously reconciling the avant-garde principle of fragment with classical harmony, he is determined not to completely reject the idea of organicity. Elaborating on the difference between the organic (symbolic) and the nonorganic (allegorical) work of art, Bürger points out that the former

> seeks to make unrecognizable the fact that it has been made. The opposite holds true for the avant-gardiste work: it proclaims itself as an artificial construct, an artifact. To this extent, montage may be considered the fundamental principle of avant-gardiste art. The "fitted" (*montierte*) work calls attention to the fact that it is made up of reality fragments; it breaks through the appearance (*Schein*) of totality. Paradoxically, the avant-gardiste intention to destroy art as an institution is thus realized in the work of art itself. The intention to revolutionize life by returning art to its praxis turns into a revolutionizing of art. (1984: 72)[26]

As I have sought to demonstrate, Adorno does not strive to return art to life and the practical sphere. The thinker of nonidentity, dissonance, and the rebellion against semblance also presents himself as an aesthetician who holds on to the notions of harmony and coherence since only they guarantee art's autonomy. It is this dialectical tension that primarily characterizes Adorno's aesthetic thought.

How can pragmatist aesthetics, as part of pragmatist humanism as anti-authoritarianism, profit from Adorno's conception of form? It can do this, as I would like to submit, by developing a post-Adornian understanding of the negation of aesthetic synthesis. We should keep the term but delink it from Adorno's critique of the historical avant-garde movements and their practice of montage. By doing so, we can give it a positive connotation and apply it to innovative and formally demanding works that demonstrate that form-giving can be regarded as an anti-authoritarian act. On Adorno's account, the autonomous artwork is not answerable to any external authority. Focusing on its formal coherence, it is anti-authoritarian and, simultaneously, as a unified, semblant whole, it is its own authority. I think it is tempting to use Adorno's aesthetic theory by redefining the negation of aesthetic synthesis as a radical form of anti-authoritarianism that characterizes fragmented and dissonant artworks that tend more toward nonorganicity than Adorno allowed. The fragmented and dissonant work in a non-Adornian sense is not answerable to any external authority, it criticizes the semblance and wholeness of the traditional autonomous artwork as forms of authority, and it lets one grasp the practice of form-giving as an anti-authoritarian act. Were pragmatist aesthetics to realize the potential use of the negation of aesthetic synthesis, there would certainly be numerous advantages. It would achieve a decidedly more complex understanding of aesthetic form in comparison with those offered by traditional versions of pragmatist aesthetics (or it would become truly interested in form in the first place). Regarding the negation of aesthetic synthesis as a form of anti-authoritarianism would not only offer the possibility of grasping the significance of dissonance and fragmentation but also that of contingency.[27]

Furthermore, it is important to see that a pragmatist aesthetics that interprets form-giving as an anti-authoritarian and idiosyncratic act does not run the danger of succumbing to formalist temptations. On the contrary, a pragmatist aesthetics that works with the negation of aesthetic synthesis in a post-Adornian sense will rather tend to refuse to accept the separation between aesthetics and everyday practice. But it will advance a critique of this separation with a more sophisticated understanding of aesthetic form than, for instance, Dewey has to offer.

It is not difficult to imagine a pragmatist aesthetician agreeing with Adorno that artworks "are the self-unconscious historiography of their epoch" (Adorno 1997: 182). As we have seen, moreover, it is stimulating when he defines aesthetic form as the "self-antagonistic and refracted" (1997: 142) coherence of the artworks ("die antagonistische und durchbrochene Stimmigkeit der Artefakte," 1973: 213). However, a pragmatist aesthetician parts company with Adorno when he draws attention to the significance of the relation between the purity of form, the radical autonomy of the avant-garde work, and its cruelty. He writes: "The purer the form and the higher the autonomy of the works, the more cruel they are. Appeals for more humane art, for conformity to those who are its virtual public, regularly dilute the quality and weaken the law of form" (1997: 50). This is one of the passages where Adorno's materialist aesthetics runs the danger of degenerating into an idealist version of aesthetics with a certain materialist bent. Instead of employing ideas such as the purity of form, the radical autonomy of the cruel works, or the law of form, a pragmatist aesthetician will be more interested in the dialectics of dissonance and coherence and in how the novelty of form-giving can have an impact on the recipient's attitudes and beliefs. Form-giving is artistic practice, a kind of poetic agency, which has effects on the artwork's recipients. Instead of talking about the purity of form and the cruelty of the avant-garde artworks, it now seems more fruitful to ask whether and how new practices of form-giving can stimulate the recipients to question or rethink traditional forms of authority. The work of form, in other words, might have an impact on what humans do and how they behave in the practical sphere (and one of their insights might be that form and form-giving have always been part of what human beings do).

While I think that pragmatist aesthetics can learn from Adorno's aesthetic theory and conception of form, Rorty would have criticized this suggestion.[28] As we saw in Chapter 3, he agrees with the proposal that pragmatist humanism can be characterized by the primacy of creative or poetic agency, but he refuses to regard the modern development from finding to making as interwoven with the history of the practice of form-giving. Rorty cannot see the possibilities offered by developing a post-Adornian understanding of the negation of aesthetic synthesis, since his pragmatist literary criticism is governed by his aversion to Kantian formalism and hence directed against the notion of a form-content dialectics. In the Rortyan framework, there is no place for the idea that the practice of form-giving might be seen as an anti-authoritarian act and a powerful means of preventing us from striving for the certainty, reliability, transhistoricity, immutability, and purity of what would be more than another human creation or invention. Rorty's insufficient grasp of the significance of form is also due to the fact that he mostly discusses literary texts that are not formally innovative (with the possible exception of Nabokov's books).

5.3 Fredric Jameson

In contrast to Adorno, Fredric Jameson has never rejected the idea and practice of realism. On the contrary, the question of a contemporary realism has preoccupied him since the 1970s. What would be the task of a new realism, Jameson asks, in a new form of capitalism?[29] He discusses the relationship between realism and modernism in pieces such as "Beyond the Cave: Demystifying the Ideology of Modernism" (1975), "The Ideology of the Text" (1976), and "Reflections on the Brecht-Lukács Debate" (1977). It should be noted that these essays are important insofar as they show that Jameson's preoccupation with the possibility of representing the total late-capitalist space, as it governs his texts on postmodernism, has a prehistory. His early pieces demonstrate that he has always been interested in thinking the possibilities, demands, and limitations of a new realism under late-capitalist conditions. Moreover, he has repeatedly criticized a reductionist understanding of realism. In "The Ideology of the Text," for instance, he advances the idea that many discussions of the dialectics of realism and modernism suffer from the fact "that whenever you search for 'realism' somewhere it vanishes, for it was nothing but punctuation, a mere marker or a 'before' that permitted the phenomenon of modernism to come into focus properly" (1976: 61). According to Jameson, realism often appears as a "negative or straw term" (1976: 61), and critics and theorists attack an "ideology of realism" (1975: 421) and its allegedly simplistic notion of representation or aesthetic of mimesis. I think his early pieces on realism and modernism demonstrate that one of the primary tasks of literary and cultural critics under late-capitalist conditions is to theorize the possibility of mediating between realism and modernism, since both aesthetic programs or frameworks have turned out to be inadequate and no longer possible (realism and modernism are thus more than period terms). Jameson writes in "Reflections on the Brecht-Lukács Debate":

> In our present cultural situation, if anything, both alternatives of realism and modernism seem intolerable to us: realism because its forms revive older experiences of a kind of social life (the classical inner city, the traditional opposition city/country) that is no longer with us in the already decaying future of consumer society; modernism because its contradictions have proved in practice even more acute than those of realism. (1977: 446)

Jameson confronts this seemingly aporetic situation by focusing on the as yet unmarked realm of a new realism. In other words, he counterbalances the standardized order realism-modernism-postmodernism with the idea of a new realism as synthesis. It is possible to interpret this new realism as a form of resistance against postmodernism as a cultural dominant in the total space of late capitalism. In a clearly Lukácsian gesture, Jameson argues that one of the main functions of this new realism would be to "reinvent" the category of totality:

> Under these circumstances, the function of a new realism would be clear: to resist the power of reification in consumer society and to reinvent that category of totality which, systematically undermined by existential fragmentation on all levels of life and social organization today, can alone project structural relations between classes as well as class struggles in other countries, in what has increasingly become a world system. (1977: 447–8)[30]

Jameson's conception of a new realism has to be seen in connection with his idea of cognitive mapping.[31] The latter term urges one to appreciate how cognition, form, and totality are interlinked and it highlights realism's claim to cognitive as well as aesthetic status. As Jameson makes clear in his analyses of postmodernism, from *Postmodernism, or, The Cultural Logic of Late Capitalism* (1991) to *The Cultural Turn* (1998), in the new postmodern space the subjects are bereft of spatial coordinates and utterly incapable of distantiation. Furthermore, capital, in the new multinational or late capitalism, has aggressively penetrated and colonized the precapitalist enclaves of nature and the unconscious that formerly functioned as realms where forms of critical thought could be developed. According to Jameson, what we "must now affirm is that it is precisely this whole extraordinarily demoralizing and depressing original new global space which is the 'moment of truth' of postmodernism" (1991: 49). In full postmodernism, as he stresses, modern aesthetic practices are useless; that is, those practices offered by, for instance, Proust, Joyce, Woolf, or Kafka are of very limited value for the attempt to represent the strictly speaking nonrepresentable.[32] We need new forms that would be capable of representing the new global late-capitalist space. Jameson holds that the first decisive steps might be taken by means of what he terms cognitive mapping. He explicitly speaks of an "aesthetic of cognitive mapping" and of a "new cultural form":

> We cannot, however, return to aesthetic practices elaborated on the basis of historical situations and dilemmas, which are no longer ours. Meanwhile, the conception of space that has been developed here suggests that a model of political culture appropriate to our own situation will necessarily have to raise spatial issues as its fundamental organizing concern. I will therefore provisionally define the aesthetic of this new (and hypothetical) cultural form as an aesthetic of *cognitive mapping*. (1991: 50–1)[33]

I do not intend to explain the Jamesonian idea of cognitive mapping in detail, but I wish to direct attention to the fact that he emphasizes that his "call for new kinds of representation is not meant to imply the return to Balzac or Brecht; nor is it intended as some valorization of content over form" (1988: 348). Cognitive mapping has a pedagogical function insofar as it teaches postmodern subjects about their position in an increasingly complex and opaque late-capitalist space; that is, it is supposed to offer spatial orientation and at the same time it prefigures a fully articulated political aesthetic practice (or it sketches the possibility of inventing this new aesthetic practice with its new forms). In his classic text, *The*

Image of the City (1960), the geographer Kevin Lynch analyzes the significance of mental maps of city space. In an original manner, Jameson extrapolates Lynch's spatial analysis to the realm of social structure. He does this by bringing together Lynch's notions of city experience and urban alienation with Althusser's famous conception of ideology:

> I have always been struck by the way in which Lynch's conception of city experience—the dialectic between the here and now of immediate perception and the imaginative or imaginary sense of the city as an absent totality—presents something like a spatial analogue of Althusser's great formulation of ideology itself, as "the Imaginary representation of the subject's relationship to his or her Real conditions of existence." (1988: 353)

By developing a new form of cognitive mapping that is appropriate to the social, political, and economic realities we inhabit in full postmodernity, the new forms of this aesthetic will eventually result in a new socialist position. On Jameson's account, "the incapacity to map socially is as crippling to political experience as the analogous incapacity to map spatially is for urban experience. It follows that an aesthetic of cognitive mapping in this sense is an integral part of any socialist political project" (1988: 353).

For our purposes, it is important to see that in order to theorize the connection between cognitive mapping and socialist politics, Jameson needs the concept of totality and the idea of form. In the 1980s, a decade that was dominated by poststructuralist and deconstructive notions of difference, heterogeneity, micropolitics, and aesthetic nominalism, he asserts: "But I do want to argue that without a conception of the social totality (and the possibility of transforming a whole social system), no properly socialist politics is possible" (1988: 355). At the end of "Cognitive Mapping," Jameson states that postmodernism does offer examples of cognitive mapping on the level of content. However, in his opinion neither the autoreferentiality of postmodern art that only plays with reproductive technology nor paranoid conspiracy fiction and films are capable of productively confronting the task that cognitive mapping has set for the new aesthetics. While the former ought to be regarded as a "degraded figure of the great multinational space that remains to be cognitively mapped," the latter "is the poor person's cognitive mapping in the postmodern age; it is a degraded figure of the total logic of late capital, a desperate attempt to represent the latter's system, whose failure is marked by its slippage into sheer theme and content" (1988: 356). By contrast, as Jameson maintains, "achieved cognitive mapping will be a matter of form" (1988: 356). In *Postmodernism*, he openly admits that he does not yet know what forms this new aesthetic will produce.[34] However, his complex discussion of Frank Gehry's house in Santa Monica, CA, in the chapter "Spatial Equivalents in the World System," already might count as a partial answer to that question. Moreover, his analyses of film in *Signatures of the Visible* (1992) and *The Geopolitical Aesthetic* (1992) would flesh out his idea of a new political aesthetic practice. While many of his texts since the early 1990s have shown that Jameson still holds that radically new forms and new modes of representing the global totality of late capitalism have to be developed, he does not often mention the idea of cognitive mapping anymore.[35]

I have briefly discussed the Jamesonian conception of cognitive mapping in order to show to what extent it is dominated by the link between cognition, form, and the concept of totality. This relation was central to his texts on postmodernism and postmodernity, roughly from the late 1970s to the mid-1990s. However, another relation, or attempt at mediation, has been even more central to Jameson's oeuvre. I wish to suggest that an appreciation of the link between narrative, aesthetic form, and totality offers an even more thought-provoking insight into this Hegelian Marxist's way of thinking (from *Marxism and Form* [1971] to *The Antinomies of Realism* [2013]). The significance of this relation becomes obvious when one considers Jameson's reading of Lukács. The former has been interested in his fellow Marxist theoretician since the 1960s.[36] Lukács has always played a central role as regards Jameson's attempt to develop a version of Marxism, and especially Marxist literary and cultural theory, which can legitimately be termed contemporary. So far as I can see, Jameson was the first theorist who called attention to the importance of the dialectics of narrative and totality for Lukács's Marxism. His chapter on Lukács in *Marxism and Form*, "The Case for Georg Lukács," and his piece "*History and Class Consciousness* as an Unfinished Project" (1998) partly develop the same argument. Both texts suggest that it would be wrong and not very productive to assume a radical break between the Lukács of *History and Class Consciousness* and his attempt to theorize a critical realism. Jameson's contention is that instead of dividing Lukács's career into early, middle, and late phases, one might contemplate the idea that there is one central aspect that preoccupied him throughout his eventful and peripatetic career—namely, narrative. Jameson intends to show "that Lukács' work may be seen as a continuous and lifelong meditation on narrative, on its basic structures, its relationship to the reality it expresses, and its epistemological value when compared with other, more abstract and philosophical modes of understanding" (1971: 163).

Jameson's argument indeed makes sense. Whether as a Hegelian (and quasi-Kierkegaardian) aesthete, a Marxist theorist of reification and alienation (with idealist inclinations), a theorist of (critical and socialist) realism, or an old man seeking to write a Marxist aesthetics and ontology—throughout his successive positions and phases one gets the impression that Lukács holds that only narrative will be capable of creatively confronting capitalist reification, alienation, and fragmentation, the reifying abstractions of science, the false objectivism of traditional epistemology, and the utter lack of poetry in people's everyday life under capitalism. Only narrative can provide a wholeness to life, it reflects the process of life in motion and in a dynamic historical context, and it offers a perspective insofar as it illuminates the real alternatives of its time. The Lukácsian notion of narrative, in other words, cannot be adequately understood without the concept of totality. Jameson submits that one ought to consider the

> possibility of conceptualizing the relationship between the idea of "totality" in *History and Class Consciousness* and the later account of realism in some other way than as break, substitution, compensation, formation. Indeed, in my opinion, what seems more plausible is rather the continuity between these two doctrines and indeed their inextricable philosophical relationship. (1998: 202)

In *History and Class Consciousness*, Lukács introduces a proletarian subject of praxis whose relationship with the world is an active one, a union of thought and action, and who because of his or her process of emancipation is capable of appreciating that the outside world must not be considered as nature but as history since it is the result of human labor. Consequently, the subject can not only in a Vichian sense understand the world, but she or he can also strive to change it. Men and women make their world, and their worldly practice and creative action in history leads to the coexistence of conflicting historical tendencies. To put it differently, one result of human labor and human action is a plurality of stories about what to do with ourselves. The abstractions of the natural sciences and the contemplative gesture of (bourgeois) philosophy, as we have seen, eventually turn out to be of only limited value for the subject of praxis who desires social change. In Lukács's account, it is only the realist novel of the nineteenth century that offers the subject of praxis, the person of creative action, the possibility of fully understanding the world in its multilayered complexity, and that thus prepares the ground for radical social change. As Jameson points out: "It was not until the nineteenth century, therefore, that what had previously been understood (and expressed) in terms of a conflict between man and destiny or nature can be narrated in the purely human and social categories of what Lukács will henceforth call *realism*" (1971: 190).

Jameson is right in maintaining that for Lukács "narration is the basic category and abstract knowledge a second best only" (1971: 195). As we have seen in the first part of this chapter, abstraction always was one of Lukács's *bêtes noires*. Abstraction necessarily entails a lack of humanist social perspective. Like the Lukácsian notion of revolutionary praxis in *History and Class Consciousness*, the realist novel depends "on those privileged historical moments in which access to society as a totality may once again somehow be reinvented" (1971: 205). From what we have discussed in this part, it should be clear that even more so than for Lukács, for Jameson narrative is intimately connected with aesthetic form. In other words, our analysis of Jameson's theoretical approach has shown that the endeavor to highlight the significance of the link between narrative, form, and totality is one possibility of establishing an important parallel between Lukács and Jameson. This link is central to their Hegelian Marxist versions of literary and aesthetic theory, and I have suggested that a pragmatist humanist will profit from contemplating the implications and consequences of this relation. Above all, they will gain a more complex and multilayered understanding of the work of aesthetic form.

5.4 Conclusion

In his long career, John Dewey did not often see the necessity of explaining his attitude toward Marxism. He freely admitted his early Hegelian inclinations, but never stated any real interest in Marxist thought. His most detailed discussion of Marxism can be found in *Freedom and Culture* (1939). In this text, Dewey's radical critique of Marxism becomes particularly obvious. His contention is that Marxism is a form of absolutism, an authoritarian, monolithic, and monistic theory, which "combines the romantic idealism of earlier social revolutionaries with what purports to be a thoroughly 'objective' scientific analysis, expressed in formulations of a single all-embracing 'law'" (1989: 65). To Dewey, and this is one of his main arguments, Marxism is profoundly antiscientific and a form of romantic absolutism that has turned out to be a hindrance to the progress of mankind. As regards his critique of Marxism, the following passage is very illuminating:

> The inherent theoretical weakness of Marxism is that it supposed a generalization that was made at a particular date and place (and made even then only by bringing observed facts under a premise drawn from a metaphysical source) can obviate the need for continued resort to observation, and to continual revision of generalizations in their office of working hypotheses. In the name of science, a thoroughly anti-scientific procedure was formulated, in accord with which a generalization is made having the nature of ultimate "truth," and hence good at all times and places. (1989: 71)

From this quote it becomes obvious that Dewey holds that Marxism is a foundationalist, essentialist, profoundly ahistorical, and antiscientific philosophy, which is moreover dominated by a metaphysical and totalizing gesture.

As a self-proclaimed disciple of Dewey, Richard Rorty shares his critical attitude toward Marxism.[37] In *Achieving Our Country*, for instance, Rorty warns his fellow Americans that "it is important not to let Marxism influence the story we tell about our own left" (1998a: 41). In "The End of Leninism, Havel, and Social Hope," he expresses his hope that "we can banalize the entire vocabulary of leftist political deliberation" (1998b: 229). Moreover, he proposes that the longing for total (Marxist or socialist) revolution seems utterly pointless after the events of 1989.[38] Marxism as a metanarrative or "grand récit" in the Lyotardian sense has become a large blurry fantasy for him, an overtheorized and ineffective way of thinking that only pretends to be capable of conceptually grasping "objects" such as "History," "Freedom," and "Capitalism." We simply have to stop using the old Marxist vocabulary, to weed out world-historical and eschatological terms:

> The events of 1989 have convinced those who were still trying to hold on to Marxism that we need a way of holding our time in thought, and a plan for making the future better than the present, which drops reference to capitalism, bourgeois ways of life, bourgeois ideology, and the working class. We must give up on the Marxist blur, as Marx and Dewey gave up on the Hegelian blur. (1998b: 233)

There has been a resurgence of interest in Marxism in the past two decades. Because of this revival of interest in Marxist thought it is not difficult to imagine intellectuals who might be inclined to advance the argument that human liberation does not consist in overcoming metaphysical thought but rather in superseding capitalism. According to them, humanism that truly deserves its name cannot ignore the predatory nature of capitalism and the dangers that it entails. Does the establishment of a postmetaphysical culture really help humans to solve the ecological crisis or to reach environmental sustainability?[39] In this context one ought to see that pragmatism strives to clear the ground for future thinking, it urges us to get rid of unnecessary baggage. Maybe future pragmatists and pragmatist humanists, *pace* Rorty, will see the necessity of arguing for a rapprochement between pragmatism and Marxism because they will appreciate that holding onto the dichotomy of overcoming metaphysics versus superseding capitalism has damaging consequences for a twenty-first-century humanism.

By substituting groundless hope for theoretical insight and by insisting upon the significance of small, concrete, banal, and local fantasies, Rorty seeks to convince his leftist readers with Marxist inclinations that they should no longer see themselves as belonging to the avant-garde. He writes:

> But now we have either to spin some new metanarrative that does not mention capitalism, yet has the same dramatic power and urgency as the Marxist narrative, or else to give up the idea that we intellectuals are notably better at holding our time in thought than our fellow citizens. Since I have no idea how to do the former, I suggest we do the latter. (1998b: 235)

I think, and hope, that future pragmatist humanists will confront the Hegelian task of "holding our time in thought" by creatively mediating between pragmatism and Marxism and by underscoring that this attempt at mediation is a more fruitful task than the Rortyan endeavor to "banalize" the vocabulary of leftist politics (including cultural politics). The urgency of today's political and ecological crises renders Rorty's modest gesture problematic.

In this chapter, I have demonstrated that one can gain a different perspective on the relation between Marxism and pragmatism by focusing on aesthetic and literary theory. Moreover, I have argued that pragmatist humanism can learn and profit from Lukács and Adorno's aesthetic theories. A consideration of the Lukácsian and Jamesonian link between narrative, form, and totality and of a post-Adornian notion of the negation of aesthetic synthesis will teach pragmatist humanists a more complex understanding of aesthetic form, or it will help them to become truly interested in the practice of form-giving, the work of form, in the first place.[40] Together with the argument that I developed in Chapter 3, this chapter has shown that pragmatist aesthetics for too long has suffered from an insufficient grasp of the significance of form. Since twentieth-century Marxist theorists, in my opinion, have offered the most convincing and stimulating theorizations of the social function of aesthetic form, of the "Gesellschaftlichkeit der Form," a dialogue between Marxist and pragmatist aestheticians promises interesting results. Furthermore, it can prepare the ground for a more detailed discussion of the possibility of bringing these two philosophies of praxis together in the twenty-first century.

6

"Nothing Is Known—Only Realized": Postcritique, Bruno Latour, and the Idea of a Positive Aesthetics

Proponents of postcritique want something new. Dissatisfied with the goals of critique and its notions of detecting, problematizing, deconstructing, and subverting, postcritics long for what might almost be termed a paradigm shift in literary and cultural studies. Critique, they maintain, is too dark, negative, gloomy, suspicious, and paranoid. At the same time, it is too predictable and mechanistic. It is joyless, anemic, and governed by the imperatives of theory. Postcritics urge one to pose the question of what would happen if the literary or cultural critic instead focused on the practices of making, creating, associating, translating, mediating, connecting, and attaching.[1] Postcritics such as Eve Sedgwick, Heather Love, and Rita Felski have proposed that a hermeneutics of suspicion should be replaced by the creativity of new constellations, a recognition of the plurality of forms of aesthetic engagement, and the endeavor to elucidate the complexity of literature's connectedness. Instead of concentrating either on literature's otherworldly status or on the literary or cultural text's potential as a form of resistance—both stances are central to modernism from Mallarmé to Adorno—the postcritic ought to illuminate that art and literature are primarily a matter of connecting, imagining, assembling, composing, and coproducing.

Critique depends on certain central dichotomies without which it cannot do its job: subject-object, word-world, text-context, truth-lie (ideology), surface-depth, and, above all, appearance-reality. The real meaning of a literary text, if one follows the (modern) critic, is hidden and hence has to be restored to the surface. To the critic, in other words, the notion of depth is indispensable. By means of his or her symptomatic or suspicious reading, the critic strives to wrest meaning from a text. To put it differently, the critic's task is to restore to the surface the history that the text represses or hides under layers of ideology. From this one can already see that the modern critic's way of speaking centers on terms such as repression, negativity, excavation, depth, depth interpretation, allegorical reading, and the really real.²

In the first part of this chapter, I discuss Felski's notion of a "positive aesthetics." What interests me is whether pragmatism will be capable of contributing to the development of this positive aesthetics. It is stimulating, I submit, to pose the question of whether this aesthetics might also entail a renewed interest in aesthetic form and the practice of form-giving. In this chapter, I also briefly discuss the role Nietzsche might play for a postcritical positive aesthetics. In the second part, I advance the argument that for Latour's philosophy of relations and radical immanence, an analysis of form runs the danger of turning into another version of formalism. Refusing to regard the agency of form as poetic agency, Latour and the postcritics prevent one from fully appreciating the relationship between the agency and contingency of aesthetic form, on the one hand, and the contingency of social and historical networks, on the other.

6.1 Rita Felski and the Idea of a "Positive Aesthetics"

In *Uses of Literature* (2008), *The Limits of Critique* (2015), and *Hooked: Art and Attachment* (2020a), Felski introduces a radically different understanding of the task of the literary or cultural critic.³ All three monographs are connected in that they develop a redescription of critique. Already in 2008, Felski was critical of the dominance of ideology critique, symptomatic reading, and the hermeneutics of suspicion in the past decades. What she wishes to offer, as she underscores on the first page of *Uses of Literature*, is "a negation of a negation, an act of yea-saying not nay-saying, a thought experiment that seeks to advocate, not denigrate" (2008: 1). In the confrontation with the omnipresence of skepticism and vigilance in literary studies, Felski instead offers "an attempt to see things from another angle, to rough out, if you will, the shape of a positive aesthetics" (2008: 22). It is precisely the introduction of this "positive aesthetics" that unites her three books and that, moreover, offers an important contribution to the debate on the state of literary studies in the twenty-first century. Calling attention to "the force of our attachments," Felski suggests that "there is no reason why our readings cannot blend analysis and attachment, criticism and love" (2008: 22).

Felski continues her argument against "the institutional entrenchment of negative aesthetics" (2008: 132) in her widely discussed *The Limits of Critique*.⁴ It ought to be noted that she does not offer a polemic against critique, and that she also does not intend to proclaim another death of theory. Moreover, she does not seek to counterbalance the reign of critique and suspicious reading with the imperative that it is high time to realize the promising potential of a new aestheticism or new formalism. Felski instead wants to represent "a close-up scrutiny of a thought style" (2015: 2), which goes hand in hand with a certain intellectual mood or disposition. According to her, critique's key elements are "a spirit of skeptical questioning or outright condemnation, an emphasis on its precarious position vis-à-vis overbearing and oppressive social forces, the claim to be engaged in some kind of radical intellectual and/or political work, and the assumption that whatever is *not* critical must therefore be *uncritical*" (2015: 2). While Bruno Latour did not yet play a role in *Uses of Literature*, he is central to the argument that Felski develops in *The Limits of Critique*. Throughout her monograph, she places a premium on creating, connecting, making, and agency (of texts), as well as on the activities or practices of redescription and recontextualization. In a central passage, for instance, she writes: "We shortchange the significance of art by focusing on the 'de' prefix (its power to demystify, destabilize, denaturalize) at the expense of the 're' prefix: its ability to recontextualize, reconfigure, or recharge perception" (2015: 17; emphasis omitted).

A positive aesthetics in Felski's sense insists that there are limits to the endlessly repeated practices of unmasking, exposing, subverting, or destabilizing.[5] Actor-network theory (ANT), as she contends, regards interpretation as a process that involves actors that create something new together. Whether seen as a form of recontextualization, a powerful mode of attachment, or a redescription within an antirepresentationalist framework, interpretation is closely linked with novelty and creativity. Felski formulates as follows: "Interpretation becomes a coproduction between actors that brings new things to light rather than an endless rumination on a text's hidden meanings or representational failures" (2015: 174; emphasis omitted).

Felski's application of Latour's ANT to literary studies contributes to an elucidation of her notion of a positive aesthetics. In the final chapter of *The Limits of Critique*, "Context Stinks!," the author defines what she terms "postcritical reading" (2015: 172–85). According to Felski, this is what a postcritical reading will refuse to do:

> Subject a text to interrogation; diagnose its hidden anxieties; demote recognition to yet another form of misrecognition; lament our incarceration in the prison-house of language; demonstrate that resistance is just another

form of containment; read a text as a metacommentary on the undecidability of meaning; score points by showing that its categories are socially constructed; brood over the gap that separates word from world. (2015: 173)

Felski understands ANT as a philosophy of relations that helps one appreciate the implications of the modern development from finding to making and that also makes one see the weaknesses and shortcomings of forms of foundationalism, essentialism, and dualistic thinking.[6] Latourian panrelationism, which was strongly influenced by William James's version of pragmatism, is incompatible with the purity of much dualistic thought. Like pragmatism, ANT radically questions the gesture of a convergence to the antecedently real, true, or pure. Both approaches confront the messiness of reality with an insistence on the significance of the creativity of action, the recognition of contingency, and the suggestions that one ought to reject the Platonic jargon and its dualisms and that the vocabulary in which the traditional problems of Western philosophy were discussed is no longer useful.[7] Latour's work, as Felski maintains, "is a sustained polemic against the urge to purify: to separate rationality from emotion, to safeguard critique from faith, to oppose fact to fetish" (2015: 179).

In a Latourian manner, Felski submits that twenty-first-century literary and cultural scholars ought to prefer "a language of addition rather than subtraction, translation rather than separation, connection rather than isolation, composition rather than critique" (2015: 182). Furthermore, she mentions the act of "multiplying actors and mediators," and she also submits that we should replace the by-now old-fashioned question "What does this text undermine?" with the decidedly more stimulating question "What does this text create, build, make possible?" (2015: 182). One ought to note that Felski's positive aesthetics, centering on this language of addition, composition, and translation and emphasizing the practices of making, creating, connecting, and multiplying, helps us to understand that the aforementioned development from finding or unmasking to making is an anti-Platonist story of poetic achievements or poetic agency that not only dismisses the correspondence theory of truth as outdated and questions the yearning for a transcultural and transhistorical truth, but also calls attention to the contingency, historicity, and creativity of the vocabularies we use.

In the introduction to *Critique and Postcritique*, Felski and Elizabeth Anker suggest that we "can no longer assume that a stance of negativity and opposition is sufficient to justify the aesthetic or social importance of literature or our practice as critics" (2017: 20). Moreover, they propose that as far as the current moment in literary and cultural studies is concerned, one can detect "a broad interest in exploring new models and practices of reading that are less beholden to suspicion and skepticism, more willing to avow the creative, innovative, world-making aspects of literature and criticism. What gets build and shaped when a critic reads? What affordances and opportunities does literary form and experience open up?" (2017: 20). This passage is important insofar as Anker and Felski make clear that their redescription of critique also concerns the significance of aesthetic form. Whereas Richard Rorty's pragmatist brand of literary criticism, as ethical criticism, almost completely ignores the question of form (as we saw in Chapter 3), Anker and Felski understand that the act of form-giving, for a literary scholar, is one of the most stimulating ways of making (and world-making). At the same time, however, one has to see that because of the influence of Latour's ANT on postcritique, proponents of the latter have not yet offered a detailed and convincing analysis of form. Latour's posthumanist focus on the redistribution of agency, as we will see further on, has left hardly any room for a new or postcritical notion of aesthetic form. Can the practice of form-giving, with its humanist connotations, be subsumed under the Latourian category of agency? What happens when one realizes the stimulating potential of a mediation between postcritique and a pragmatist version of humanism and at the same time notes that both have failed to offer a convincing discussion of form? How can one productively use the insight that while both ANT and pragmatism are governed by the supremacy of the agent's point of view and by an emphasis on the contingent plurality of actions in a world that is in the Jamesian sense in the making, the creativity of artistic form-giving does not have an exceptional status?[8]

In her latest study, *Hooked*, Felski explicitly states that she intends to "build an aesthetic that is premised on relation rather than separation, on attachment rather than autonomy" (2020a: viii). Thus, she continues her endeavor to develop a positive aesthetics and illuminate the possibilities of a language of attachment. Another important influence of Latour's philosophical stance on Felski's aesthetics is the critical attitude toward traditional epistemology. In epistemology, as Latour and the pragmatists demonstrate, detachment is seen as a precondition for knowledge. In other words, there is an intimate relation between knowledge, detachment or distance, and the coherence of epistemological theories. This intimate link is rejected by Felski's postcritical approach and by Latour's philosophy of associations or version of empiricism; both criticize the view from nowhere (Thomas Nagel) and the quest for certainty (Dewey). Latour's imperative to follow the actors and describe what they do and Felski's notion of poetic agency indirectly question the necessity for a coherent grand theory. Felski points out in this context: "The coherence of critical theories is their forte but also their frailty; while intellectually appealing and morally compelling, they can be a poor fit for the messiness of reality—or of art" (2020a: 11). ANT's flat ontology and its critique of epistemology indeed offer the possibility of approaching the "messiness of reality." ANT's framework leaves room for contingency, the unpredictable moves of actors, their quirks and idiosyncrasies, and for the often unexpected forms of networks. Nothing, it seems, is already given. In a world of relations without foundations and essences, the notion of an "enframing reality that is already given" seems no longer useful. Felski stresses that "we cannot know in advance which networks will count. ANT's tracing of relations differs from a traditional view of context, as an enframing reality that is already given, that precedes—historically and analytically—the phenomenon being analyzed, which only needs to be shoehorned into the relevant container" (2020a: 140).

6.2 Bruno Latour, Postcritique, and the Critique of Epistemology

How can one describe Latour's version of ANT?[9] Is it a radically relationist philosophy? A radical empiricism in the Jamesian sense? A process philosophy in the Whiteheadian sense? A new brand of realism? Or is it a thought-provoking mixture of these influences? After the reign of high (French) theory, Latour's ANT has had a profound influence on more and more humanist scholars since the beginning of the twenty-first century. His essay "Why Has Critique Run Out of Steam?" played a crucial role in this context. There is no need to offer another detailed discussion of the argument Latour develops in this piece. However, as regards his own position, one ought to see that his contention is that the "question was never to get *away* from facts but *closer* to them, not fighting empiricism but, on the contrary, renewing empiricism" (2004: 231). Furthermore, he underlines that if the critical mind wishes to renew itself and become more relevant, then it ought to strive for "the cultivation of a *stubbornly realist attitude*—to speak like William James—but a realism dealing with what I will call *matters of concern*, not *matters of fact*" (2004: 231). It is precisely this "second empiricism, this return to the realist attitude" (2004: 232) that this French philosopher offers as a means of dealing with the drastically reduced significance, or uselessness, of critique. The modern critic alternately presented himself as an iconoclast or antifetishist, a positivist, or a realist.[10] He did not see a mismatch of these contradictory frameworks, since he used them to approach and conceptually grasp different topics. His dualistic thought made it easy to categorize and thus separate things and phenomena; that is, his dichotomous thinking stabilized the notion of purity that did not offer the possibility of accentuating the importance of the realm of the in-between (as a realm of hybrids or quasi-objects).[11] The modern critic's understanding of matters of fact now seems obsolete, and it has continually promised something that it could not deliver. What is needed instead, according to Latour, is "a multifarious inquiry launched with the tools of anthropology, philosophy, metaphysics, history, sociology to detect *how many participants* are gathered in a *thing* to make it exist and to maintain its existence" (2004: 246).

What, if one follows Latour, is the task of the critic after the conceptions of modernity and modernism have proven to be severely limited? In other words, the question arises as to what the task of the critic is after we have reached the conclusion that "critical theory died away long ago" (2004: 248)? Criticism, in his opinion, should be associated with "a whole set of new positive metaphors, gestures, attitudes, knee-jerk reactions, habits of thought" (2004: 247). In other words, the new version of critique or inquiry "could be associated with *more*, not with *less*, with *multiplication*, not *subtraction*;" it is a task associated with "mediating, assembling, gathering" (2004: 248). In Latour's account, the critic is the one who creatively makes, who establishes connections, worries about the possibility of new mediations, traces associations, and creates new assemblies. He or she does not concentrate on finding, discovering, detecting, or unmasking:

> The critic is not the one who debunks, but the one who assembles. The critic is not the one who lifts the rugs from under the feet of the naïve believers, but the one who offers the participants arenas in which to gather. The critic is not the one who alternates haphazardly between antifetishism and positivism like the drunk iconoclast drawn by Goya, but the one for whom, if something is constructed, then it means it is fragile and thus in great need of care and caution. (2004: 246)

Latour's idea of a positive alternative to critique also plays a central role in his "An Attempt at a 'Compositionist' Manifesto.'" What he terms "compositionism" could function as an alternative to critique. In this context, it is of particular interest how Latour draws attention to the degree to which critique is governed by the appearance-reality distinction. In his opinion, critique has exhausted its possibilities, since it was "predicated on the discovery of a true world of realities lying behind a veil of appearances. This beautiful staging had the great advantage of creating a huge difference of potential between the world of delusion and the world of reality" (2010: 475). Compositionism is intimately linked to Felski's positive aesthetics, since both elucidate the significance of making, creating, assembling, and of positive knowledge. By contrast, modern critique combines its ethos of negativity, its omnipresent skepticism, with its obsession with the dialectics of appearance and reality. On Latour's account, critique works with the notion of "a real world of the beyond," that is, the really real. It is the critic's task to discover this really real behind the veil of appearances. The modern critic holds that because of the sophistication of their conceptual tools they have "a privileged access to the world of reality behind the veil of appearances." What this boils down to, if one follows Latour, is that the modern critic, contrary to their self-understanding, continues the Platonic tradition of transcendence.[12] Whereas the critic still relies on transcendence, the Latourian world is characterized by its immanence and its notion of absolute concreteness. The respective passage is worth quoting in full:

> Ironically, given the Nietzschean fervor of so many iconoclasts, critique relies on a rear world of the beyond, that is, on a transcendence that is no less transcendent for being fully secular. With critique, you may debunk, reveal, unveil, but only as long as you establish, through this process of creative destruction, a privileged access to the world of reality behind the veils of appearances. Critique, in other words, has all the limits of utopia: it relies on the certainty of the world *beyond* this world. By contrast, for compositionism, there is no world of beyond. It is all about *immanence*. (2010: 475)

It is indeed ironic that modern critics, on the one hand, present themselves as Nietzschean iconoclasts and, on the other, still rely on the appearance-reality dichotomy. One of the primary targets of Nietzsche's naturalism was precisely this appearance-reality distinction. He advances the idea that the traditional philosopher constantly sought to make the natural and historical world, the world of practice as the only world we have, look bad. In *The Will to Power*, Nietzsche states that the traditional philosopher "invents a world so as to be able to slander and bespatter this world: in reality, he reaches every time for nothingness and construes nothingness as 'God,' as 'truth,' and in any case as judge and condemner of *this* state of being" (1968, sec. 461). In this context, one should also remember how Nietzsche summarizes the process of detranscendentalization in "How the 'True World' Finally Became a Fable" in *Twilight of the Idols* (1889).[13] If one thinks of the fact that French anti-Hegelianism can be understood as a form of Nietzscheanism (from Bataille and Blanchot to Barthes, Foucault, and Derrida), then Latour's diagnosis of the malaise of postmodernism gains in importance. Abhorring the postmodern specter, Latour suggests that the situation is even worse for the postmodern critic who, after the process of deconstruction, has to discover that there is nothing real behind the layers of appearances. This is the kind of nihilism dominating too many versions of poststructuralism and deconstruction: "For the hammer of critique can only prevail if, behind the slowly dismantled wall of appearances, is finally revealed the netherworld of reality. But when there is nothing real to be seen behind this destroyed wall, critique suddenly looks like another call to nihilism" (2010: 475).[14] In spite of its anti-Platonic gesture and antifoundationalist stance, modern and postmodern critique is still dominated by a desire for transcendence, and the latter can be detected in the critics' incapability of getting rid of the appearance-reality distinction even when the results of their conceptual work repeatedly have turned out to be a paralyzing and stultifying nihilism.

It is noteworthy that Latour, in contrast to most postmodern critics, does not radically reject the concept of truth. Compositionists, as he emphasizes, "want immanence *and* truth together. Or to use my language: we want *matters of concern*, not only *matters of fact*. For a compositionist, nothing is beyond dispute. And yet, closure has to be achieved. But it is achieved only by the slow process of composition and compromise, not by the revelation of the world of beyond" (2010: 478). In this context, I wish to briefly come back to Latour's critique of epistemology. The complexity of his position becomes obvious when one compares his emphasis on "immanence *and* truth" with his attitude toward truth in *Irréductions*. The latter is still one of his most fascinating texts.[15] It is undoubtedly one of his most systematic books, although not striving for the crystalline purity of Wittgenstein's *Tractatus*, and at the same time a partly confusing text. For our purposes, it is interesting to note that there are many passages in *Irréductions* that could be interpreted as being part of a pragmatist manifesto. Latour comments on the adjective "true" as follows: "A sentence does not hold together because it is true, but *because it holds together* we say that it is 'true'" (1988: 185). While Rorty would advance the idea that one should no longer consider truth to be a philosophically interesting topic, he would also contend that Latour in the 1980s contributed to the endeavor to get out from under Platonism. Latour's following comments on truth also strongly remind one of Rorty's pragmatist position: "One form of know-how is no more 'true' than another. [...] The word 'true' is a supplement added to certain trials of strength to dazzle those who might still question them" (1988: 227). In the context of the central Latourian idea that reality is primarily resistance or that what resists is real, he asserts: "We can say that whatever resists is real. The word 'truth' adds only a little supplement to a trial of strength" (1988: 227). The notion of truth here no longer has anything to do with correspondence or coherence theories of truth, it is rather located in a series of translations and mediations between actors. Whereas Latour maintains that the more connected an actor or actant is, the more real it is and the higher the probability that one would use the adjective "true" in one's description of it, a pragmatist—as humanist—would claim that "true" ought to be regarded as a compliment one pays to a human practice or set of social practices or man-made form of normativity that have proven to be useful or led to desired consequences.[16]

As we have seen, Latour's world is a world of immanence. There are only trials of strength (or weakness). It is a world of forces or entelechies or actants; a world of negotiations, alliances, mediations, or translations between those forces. Moreover, it is a world of utter concreteness where everything happens only once, at a specific time, and in one specific place. Consequently, the Latourian world is less a Deleuzian world of becoming than one of specific events. Simply put, this world no longer has need for epistemology, since its inhabitants no longer have to bridge the gap between subject and object or humans and a world out there. As Graham Harman formulates: "Whereas Latour places all human, nonhuman, natural, and artificial objects on the same footing, the analytics and continentals both still dither over how to bridge, ignore, deny, or explain away a single gap between humans and world" (2009: 16).[17] Latour's rejection of epistemology also becomes clear when one considers one of the most important sentences he ever wrote: "Nothing is known—only realized" (1988: 159). Another quasi-pragmatist motto. According to Latour, epistemology is governed by a desire for transcendence that is neither needed nor wanted in a world of human and nonhuman practices, trials, or experiments. Striving to discover or find a static world of immutable and eternal truth, the really real, behind this world of practices and trials, which is contingent and unpredictable, only seems possible when one holds that there is a special activity called thinking that offers humans the possibility of reaching a transcendent position. By contrast, in Latour's object-oriented philosophy, illuminating the notion of a democracy of objects, there is no special place for the thinking subject.

Elucidating the intimacy of the link between knowledge and transcendence, Latour claims that "nowhere more than in the evocation of this kingdom of knowledge do we create the impression that there is another transcendental world. It is only here that there is sanctuary. Politics has no rights here, and the laws that rule the other worlds are suspended" (1988: 215). In its ideal form, this dualistic world is pure, static, and uncontaminated by history. Latour writes: "All the failings of epistemology—its scorn of history, its rejection of empirical analysis, its pharisaic fear of impurity—are its only qualities, the qualities that are sought for in a frontier guard" (1988: 216). Again in a pragmatist manner, he avers that "knowledge does not exist—what would it be? There is only know-how. In other words, there are crafts and trades" (1988: 218). The aforementioned idea that "nothing is known—only realized" has to be seen in connection with his suggestion that there "is no such thing as 'knowledge', but it is possible to realize, that is, to make real, to understand" (1988: 226).

In numerous of his texts, Nietzsche works with the dualism finding versus making. In his opinion, the "reverence for truth is already an illusion." Consequently, "one should value more than truth the force that forms, simplifies, shapes, invents" (1968: sec. 602). The original speaks of "die bildende, vereinfachende, gestaltende, erdichtende Kraft." He continues his argument in section 605 where he suggests that the "ascertaining of 'truth' and 'untruth,' the ascertaining of facts in general, is fundamentally different from creative positing, from forming, shaping, overcoming, willing, such as is of the essence of philosophy" (1968). For our purposes, it is of the utmost importance to appreciate that in contrast to Latour and the pragmatists, Nietzsche directs attention to the significance of humans' creative acts of form-giving (see Section 7.4).[18] Latour's posthumanism and object-oriented philosophy cannot accept Nietzsche's idea that only we have created the world that has value and that concerns us as human beings, while pragmatist aesthetics has never offered a convincing analysis of form (see Chapter 3).[19] What this boils down to is that Nietzsche helps us understand how much the Latourian and pragmatist suggestion that "nothing is known—only realized" has to do with creative acts of form-giving or with the contingency, particularity, and historicity of aesthetic form. Opposing the "will to truth" of the metaphysicians and representationalists to the "will to create" of the experimenters and new philosophers, Nietzsche's contention is that one ought to regard the "will to truth" "*as the impotence of the will to create*" (1968: sec. 585).

Crucially, Nietzsche has so far played no role for the postcritical attempt to develop a positive aesthetics. This is deplorable. In *The Limits of Critique*, for instance, Felski only briefly mentions Nietzsche in the context of her discussion of Ricoeur's idea of a "hermeneutics of suspicion" (Felski 2015: 31–2) and completely ignores the later Nietzsche's suggestion that art is primarily a means of enhancing life. The point here is not that Ricoeur's interpretation of Marx, Nietzsche, and Freud was too undifferentiated to begin with, but rather that Nietzsche's advocacy of art's positive mission and his desire to link art and the self-affirmation of life could have strengthened Felski's argument. Hardly any philosopher has introduced an aesthetics as radically positive as that of the later Nietzsche. In his "Attempt at Self-Criticism," a harsh self-critique of his first book, *The Birth of Tragedy* (1872), he unequivocally makes clear that art is this-worldly, and he opposes "the art of comfort *in this world*" (1999: 12) to a metaphysical understanding of the task of art. Art, as he underscores in *Twilight of the Idols*, is "the great stimulus to life" ("Skirmishes," sec. 24). For Nietzsche, art affirms. Hence, there is no such thing as pessimistic art. In a programmatic sentence in *The Will to Power*, he maintains that what "is essential in art remains its perfection of existence, its production of perfection and plenitude; art is essentially *affirmation, blessing, deification of existence*" (1968: sec. 821). The later Nietzsche directs attention to the following question: "Is art a consequence of *dissatisfaction with reality*? Or an expression of *gratitude for happiness enjoyed*?" (1968: sec. 845).

Radically criticizing the will to truth, to reality, and the notion of "mere" appearance, he asserts that art stands for life, appearance, becoming, change, and the will to create (which we would interpret as the will to power as the will to form-giving). According to Nietzsche, Christian morality introduced a way of thinking that has turned out to be deeply hostile to art and life. It is characterized by "hatred of the 'world', a curse on the passions, fear of beauty and sensuality, a Beyond, invented in order better to defame the Here-and-Now, fundamentally a desire for nothingness, for the end" (1999: 9). Nietzsche's aesthetics simultaneously critiques Christian morality (eventually culminating in a form of nihilism), an aesthetics of decadence, and the notion of *l'art pour l'art*. However, this Nietzschean critique is not critique in the sense of what postcritics argue against, but rather an exalted and partly frivolous celebration of art's potential to creatively shape our lives and to make them endurable and worth living. Art, as the later Nietzsche holds, makes life possible: "Art and nothing but art! It is the great means of making life possible, the great seduction to life, the great stimulant of life. / Art as the only superior counterforce to all will to denial of life, as that which is anti-Christian, anti-Buddhist, antinihilist *par excellence*" (1968: sec. 853). From today's perspective, Nietzsche's exalted view of art may seem somewhat too much and partly naïve. However, one should see what the later Nietzsche's positive aesthetics combines: an emphasis on the will to create, a celebration of art as a means of enhancing life, noncognitivism (that is, a refusal to accept the idea that art has major cognitive significance and that it can tell us the truth about reality), an understanding of art as the good will to appearance (and hence a questioning of the idea of digging deep), and the desire to highlight the significance of the act of form-giving.[20] It is unclear why postcritics so far have refrained from using the potential of this combination.

In *Irreductions*, Latour underscores how far-reaching his anti-Platonism is: "But there is no 'theory,' no 'contemplation,' no 'speculation,' no 'prevision,' no 'vision,' and no 'knowledge.' Plato's sun neither burns nor turns in the sky" (1988: 228). We have seen that of the Latourian, pragmatist, and Nietzschean versions of anti-Platonism only the latter forces one to contemplate the implications of the idea that the will to create is synonymous with the action of creative form-giving—the work of form. What is the impact on our understanding of form when Latour advances the radical argument that there is no theory, or that "in theory, theories exist. In practice, they do not" (1988: 178)? When "practice lacks nothing" (1988: 179), does this signify that an analysis of form would be an abstract discussion of an abstract process that transforms empirical problems into purely formal issues and hence inevitably strengthens the theoretical over the practical? Does form, as the general, universal, or necessary, transcend the impure world of associations and translations, the world of immanence in the Latourian sense, and can it thus be regarded as part of the quest for certainty?

For both Latour and the pragmatist Rorty, an analysis of form too easily degenerates into another version of formalism, and the latter is part of the Kantian baggage we have to finally get rid of. Kant's First and Third *Critiques* established a stark subject-object dichotomy that, according to actor-network theorists and pragmatists, has had severely damaging consequences.[21] Latour's notions of a flat ontology and a democracy of objects and the Deweyan insistence on a continuity between nature-subject-society have had an impact on their followers' appreciation of the work of form. Since many postcritics have been influenced by Latour's version of ANT, they seemingly have been reluctant to engage in discussions of aesthetic form. How can one confront their limited interest in form? Too many postcritics seem to refuse to realize the implications of the following dialectical tension (which might also be due to the fact that they consider dialectics as belonging to the old-fashioned conceptual framework of critique):

> The specificities of historical contingency become intelligible in their forms of articulation. Actions of form are enmeshed in, and even exercise agency within, networks of social and historical conditions. So if an investigation of cultural formations will improve our sense of the production of literary forms, reading for form will also improve our sense of how cultural forms are produced. (Wolfson 2006: 12)

6.3 Conclusion

In this book, I have argued that pragmatist humanism can develop an aesthetics and literary criticism that will be capable of illuminating this intimate relationship between the agency and contingency of aesthetic form, on the one hand, and the contingency of social and historical networks, on the other. A positive aesthetics, which pragmatism is in a unique position to develop, needs a multilayered notion of the agency of form. Ironically enough, as we have seen in Chapter 5, particularly Adorno's dark aesthetics plays an important role in this context.

Within the framework of his ANT, Latour elucidates to what degree his idea of a nonmodern constitution is governed by a redistribution of agency. Seeking to avoid the reductionism of modern humanists, he proposes that the new constitution offers the possibility of appreciating that the "human is in the delegation itself, in the pass, in the sending, in the continuous exchange of forms" (1993: 138). In *Irreductions*, he pointedly states: "No matter how far we go, there are always forms" (1988: 161). For a pragmatist aesthetics, as part of a humanist philosophy, these ideas of "the continuous exchange of forms" and of the omnipresence of forms are too vague. They do not illuminate the work of form as poetic agency. Admittedly, one might be inclined to advance the argument that these ideas to a certain degree are compatible with the conception of form that Dewey introduces in *Art as Experience*. However, as I have argued, Dewey's understanding of form is the weakest part of his aesthetics. We need more than Latour and Dewey are willing to offer.

7

"I Turned to the Poets": Humanist Stories of Progress

When Socrates goes to the poets, he is profoundly disappointed. At the beginning of the *Apology*, Plato tells us about Socrates's reaction when he hears that the oracle at Delphi said that he was the wisest man on earth. Socrates seeks to verify whether the oracle is right by talking to men who he thinks are wiser than him. After having talked to the politicians, he converses with the poets: "I turned to the poets, dramatic, lyric, and all the rest" (22a-b). The latter do not teach Socrates anything. He does not learn from them. Socrates thinks that "it was not wisdom that enabled them to write their poetry, but a kind of instinct or inspiration, such as you find in seers and prophets who deliver all their sublime messages without knowing in the least what they mean" (22c). Furthermore, he maintains "that the very fact that they were poets made them think that they had a perfect understanding of all other subjects, of which they were totally ignorant" (22c). In the *Apology*, the poets are no help at all; they do not look good. In a Rortyan postmetaphysical or poeticized culture, their status would be different. By introducing a new way of speaking or a new set of metaphors, or by bringing together two hitherto isolated sets of metaphors, the poet—in the broad sense—might prepare the ground for cultural change. As we have seen, Rorty intends his literary or poeticized culture to be the final stage of the process of secularization. His antifoundationalist and antirepresentationalist story of progress ends here. One of the questions that are central to a Rortyan postmetaphysical culture is the following: What can we learn from the poets? For our purposes, it is crucial to note that pragmatist humanism as anti-authoritarianism urges one to confront the same question.

In this final chapter, I will seek to elucidate that Rorty's poeticized culture and the idea of a pragmatist humanism have a nineteenth-century prehistory. Discussing authors as varied as Emerson, Whitman, William James, and Nietzsche will further illuminate the contours of pragmatist humanism. From a Rortyan perspective, these authors tell humanist stories of progress.

Moreover, they directly answer the question of what one can learn from the poets. Having helped prepare the establishment of a Rortyan poeticized culture, these authors might also aid us in our endeavor to realize how pragmatism, humanism, anti-authoritarianism, and postmetaphysics are interlinked. Rorty's postmetaphysical culture and the notion of pragmatist humanism as anti-authoritarianism are supposed to show the implications of the aforementioned idea that the search for God was replaced by the striving for Truth and that the latter has finally been replaced by the search for novelty, by an emphasis on the power of the imagination, and by the realization that one must no longer think that "the ultimate source of our responsibilities and obligations lies outside of us, in something non-human, in the way things anyway are, apart from and independently of our practical activities and attitudes" (Brandom 2021: viii). Emerson, Whitman, James, and Nietzsche, I submit, can help one to better understand this development.

David Hall convincingly characterizes a Rortyan literary or poeticized culture as follows: "The real triumph of the Enlightenment is, ironically, its transmogrification into a pragmatic vocabulary which best expresses a de-theologized, but also de-scientized and de-philosophized secularity. Thus, the end of enlightenment would not be a scientized but a poeticized culture" (1994: 16). Curiously enough, in Rorty studies his notion of a poeticized culture has played hardly any role so far. This is problematic because, as Christopher Voparil correctly points out, "by the late 1980s, Rorty's depiction of a poeticized, post-metaphysical culture is in full swing" (2010: 29). In *Romanticism and Pragmatism* (2015), I offered the first detailed discussion of this Rortyan idea. I hope that this final chapter not only functions as a coda but will also be capable of establishing a dialogue with my previous study, adding to the prehistory of this idea of a postmetaphysical culture. In my opinion, the notion of a poeticized culture is at the heart of Rorty's pragmatist humanism, and one should therefore strive to appreciate its multilayered complexity.

7.1 Emerson

Together with the liberal ironist, the poet in the broad sense of someone who wants to make it new, the maker of new words or the shaper of new and exciting languages, is the hero of Rorty's poeticized culture. The strong poets in the Bloomian and Rortyan sense are provocative, innovative, and stimulating insofar as they constantly long to redescribe many things in new ways, use words as they have never been used before, and desire to expand the power of the human imagination.[1] In other words, the strong poets make one realize the importance of self-creation, self-fashioning, and redescription in a literary or poeticized culture. In a Nietzschean manner, Rorty contends that the strong poet who desires to achieve self-renewal and self-creation must never accept somebody else's description of himself. The Emersonian poet also does not accept, and does not need, someone else's description of himself. He is the self-reliant namer of things, the inventor of a new language, the destroyer of traditional forms, the teller of new experiences; he is representative of man and at the same time a liberating god. The poet, it seems, is the exact opposite of the "meek young men [who] grow up in libraries" (1837: 56) of whom Emerson speaks in "The American Scholar." Like the American scholar, the Emersonian strong poet does not accept dogmas, traditional book-knowledge and education, the security of the past, popular opinion, systems of knowledge, and conformity. Furthermore, the scholar and the strong poet are both creative inventors of new languages and sets of metaphors, both are self-reliant redescribers who long for self-creation, self-trust, and self-overcoming. Both, moreover, want to leave their impressions on others and thereby change their minds. In the Rortyan sense they aim to redescribe things and persons, and by doing so they wish to convince or persuade others to adopt this new vocabulary. Concerning the American scholar's power of redescription, Emerson states that they "are the kings of the world who give the color of their present thought to all nature and all art" (1837: 65). This idea of "giv[ing] the color of their present thought to all nature and all art" is the typical gesture of the Emersonian, Nietzschean, and Bloomian strong poet who desires to be more than a mere replica.[2]

In "Self-Reliance," there are many passages that one might use in order to characterize the strong poet. Emerson, for instance, elaborates on the importance of nonconformity and the integrity of one's own mind. He also warns against the sin of imitation: "Insist on yourself; never imitate" (1841b: 160). The scholar is no imitator; that is, he does not emulate old ways of speaking. On the contrary, in a Nietzschean manner he seeks to "recreat[e] all 'it was' into a 'thus I willed it'" (Rorty 1989: 29). Emerson's American scholar, like the poet, creates the language and the criteria by which he will be judged by posterity. He lives fully in the present and accepts the contingency of his language, his self, and his community, but he does not let the circumstances of his time and place govern him. By acknowledging contingency, he does not inherit a world, a world that is beyond his creative power and grasp, but gives voice and a form to his own world.³

The true poet, as Emerson claims in "The Poet," "stands among partial men for the complete man" (1844: 242). Moreover, he "traverses the whole scale of experience, and is representative of man" (1844: 243). The true poet, as Emerson sees him, is "the sayer, the namer, and represents beauty. He is a sovereign and stands on the centre" (1844: 244). In contrast to traditional and conventional poets, for whom "the finish of the verses is primary" (1844: 245) and for whom meter and form are of the utmost importance, the original poet is supposed to forever change our perspective by articulating a new and passionate thought, by singing a radically new experience. By constructing his own mind, the strong poet creates his own language, his own idiosyncratic set of metaphors. He does not care, or rather pretends not to care, about the vocabularies other human beings have left behind. The strong poet, in his Emersonian version, sings about his own time and place in his own words, and he waits for his readers to follow him along hitherto untrodden paths: "The poet has a new thought; he has a whole new experience to unfold; he will tell us how it was with him, and all men will be the richer in his fortune. For the experience of each new age requires a new confession, and the world seems always waiting for its poet" (1844: 245).⁴

In "The Poet," Emerson repeatedly underlines the power of the true poet as far as his use of language is concerned. Not only does the poet make the old use of symbols forgotten, or fills those symbols with new life, he is also capable of stepping nearer to things than his fellow human beings. Since he can see the higher form within the form everyone else perceives, he can represent and communicate with the ideal. In other words, the poet can depict the essence of the higher form by means of his innovative and creative language. The point here is not that in some of his essays Emerson's idealism is grounded in an appearance-reality/essence distinction, a distinction that Rorty, for instance, had severely criticized since his early texts, but rather the former's suggestion that the poet's "speech flows with the flowing of nature" (1844: 252). The Emersonian poet sings the real nature of things, and he expresses the divine aura that shows itself in the aforementioned higher forms. To Emerson, "the poet is the Namer or Language-maker, naming things sometimes after their appearance, sometimes after their essence, and giving to every one its own name and not another's, thereby rejoicing the intellect, which delights in detachment or boundary" (1844: 252). In order to get close to the real nature of things, the poet as language-maker, this

Adam-like figure or American Adam, must recognize "that he speaks adequately then only when he speaks somewhat wildly" (1844: 255).

It is noteworthy that already in his first book, *Nature* (1836), Emerson directs attention to the Romantic idea that we create our own world. It is the poet who demonstrates the power and worth of human activity and highlights the significance of poetic agency. Whereas "the sensual man conforms thoughts to things; the poet conforms things to his thoughts. The one esteems nature as rooted and fast; the other, as fluid, and impresses his being thereon. To him the refractory world is ductile and flexible; he invests dusts and stones with humanity" (1836: 35). In spite of their differences, the one proposing beauty as his main end and the other striving to reach truth, the poet and the philosopher are united in their world-shaping power:

> It is, in both cases, that a spiritual life has been imparted to nature; that the solid seeming block of matter has been pervaded and dissolved by a thought; that this feeble human being has penetrated the vast masses of nature with an informing soul, and recognized itself in their harmony, that is, seized their law. (1836: 37)

According to Emerson, "the plastic power of the human eye" is amplified in "the passions of the poet" (1836: 13, 35). The singing of Emerson's "Orphic poet" (1836: 47) dominates the final pages of *Nature*. The song of this Orphic poet seeks to convince us to believe in our creativity and world-shaping power and to appreciate that the world exists for us:

> Then shall come to pass what my poet said: 'Nature is not fixed but fluid. Spirit alters, moulds, makes it. The immobility or bruteness of nature is the absence of spirit; to pure spirit it is fluid, it is volatile, it is obedient. Every spirit builds itself a house, and beyond its house a world, and beyond its world a heaven. Know then that the world exists for you. (1836: 49)

It would undoubtedly be too simplistic to advance the idea that Emerson's *Nature* once again confirms that American transcendentalism was but a slightly modified version of Kantian idealism (with an interesting materialistic bent). Instead, I wish to submit that one should regard Emerson's Romanticism as a version of humanism that highlights the significance of poetic agency and the development from finding to making and therefore can be interpreted as being central to pragmatism's antifoundationalist story of progress and emancipation. In other words, Emerson helps one grasp that what unites the Romantics with Nietzsche and the pragmatists is the idea that the human subject does not have to answer to the world; that is, it had better stop considering the idea of human answerability to something nonhuman. Although it is true that divinity is omnipresent in Emerson's thinking and there is an influx of the divine mind into the human subject's mind, in his most thought-provoking moments he critiques the gesture of a convergence to the antecedently real or true and hence the quest for certainty. Instead of claiming that our rational beliefs and sentences ought to be world-directed and ought to correspond to reality as it really is, we should understand the implications of the notion that "we animate what we can, and we see only what we animate" (1981: 269). In "Spiritual Laws," Emerson formulates as follows: "Not in nature but in man is all the beauty and worth he sees. The world is very empty, and is indebted to this gilding, exalting soul for all its pride" (1981: 197).

Is it possible to argue that the Emersonian suggestion, in "Experience," that "the universe wear[s] our color" (1981: 286) goes further than Kant's *Critique of Pure Reason*? To put it differently, the question arises as to whether there is a link between Kant's rationalism and its categories and Emerson's transcendentalism and its humanistic idea that we see only what we have animated. In his discussion of F. C. S. Schiller's version of humanism, William James admits that there is a superficial resemblance between the latter and Kant's idealism. However, as James underscores, "between categories fulminated before nature began, and categories gradually forming themselves in nature's presence, the whole chasm between rationalism and empiricism yawns" (1907: 595). Emerson also rejects the idea of a priori categories, and his insistence on poetic agency and creative making lets him prefer the notion that the subject creates its categories in the confrontation with particular tasks in certain historical situations. This critique of apriorism unites Emerson with Nietzsche and James.[5]

For our purposes, it is important to note that there is an intimate connection between Emerson's emphasis on the world-shaping power of the poet, the Nietzschean suggestion that only we have created the world that concerns us as human subjects, and James's "humanistic principle" (James 1907: 598). To what degree Emerson prepared the ground for Nietzsche and James's radical humanism becomes especially clear in "Circles," which is still one of Emerson's most interesting essays. In this piece, he alternately presents himself as a Romantic, a process philosopher, an antifoundationalist and antiessentialist, and a nominalist historicist. "There are no fixtures in nature," as Emerson contends, and the "universe is fluid and volatile. Permanence is but a word of degrees" (1841a: 229). Moreover, there "are no fixtures to men, if we appeal to consciousness" (1841a: 231). In an almost Deleuzian manner, Emerson combines the plasticity of the world with the unpredictable creativity and contingent way of speaking of the subject. One of Emerson's most far-reaching sentences, in all of his oeuvre, is the following: "All that we reckoned settled shakes and rattles; and literatures, cities, climates, religions, leave their foundations and dance before our eyes" (1841a: 234). Who makes them dance? A Nietzschean, and Rortyan, reading of "Circles" would highlight Emerson's emphasis on the power of the imagination and thus on the poet's invention and introduction of new vocabularies or new sets of metaphors. Regarding the adoption of new vocabularies by humans and institutions as the motor of history, an Emersonian story of progress has to focus primarily on linguistic change, the change of linguistic practices or the replacement of one (final) vocabulary by another. Furthermore, this kind of story would use "Circles" in order to draw attention to the contingency and fragility of our final vocabularies as poetic achievements, or to the transitory nature of our webs of beliefs and desires. Realizing the importance of creative and imaginative redescriptions and of the idea that these are all we have, this story would try to elucidate what unites the Emersonian understanding of self-creation and self-reliance, the Nietzschean notion of self-overcoming, and James's idea of the infinite malleability of human beings.

Not only does Emerson's "Circles" underline the distinctly aesthetic component of modern subjectivity, and thus the diversity of private purposes and the radically poetic character of individual lives, it also argues that there is "no circumference" to human beings: "Every ultimate fact is only the first of a new series. Every general law only a particular fact of some more general law presently to disclose itself. There is no outside, no inclosing wall, no circumference to us" (1841a: 230). This is the Romantic notion of progress. Nothing is static, everything can be creatively redescribed, and in "the thought of tomorrow there is a power to upheave all thy creed, all the creeds, all the literatures of the nations, and marshal thee to a heaven which no epic dream has yet depicted" (1841a: 230–1). However, the idea that there is "no circumference" and "no inclosing wall" shows that in his most radical moments Emerson also rejects the notion of the Real. There is nothing to which our various ways of speaking and creative recontextualizations have to be adequate. There will never be a description that perfectly depicts the Real and hence makes further (linguistic) progress unnecessary. Moreover, there is no such thing as the intrinsic nature of reality that our vocabularies will help us find and represent. By (indirectly) criticizing the appearance-reality distinction, Emerson in his best moments makes the gesture of a convergence to the antecedently real or true seem outdated.[6] Instead of concentrating our energies on being adequate to what was invented in the past (or assuming that it was presented to us by a higher being), we should focus on imagining new forms of poetic agency in the future. Emerson's contention is that any certainty that a vocabulary, or way of thinking, offers will only be temporary. The "entire system of human pursuits" will look different after the invention of a new vocabulary; that is, after the poet, in the broadest sense, has suggested a new set of metaphors with revolutionary effect: "The things which are dear to men at this hour are so on account of the ideas which have emerged on their mental horizon, and which cause the present order of things, as a tree bears its apples. A new degree of culture would instantly revolutionize the entire system of human pursuits" (1841a: 233).

I wish to complicate my (Rortyan) reading of Emerson by calling attention to a sentence in "The Poet" that is too often overlooked: "[The poet] uses forms according to the life, and not according to the form" (1844: 252). From what we discussed in Chapter 3, it should be clear that this sentence could be taken directly from Dewey's *Art as Experience*. It seems that Emerson, like Dewey, holds that the general conditions of aesthetic form "are objective in the sense of belonging to the world of physical materials and energies" (Dewey 2008a: 151).[7] In a Deweyan sense, using forms "according to the life" could signify that they have their origin in the physical world and reflect the rhythmic pattern in experience that grows out of the interactions of the live creature and its environment. Using forms "not according to the form" might be interpreted as an early warning against what would later be termed formalism and aestheticism. This relationship between Emerson and Dewey as far as the question of aesthetic form is concerned is critical for the argument developed in this book, since it shows that pragmatism's insufficient appreciation of form at least partly goes back to this American transcendentalist. Establishing an intimate relation between form and life, as we have seen, deprives pragmatist aesthetics of fully grasping the significance of modern art and literature. Although Emerson also speaks of "the divine aura which breathes through forms" (1844: 255), he makes clear that he thinks of the poet as a man of action and that he is moreover willing to consider the link between form and action: "Every thought is also a prison; every heaven is also a prison. Therefore we love the poet, the inventor, who in any form, whether in an ode or in an action or in looks and behavior, has yielded us a new thought. He unlocks our chains and admits us to a new scene" (1844: 259).

While I have underlined that the practice of form-giving is a central part of the development from finding to making, I have also advanced the argument that it is problematic to employ the notion of using aesthetic forms "according to the life" when approaching modern artworks.

There is another important parallel between Emerson and Dewey that I wish to highlight. This parallel also complicates my Rortyan reading of Emerson. It is in his essay "Art," from *Essays: First Series*, that Emerson develops a critique of the distinction between the fine and the useful arts that reminds one of Dewey's position in *Art as Experience*. Emerson demands that "beauty must come back to the useful arts, and the distinction between the fine and the useful arts be forgotten" (2000: 282). In *Art as Experience*, Dewey famously inveighs against the "museum conception of art" and "the compartmental conception of fine art" (2008a: 12, 14). He holds that theory "can start with and from acknowledged works of art only when the esthetic is already compartmentalized, or only when works of art are set in a niche apart instead of being celebrations, recognized as such, of the things of ordinary experience" (2008a: 16). In Dewey's opinion, as he pointedly formulates, "the trouble with existing theories is that they start from a ready-made compartmentalization, or from a conception of art that 'spiritualizes' it out of connection with the objects of concrete experience" (2008a: 17). Intending to reestablish this connection with the qualities of ordinary experience and to recover the continuity of aesthetic experience with normal and everyday processes of living, Dewey warns against the attempt to isolate art in its own sphere and thereby to emphasize the contemplative character of the aesthetic.

Emerson introduces a comparable argument in "Art." I am not interested in the fact that there are contradictions between his ideas in "Art" and his more radical positions in, for instance, "The Poet" or "Circles." I just wish to draw attention to his Deweyan moments in the former piece. What Emerson demands from art is not the fantastic and ostentatious, the daring new style, but "the simple and true," the "familiar and sincere," and "the old, eternal fact I had met already in so many forms" (2000: 279). In other words, he requires of all pictures "that they domesticate me, not that they dazzle me. […] Nothing astonishes men so much as commonsense and plain dealing. All great actions have been simple, and all great pictures are" (2000: 279). As in Dewey, this is not exactly a call for radical formal experiments. According to Emerson, art has a moral and practical task to fulfill. Among other things, its task is to delight and motivate those who hitherto have had no contact with art, that is, the poor and uneducated: "Art has not yet come to its maturity if it do not put itself abreast with the most potent influences of the world, if it is not practical and moral, if it do not stand in connection with the conscience, if it do not make the poor and uncultivated feel that it addresses them with a voice of lofty cheer" (2000: 280). Emerson makes clear in his essay that he thinks that the theorist's focus on form is wrong, it leads in the wrong direction. His contention is that "picture and sculpture are the celebrations and festivities of form. But true art is never fixed, but always flowing" (2000: 281). Moreover, he asserts that "all works of art should not be detached, but extempore performances" (2000: 281). One might be inclined to surmise that Emerson's idea of "extempore performances" inevitably entails an insistence upon the idiosyncratic and unpredictable practices of form-giving, the permanent desire to make it new, or the radical will to break with tradition. However, this is not the case, since he stresses that the "fountains of invention and beauty in modern society are all but dried up" (2000: 281).

This is a far-reaching sentence; especially in view of the fact that Emerson writes at the end of the period we have termed Romanticism. Like Dewey, Emerson in "Art" does not underscore the necessity of formal innovation and experiment, but instead strives to make his readers appreciate how crucial it is to forget the distinction between the fine and the useful arts. When the artist is "drunk with a passion for form which he could not resist," all he will produce are "fine extravagances" (2000: 281). These are useless and frivolous. Emerson tries to convince the person who seeks beauty in the present time that "high beauty is no longer attainable by him in canvas or in stone, in sound, or in lyrical construction; an effeminate, prudent, sickly beauty, which is not beauty, is all that can be formed" (2000: 282). This "sickly beauty," it seems, is the necessary result of the endeavor to radically isolate art from everyday life and from nature. Art that is too refined, obsessed with form, and esoteric, as Emerson and Dewey argue, is useless, since it will never have anything to do with real people and their everyday lives. It is like reading Proust in Kansas. According to Emerson, artists who "reject life as prosaic [...] create a death which they call poetic" (2000: 282). In "Art," he does not praise the virtues of the strong and self-reliant poet who radically rejects tradition and desires artistic novelty. Like Whitman, Emerson contains multitudes, and the fact that there are contradictions between his positions in several essays indicates that it might be possible to argue that he, in a stimulating manner, demarcates a space between Dewey and Rorty.

7.2 Whitman

Whitman presented himself as the Emersonian singer, the American bard who speaks wildly about his own time and place. He did everything he could in order to fulfill the Emersonian role of the solitary singer as namer, sayer, wanderer, and reconciler. Whitman sang America, and he did this by radically rejecting the conventional understanding of meter and aesthetic form. In the "Preface" to *Leaves of Grass* (1855), he asserts that "nothing is finer than silent defiance advancing from new free forms" (1855: 14), whereas in "A Backward Glance O'er Travel'd Roads," he claims that "new poetic messages, new forms and expressions, are inevitable" (1888: 300). In many respects, Whitman was the paradigmatic strong poet who demonstrated the possibilities and the power of self-creation, of a self-reliant individual inventing himself. The Romanticism that unites Emerson, Whitman, and Rorty is not only grounded in the idea that poets—as redescribers—are the true legislators of the world, but can also be detected in the strong emphasis on the importance of (Nietzschean) self-creation and contingency. The genuinely protean self of Whitman's "Song of Myself," for instance, continually rewrites and reinvents itself. It embraces contingency and contradiction and longs to bring a new form of life into being just by means of its creative and innovative use of words. America is in permanent flux, or so Whitman seems to hold, and the songs of the Romantic radical redescriber are supposed to shape that which is yet to come. To Whitman, the poet as radical redescriber and prophet of continual self-invention is always a poet of democracy. While Whitman often changed his ways of expressing his democratic sympathies, from his expansive vision of democracy and his notion of populist democracy in the 1840s and 1850s to the decidedly gloomier picture he painted in the 1870s (e.g., in *Democratic Vistas*), he always made unequivocally clear that the crucial ideas of a democratic personality and a democratic soul could only be realized in the United States.

Whitman's most Emersonian prose text is presumably his "Preface" to the first edition of *Leaves of Grass*. In this "Preface," he describes the tasks the American poet has to fulfill and the standards he has to meet. Emerson's suggestion that "America is a poem in our eyes" (1844: 262) becomes Whitman's claim: "The United States themselves are essentially the greatest poem" (1855: 5). Whitman's contention is that "of all nations the United States with veins full of poetical stuff most need poets and will doubtless have the greatest and use them the greatest"

(1855: 9). He characterizes the great poet, who is apparently yet to come (or who has just presented himself in the person of Whitman himself), as follows: "He is the arbiter of the diverse and he is the key. He is the equalizer of his age and land … he supplies what wants supplying and checks what wants checking" (1855: 9). Emerson's notions of self-reliance and self-trust, as well as his idea that the true poet is capable of seeing the higher forms and thus of communicating with the ideal, are expressed in the following passage from the "Preface":

> The greatest poet hardly knows pettiness or triviality. If he breathes into any thing that was before thought small it dilates with the grandeur and life of the universe. He is a seer … he is individual … he is complete in himself … the others are as good as he, only he sees it and they do not. He is not one of the chorus … he does not stop for any regulations … he is the president of regulation. (1855: 10)

It is interesting to see that Whitman's text contains some passages that could almost have been written by Rorty in his description of the characteristics and advantages of a literary culture. The first parallel that ought to be mentioned concerns the question of contingency. Just like the Rortyan strong poet or literary intellectual or liberal ironist, the Whitmanian great poet is not afraid of contingency. He handles it well: "He consumes an eternal passion and is indifferent which chance happens and which possible contingency of fortune or misfortune and persuades daily and hourly his delicious pay" (1855: 12). It is undoubtedly true that one might argue that there are sentences in the "Preface" that show that Whitman's poet is still a metaphysician or Platonist who is incapable of leaving foundationalist epistemology and essentialist thinking behind. Whitman maintains, for instance: "The poets of the kosmos advance through all interpositions and coverings and turmoils and stratagems to first principles" (1855: 19). In addition, one sometimes gets the impression that his statements are at least partly shaped by a mimetic understanding of art. Yet, one should also recognize that a sentence like "Whatever satisfies the soul is truth" (1855: 23) is pragmatist and antifoundationalist all the way down. This understanding of truth is almost Jamesian in the radical nature of its critique of traditional definitions of this concept.

The degree to which Whitman's "Preface" prefigures the Rortyan notion of a literary or poeticized culture becomes especially obvious when the author explicates that the work of the priest is no longer needed; that is, that the search for God has been replaced by the search for a different kind of redemption.

Whitman writes: "There will soon be no more priests. Their work is done. They may wait awhile ... perhaps a generation or two ... dropping off by degrees. A superior breed shall take their place ... the gangs of kosmos and prophets en masse shall take their place" (1855: 25). One ought to note that the idea of this replacement still preoccupies him in *Democratic Vistas*. There he formulates this thought as follows: "The priest departs, the divine literatus comes. Never was anything more wanted than, today, and here in the States, the poet of the modern is wanted, or the great literatus of the modern" (1871: 321). The role Whitman attributes to literature as far as the strengthening of American democracy is concerned cannot be overestimated. His ideal society seems to be a (secularized) literary culture governed by self-reliant strong poets, "the great literatus[es] of the modern," who illuminate that social and religious problems and ills can be treated by literature and who also elucidate how American literature shapes American moral identity. Regarding the power of literature, Whitman underscores that it "penetrates all, gives hue to all, shapes aggregates and individuals, and, after subtle ways, with irresistible power, constructs, sustains, demolishes at will" (1871: 321). He moreover points out that "in the civilization of today it is undeniable that, over all the arts, literature dominates, serves beyond all—shapes the character of church and school—or, at any rate, is capable of doing so. Including the literature of science, its scope is indeed unparalleled" (1871: 322–3).

Democratic Vistas also contains a passage that can be interpreted as nicely illustrating the power of redescription in a Rortyan sense. By creatively expressing a new thought or by inventing a new way of speaking, as Whitman makes us aware, the strong poet may cause what we today would term a paradigm shift in a Kuhnian sense. Radical redescription, in other words, may cause radical changes; that is, changes that even the great literatus could not have imagined or foreseen. The inhabitants of a literary or poeticized culture, having grown accustomed to the constant gestalt switches of the strong poet, welcome those changes and creatively put the new thoughts, the new vocabulary, to work. As Whitman puts it:

> Yet, it may be, a single new thought, imagination, abstract principle, even literary style, fit for the time, put in shape by some great literatus, and projected among mankind, may duly cause changes, growths, removals, greater than the longest and bloodiest war, or the most stupendous merely political, dynastic, or commercial overturn. (1871: 322)

In this utopian scenario of a literary culture it will be perfectly natural to accept the Shelleyan idea that the strong poets are the true legislators of the world. People will be prepared to appreciate and honor the strong poets' attempt to make old and conventional vocabularies look bad by introducing a radically new way of speaking.

In order to illuminate the radical gesture of the early Whitman, one should not only analyze the first preface to *Leaves of Grass* but also that to the second edition of 1856. This preface, which has the form of an open letter to Emerson (after the latter's famous letter to Whitman in 1855), is often overlooked. The rhetoric of this preface-letter is still that of the 1855 preface. It is the rhetoric of the radical redescriber, the American strong poet, who desires to make it new. As in the first preface, Whitman asks for self-reliant authors who produce an independent American literature written in American English. Whitman's advice to America does not leave much room for interpretation: "Strangle the singers who will not sing you loud and strong" (1856: 639). Emerson's wild speaking here becomes the loud and strong singing of the American rough. It goes without saying that Whitman's status as one of the most important modern poets is not only due to the new content of his poetry, but is also based on his being a radical innovator of form. The prose-like quality of his poetry, his long, run-on lines and innovations in metrics, his radical rejection of a conventional rhyme scheme, and his use of everyday language, slang, and specific terminologies from the various worlds of work—these are only some of the formal aspects of his poetry that still deserve our attention. In the preface-letter of 1856 Whitman speaks of "new arts, new perfections, new wants" (1856: 639). In an almost Adornian manner, he seeks to make his readers understand that new arts need new forms. Whitman, seemingly effortlessly, provided those forms. This is the primary reason that he is important as regards the prehistory of pragmatist humanism. The early Whitman makes his readers appreciate the humanist and anti-authoritarian implications of the practice of form-giving.

Whitman's radical rejection of the past becomes especially obvious in the 1856 preface. The author even goes so far as to use the verb "to destroy" in this context. He writes: "Authorities, poems, models, laws, names, imported into America, are useful to America today to destroy them, and so move disencumbered to great works, great days" (1856: 641). This is one of the few moments when it becomes clear that the strong poet as redescriber might even be considered a destroyer of the old and conventional. Most presumably, this is one of Whitman's most un-Hegelian, nondialectical moments. Apart from the fact that the idea of a destruction of everything imported into America is a gesture somewhat too sweeping and undifferentiated, it also seems much less productive than the proposal that the redescriber productively uses, or creatively plays with, old vocabularies and ways of speaking. If one concentrated exclusively on the idea of destruction, one would not be able to grasp that the strong poet is also always an elegant rhetorician. One does not necessarily need rhetoric for destruction, yet it is urgently needed if one intends to make something new look good and if one wants others to adopt one's new perspective and vocabulary.

From what I have discussed thus far it should be obvious that Whitman is truly important for Rorty's pragmatist humanism. The latter reads this poet of the American Renaissance as a radical democrat and secular poet. I will argue that this interpretation is problematic, since one needs to clearly differentiate between the early and the later Whitman. According to Rorty, as he writes in *Achieving Our Country*, both Whitman and Dewey "viewed the United States as an opportunity to see ultimate significance in a finite, human, historical project, rather than in something eternal and nonhuman" (1998a: 17). Furthermore, Rorty's contention is that Whitman and Dewey regard the terms "America" and "democracy" as "shorthand for a new conception of what it is to be human—a conception which has no room for obedience to a nonhuman authority, and in which nothing save freely achieved consensus among human beings has any authority at all" (1998a: 18). From these quotes it becomes obvious that Rorty holds that Whitman and Dewey's most important characteristic is their "thoroughgoing secularism" (1998a: 15). America, as the first radical experiment in national self-creation, will be the first nation-state courageous enough to renounce hope of justification from something or someone that transcends human practices. Whitman's radical anti-authoritarianism regards the United States as essentially the greatest poem; there is nothing nonhuman and eternal that has any power over this new country. As Rorty reads Whitman, this new experiment lets the gesture of a convergence to the antecedently real and holy appear as utterly unnecessary. What counts, by contrast, is America's future orientation and its notion of free consensus achieved by social practices whose ideals are not obedience or faithfulness but growth, diversity, and change. Rorty interprets Whitman's secularism as a form of anticlericalism; that is, as an attack on religion as an institution (directed against the power of churches and priests, as well as churches that get involved in political matters).[8] However, Rorty also regards Whitman's religion as a religion of love that can easily be privatized, or rather, that should be privatized. Instead of seeking to discover God's will, or establishing the moral law, or discovering the real nature of human beings, Whitman, as Rorty understands him, wants his fellow Americans to be curious about each other and to develop new forms of social practices that would offer them the possibility of inventing a radically new understanding of national identity.[9]

Rorty finds justification for his reading of Whitman, for instance, in the following passage from the "Preface 1855": "The whole theory of the special and supernatural and all that was twined with it or educed out of it departs as a dream.... It is not consistent with the reality of the soul to admit that there is anything in the universe more divine than men and women" (quoted in Rorty 1998a: 21–2). The problem with Rorty's interpretation of Whitman is that he refuses to acknowledge the later Whitman's idealism. In the 1870s, Whitman is no longer a secular poet who propagates a religion of love that does not leave room for obedience to a nonhuman authority, but he demands a decidedly stronger and more central role for religion. Democratic social practices and the ideal of democratic consensus have to be shaped and governed by what in the "Preface 1872—A Strong Bird on Pinions Free" he calls "one deep purpose," namely, "the Religious purpose" (1872: 650). Rorty's pragmatist humanism not only wants us to privatize religion, it also strives to convince us to give up even secularist ways of telling ourselves that our life would be easier, truer, more moral, and more beautiful if something large and powerful were on our side. In *Achieving Our Country*, he uses Whitman for this endeavor and thereby reduces the complexity of this poet's development. What makes Whitman Romantic—and the same could be said about Emerson, Thoreau, Shelley, and the early Wordsworth—is the tension between metaphysical need and postmetaphysical desire.[10] It is this tension that allows one to regard these poets as part of a pragmatist genealogy, and at the same time it forces one to appreciate that they were not yet pragmatist all the way down. The later Whitman certainly valued "the secular, antiauthoritarian vocabulary of shared social hope" (Rorty 1998a: 32) that had gained in popularity in the 1860s and 1870s, but he also gave voice to the profound need for a religion that would not be confined to the private sphere and that would connect one to a universal order.[11]

In the "Preface 1872," Whitman speaks of "the New Theology" and he maintains that "the supreme and final Science is the Science of God" (1872: 650). Whitman's anticlericalism becomes obvious when he suggests that religion is "too important to the power and perpetuity of the New World to be consigned any longer to the churches, old or new, Catholic or Protestant" (1872: 651). Insisting on the crucial nature of "scientism," Whitman, in the "Preface 1876—*Leaves of Grass* and *Two Rivulets*," chooses a curious formulation when he points out that one's religious beliefs, one's idealism, are to be seen as "absolute" and materialist, as it were: "To me, the worlds of Religiousness, of the conception of the Divine, and of the Ideal, though mainly latent, are just as absolute in Humanity and the Universe as the world of Chemistry, or any thing in the objective worlds" (1876: 659–60). The idea of something being "latent" also plays an important role in the next paragraph of this Preface. In the following passage, I submit, it becomes clear that the former poet of the immanence of praxis, of finite experiences, and of making has developed a new self-understanding. Central to his argument now is the Platonic appearance-reality distinction:

> To me, the crown of Savantism is to be, that it surely opens the way for a more splendid Theology, and for ampler and diviner Songs. No year, nor even century, will settle this. There is a phase of the Real, lurking behind the Real, which it is all for. There is also in the Intellect of man, in time, far in prospective recesses, a judgment, a last appellate court, which will settle it. (1876: 660)

The idea that there is something "behind the Real," as well as "a last appellate court," might indicate, *pace* Rorty, that Whitman in the 1870s needed the certainty, profundity, immutability, and purity of something that would be more than another human creation. Is the author of the "Preface 1876" still someone who rejects any form of nonhuman authority? Is what is "behind the Real" the really real? I think it is legitimate to advance the argument that Whitman in the 1870s intellectualizes, or theorizes, the appearance-reality distinction.

The priest departs, he is no longer needed, his time is up. As Whitman stresses in the "Preface 1855" and in *Democratic Vistas*, the priest is replaced by the poet, the poet of the modern, the self-reliant Emersonian poet and redescriber. One of the most important sentences in *Democratic Vistas*, this partly bitter and dark text, is: "The priest departs, the divine literatus comes" (1871: 321). This sentence is of the utmost importance for our discussion, since it shows the aforementioned tension between metaphysical need and postmetaphysical desire that governs especially the later Whitman's texts. Whitman's anticlericalism and his ideal of a religious democracy have no use for the authoritative figure of the priest anymore. Nonetheless, the priest is replaced by a poet who is "divine;" that is, whose verses connect his readers with the transcendental realm, with the universal, with the All. In other words, the verses of this "divine literatus" will offer his readers the possibility of escaping from a world of appearances to an enduringly real world in which humans will approach an almost God-like status and in which the True and the Good are One. What I wish to underscore in this context is that only in a genuinely postmetaphysical culture one would realize how scandalously oxymoronic the term "divine literatus" is. Rorty purposely overlooks that Whitman is not yet capable of appreciating the full implications of this term, since he only helps prepare the establishment of a postmetaphysical culture without being able to leave metaphysics completely behind.[12]

There are many passages in *Democratic Vistas* that contradict Rorty's reading of Whitman and that confirm our idea that religion plays a decidedly more significant role for the later Whitman. At the core of democracy, as Whitman unequivocally states, "is the religious element" (1871: 337). Furthermore, the former poet of praxis who relentlessly praised the virtues of a contingent plurality of actions, occupations, and novelties has completely changed the character and direction of his thought when he speaks of "the immortal, the unknown, the spiritual [as] the only permanently real" (1871: 358). This quest for an enduringly real "behind the Real" makes it difficult to advance the idea that Whitman is a proto-pragmatist. His thoughts in *Democratic Vistas* culminate in his idea of "a new Metaphysics" (1871: 372). The task of this new metaphysics is to mediate between Whitman's belief in the power of the creative and innovative individual, in the power of literature—and especially poetry—to shape the rest of American culture, and in the power of scientific innovation, on the one hand, and his belief in the divine idea of All, in the spiritual cosmos, and in the power of religion, on the other. Whitman's idealism, this confusing and stimulating mixture of American transcendentalism, unitarianism, mysticism, and materialism, puts an emphasis on the idea that "the religious tone, the consciousness of mystery, the recognition of the future, of the unknown, of Deity over and under all, and of the divine purpose, are never absent, but indirectly give tone to all" (1871: 372). How far-reaching Whitman's notion of a new metaphysics is becomes obvious in the following quotation where he, standing on "the highest, only permanent ground," condemns those literary, philosophical, and moral texts and ideas that "violate" or "ignore" the religious imperative:

> Standing on this ground—the last, the highest, only permanent ground—and sternly criticizing, from it, all works, either of the literary, or any art, we have peremptorily to dismiss every pretensive production, however fine its aesthetic or intellectual points, which violates or ignores, or even does not celebrate, the central divine idea of All, suffusing universe, of eternal trains of purpose, in

the development, by however slow degrees, of the physical, moral, and spiritual cosmos. (1871: 373)

These are the words of an American prophet, who has not yet completely lost faith in his fellow Americans' power to shape their future. However, these are also the words of a Romantic poet with metaphysical inclinations. This tension indicates the multilayered complexity of Romanticism.

The early Whitman's emphasis on the significance of the idiosyncrasies of aesthetic form makes him part of the genealogy of pragmatist humanism as anti-authoritarianism. By contrast, the later Whitman's idealism demands a central role for religion. Making the Platonic appearance-reality distinction central to many texts, the later Whitman surmised that there was something "behind the Real." Consequently, the question arises as to whether the later Whitman still was a poet and intellectual who rejected or critiqued any form of nonhuman authority. In spite of his metaphysical inclinations, however, his poetry and prose illuminated the contours and promising potential of a postmetaphysical culture.

7.3 James

We saw in Chapter 3 to what degree James shaped our understanding of pragmatist humanism. His pragmatism as humanism is a worldly philosophy.[13] In order to understand the worldliness of his brand of pragmatism, one has to note that James functioned as a public philosopher in his time. Like, for instance, Cornel West and Edward Said after him, James accepted responsibility for addressing public problems; that is, he grappled with cultural, social, and political forces in the public sphere (think of his vehement anti-imperialist stance). He was not content with presenting himself exclusively as a professional philosopher solving abstract problems, but he always put a premium on the importance of a fruitful tension between technical work and public issues, the professional and the popular. As so very often, James saw his primary role as *mediator*, here someone who tried to creatively blur the traditional lines between professional and public philosophy. He did, of course, not declare the demand for philosophical depth as obsolete, but instead sought to balance it with the needs of a public presence, an oppositional voice in the public sphere. Applying insights from his complex technical work to public issues and problems, James's texts show that these popular concerns and public issues in turn also had a strong impact on his professional philosophy. Especially during his most successful period as professional and public philosopher, from 1890 to 1910, this reciprocity could be detected in his work. Of primary concern here ought to be his constant attempt to call attention to the interplay of theory and practice or the fruitful and productive tension between professional and partly abstract philosophy, on the one hand, and public philosophy as political practice, on the other.

Since James sought to present his thinking in accessible fashion in his numerous lectures, he had to pay a price that would have been much too high for traditional, rationalist and abstract, philosophers. Yet to James, the lack of systematization, technical exactitude, and logical rigor did not appear as a disadvantage or problem. As a public philosopher, attempting to confront worldly problems in their historical and cultural specificity, he was highly critical of the pretensions of professional philosophy and its desperate search for that which is more than another human invention.

James's public philosophy and his thinking in general were of great importance to many turn-of-the-century political theorists and reformers. James's radical theory of knowledge, meaning, and truth, that is, his antifoundationalist critique of traditional epistemology, proved useful and suggestive to those who fought for progressive change in America around 1900. His meliorism, voluntarism, future orientation, and his emphasis on concerted action apparently corresponded with the reform agenda of American progressives and social democrats that steadily gained power in the first decade of the twentieth century. Contributing to a willingness to reform and to an acceptance of change in the social and political realm, James helped to create a new political sensibility that would eventually reach fruition in Dewey's writings and that of other reformers and radicals. One only has to think of James's influence on W. E. B. Du Bois and Alain Locke, two of his students at Harvard.[14]

James never intended to present an elaborate and sophisticated pragmatist political theory. Rather, he wanted his worldly philosophy to become an influential part of the public conversation and thereby to strengthen the community. The work of the poet plays an important role in this context. In his discussion of ethics in "The Moral Philosopher and the Moral Life," James not only maintains that no ethical philosophy in the traditional, dogmatic, and a priori sense is possible, he also contends that in some rare cases (public) conversation might be shaped by the revolutionary thought or action of what we today would call a strong poet in the Bloomian or Rortyan sense. He writes:

> Every now and then, however, someone is born with the right to be original, and his revolutionary thought or action may bear prosperous fruit. He may replace old "laws of nature" by better ones; he may, by breaking old moral rules in a certain place, bring in a total condition of things more ideal than would have followed had the rules been kept. (1891: 258)

Undoubtedly, one might argue that these sentences can be applied to James himself. As a public philosopher he was at the same time a (Romantic) strong poet, offering creative and innovative redescriptions and, within the framework of his worldly pragmatism, never forgetting about the "howling mob of desires" (1891: 255) shaping our ideals, judgments, and decisions.

The complexity of the relationship of individual and community is of course central to the thought of all classical pragmatists. While it is impossible to fully appreciate James's brand of pragmatism without paying attention to the crucial role of the community in his texts, it seems interesting to see him, together with Emerson and Whitman, as a strong poet who prepared the establishment of a postmetaphysical literary or poeticized culture. For our present purposes, it suffices to recognize that an essay like James's "Great Men and Their Environment" can be interpreted as illustrating the power of the poet in the Rortyan sense. According to James, the mutations of societies are primarily due to the acts of creative and innovative individuals. These individuals often appear as an example that others strive to imitate. In *Pragmatism*, James speaks of "men of radical idiosyncrasy" with a "strong temperamental vision" (1907: 489). The genius of these individuals, whom we interpret as strong poets, "was so adapted to the receptivities of the moment, or whose accidental position of authority was so critical that they became ferments, initiators of movement, setters of precedent or fashion, centres of corruption, or destroyers of other persons, whose gifts, had they had free play, would have led society in another direction" (1880: 227).

This passage beautifully highlights the potential power James grants to the extraordinary individual. Well aware of the potential dangers of aggression, corruption, or destruction in connection with the reign of the strong individual or poet, James also puts a particularly strong emphasis on the fermentative influence of the new genius. He or she proves to be capable of causing changes in the direction of social evolution. His or her contingent gestalt switches have a profound impact on the development of the community. In "Great Men and Their Environment" James draws attention to the aforementioned relation between the individual and the community when he famously formulates as follows: "The community stagnates without the impulse of the individual. The impulse dies away without the sympathy of the community" (1880: 232). A certain genius may of course eventually turn out to be incompatible with his or her surroundings, with no possibility of influencing and creatively changing them, but this only means, if we follow James, that this community is still under the influence of some previous poet or redescriber. There are two things I want to underline with regard to James's essay. First, his stress on "the vital importance of individual initiative" (1880: 245). Second, his wish that the energy and creativity of the individual ought to form and change the world of practice. The strong poet in the Jamesian sense is not an anemic and unworldly man of abstraction or speculation. He does offer new forms of abstraction, yet his main concern is the seemingly spontaneous offer of a new way of thinking (and speaking), and thus of coping with our daily practice. The Jamesian genius seems to propose: "Try to think of things in this radically new and at first surprising way, and find out whether it is not only stimulating and exciting but also useful for you in your continuous attempt to cope with the messy world of practice." The following passage sounds almost Rortyan in its explanation of the poet's desire to make it new:

> Instead of thoughts of concrete things patiently following one another in a beaten track of habitual suggestion, we have the most abrupt cross-cuts and transitions from one idea to another, the most rarefied abstractions and discriminations, the most unheard-of combinations of elements, the subtlest associations of analogy; in a word, we seem suddenly introduced into a seething caldron of ideas, where everything is fizzling and bobbing about in a state of bewildering activity, where partnerships can be joined or loosened in an instant, treadmill routine is unknown, and the unexpected seems the only law. According to the idiosyncrasy of the individual, the scintillations will have one character or another. They will be sallies of wit and humor; they will be flashes of poetry and eloquence; they will be constructions of dramatic fiction or of mechanical device, logical or philosophic abstractions, business projects, or scientific hypotheses, with trains of experimental consequences based thereon; they will be musical sounds, or images of plastic beauty or picturesqueness, or visions of moral harmony. (1880: 248)

James's pluralism urges one to understand that the world of practice and the world of poetry do not necessarily have to be mutually exclusive; that is, the "flashes of poetry and eloquence," going back to the idiosyncratic vocabulary of the genius or strong poet, may cause contingent changes in the world of practice.[15] In other words, we might be shocked and disoriented in our first confrontation with this new set of metaphors, this new way of speaking, but eventually we might find out, surprisingly enough, that it helps us cope with the multitudinous, messy, and tangled world of everyday life. Clearly, the quotation given earlier, with its emphasis on "the most unheard-of combinations of elements, the subtlest associations of analogy," "the seething caldron of ideas," and "the state of bewildering activity" where "the unexpected seems the only law," depicts the exact opposite of the world described by absolute idealists, monists, or rationalists as metaphysicians (or vulgar materialists, for that matter). This, I submit, is a description of a literary or poeticized culture, a pluralistic world governed by novelty, contingency, and the desire for constant redescriptions—a world, that is, in which humans no longer see the necessity of escaping from the temporal to the eternal and transcendental and in which they are satisfied with the horizontality of contingent and historical practices.

7.4 Nietzsche

In *The Will to Power*, Nietzsche suggests that "before 'thought' is possible, 'poetizing' must first have done its work" (2017: sec. 544). From what we have discussed thus far in this study, it should be clear that his idea that the practice of "poetizing" comes before cognition is central to the modern development from finding to making as well as to the antirepresentationalist story of progress and emancipation as it characterizes pragmatist humanism.[16] Poetry, in this context, ought to be regarded as shorthand for the contingency of agency and the necessity of always considering the primacy of social practices. Throughout his career, Nietzsche uses the work of the poet for his endeavor to detranscendentalize or "humanize" (Nietzsche 1968: sec. 614) the world. The poet, he thinks, might help humans appreciate that they must not try to get beyond their contingent practices to a nonhuman authority. In *Beyond Good and Evil*, Nietzsche makes unequivocally clear that he desires to contribute to "the artistic refashioning of *mankind*" (2003: sec. 62). In this context, it ought to be noted that the early Nietzsche, in his radical critique of the concept of truth, argues that humans create their world; that is, they create a world that concerns them. They do this by creating metaphors. In a Protagorean sense man is the measure of all things. However, Nietzsche states that humans tend to forget to what degree their perception is governed by their own set of metaphors, their idiosyncratic vocabularies. Too often, humans think that they confront the things themselves, but this forgetting of their position as *"artistically creative* subject[s]" also offers them a feeling of security and certainty:

> Only by forgetting this primitive world of metaphor, only by virtue of the fact that a mass of images, which originally flowed in a hot, liquid stream from the primal power of the human imagination, has become hard and rigid, only because of the invincible faith that *this* sun, *this* window, this table is a truth in itself—in short only because man forgets himself as a subject, and indeed as an *artistically creative* subject, does he live with some degree of peace, security, and consistency; if he could escape for just a moment from the prison walls of this faith, it would mean the end of his "consciousness of self." (1999: 148)

Even in his early texts and those of his middle period, Nietzsche always considers the enormous significance of "the primal power of the human imagination" and of the "*artistically creative* subject." This of course unites him with the Romantics and their idea that truth is made rather than found, as well as with their suggestion that the human self is not adequately or inadequately expressed in a vocabulary but rather created by the use of a vocabulary. Bringing naturalism and aestheticism together, Nietzsche's "artistic refashioning of *mankind*" desires a postmetaphysical culture in which people would delight in the stimulating plurality of metaphors and new ways of speaking that do not pretend to offer a single, firm, unequivocal, and transhistorical truth and that critique the idea that there is a permanent reality to be found behind the many temporary appearances (something, that is, which is more than another human creation). While Nietzsche famously maintained in *The Birth of Tragedy* that "the existence of the world is *justified (gerechtfertigt)* only as an aesthetic phenomenon" (1999: 8), he chooses a comparable formulation in *The Gay Science* in order to draw attention to the significance of art: "As an aesthetic phenomenon existence is still *bearable* for us, and art furnishes us with eyes and hands and above all the good conscience to be able to turn ourselves into such a phenomenon" (1974: sec. 107).

What makes "Upon the Blessed Isles" one of the most stimulating parts of *Thus Spoke Zarathustra* is not only Nietzsche's suggestion that creation "is the great redemption from suffering, and life's growing light" (1982a: 199), but also his endeavor to prepare the ground for the establishment of a humanist culture. The will to truth, as Zarathustra advises his disciples, "should mean to you: that everything be changed into what is thinkable for man, visible for man, feelable by man" (1982a: 198). And Zarathustra goes on in a manner that reminds one of section 301 in *The Gay Science*, which is central to the argument that I have developed in this study: "And what you have called world, that shall be created only by you: your reason, your image, your will, your love shall thus be realized. And verily, for your own bliss, you lovers of knowledge" (1982a: 198). In a Nietzschean postmetaphysical and humanist culture, it would become obvious that art offers possibilities of self-creation and self-overcoming that no other sphere provides.[17] Moreover, it is especially in *The Gay Science* that Nietzsche argues that artistic self-creation offers an effective means of confronting the dangers of moral dogmatism, epistemological foundationalism, and ontological essentialism. According to Nietzsche, "we need all exuberant, floating, dancing, mocking, childish, and blissful art lest we lose the *freedom above things* that our ideal demands of us" (1974: sec. 107). This "freedom above things," in the moral sphere, means that art teaches us that there are many values, that they are, like everything else, man-made and hence can be incompatible, and that we necessarily have to live with the imperfection of all human answers, arrangements, and forms of normativity. This "exuberant," "dancing," and "blissful" art helps one appreciate that no single answer that claims to be perfect and true can in principle be perfect and true.

On Nietzsche's account we "have arranged for ourselves a world in which we can live—by positing bodies, lines, planes, causes and effects, motion and rest, form and content; without these articles of faith nobody could endure life" (1974: sec. 121). Whereas this already confirms the subject's creativity, humans have to go further by learning from artists. Nietzsche proposes that artists can help one to answer the following question: "How can we make things beautiful, attractive, and desirable for us when they are not?" (1974: sec. 299). As he insists, answering this question has much to do with considering the significance of perspective and with understanding that we in the Jamesian sense add to what we perceive ("and there is much that our eye has to add [to the things] if we are still to see them at all," [1974: sec. 299]). However, he also emphasizes that one has to go farther than the artists insofar as their "subtle power" is only effective in the sphere of art, whereas we ought to strive to become "die Dichter unseres Lebens." Art and the practice of artistic self-creation should have a direct impact on our daily lives: "For with [the artists] this subtle power usually comes to an end where art ends and life begins; but we want to be the poets of our life—first of all in the smallest, most everyday matters" (1974: sec. 299).

Nietzsche continues this thought in one of his most important and stimulating aphorisms, "Wahn der Contemplativen/The fancy of the contemplatives" (1974: sec. 301). In this aphorism, he describes the complex situation of what he terms "the higher human being," who is a poet and also plagued by a delusion. Instead of taking pride in his artistic creativity, his world-making activity, he thinks "that he is a *spectator* and *listener* who has been placed before the great visual and acoustic spectacle that is life; he calls his own nature *contemplative* and overlooks that he himself is really the poet who keeps creating this life" (1974: sec. 301). As a poet, he combines the *vis contemplativa* and the *vis creativa*, and on Nietzsche's account, the latter, which the normal man or woman of practice lacks, ought to be regarded as the most important aspect of his character. Contrary to public opinion, it is the higher human beings as poets who are the makers, who constantly create something new, and who invent the world that concerns us as human beings. This world ("This poem that we have invented") is then studied by "practical human beings" who translate it into everyday existence:

> We who think and feel [die Denkend-Empfindenden] at the same time are those who really continually *fashion* something that had not been there before: the whole eternally growing world of valuations, colors, accents, perspectives, scales, affirmations, and negations. This poem that we have invented is continually studied by the so-called practical human beings (our actors) who learn their roles and translate everything into flesh and actuality, into the everyday. Whatever has *value* in our world now does not have value in itself, according to its nature—nature is always value-less, but has been *given* value at some time, as a present—and it was *we* who gave and bestowed it. Only we have created the world *that concerns man*! (1974: sec. 301)

Nietzsche's philosophy of creativity wants us fully to appreciate the far-reaching implications of the idea that we have created and invented the world that concerns men and women. If we underestimate ourselves, or so he seems to hold, we will never free ourselves from the clutches of metaphysics and ontotheology. It should have become clear that Nietzsche's combination of naturalism and aestheticism elucidates the significance of the modern antifoundationalist story of progress and emancipation by arguing that a new postmetaphysical culture, shaped by poets in the broadest sense and by new philosophers or "experimenters" (2003: sec. 210), would be characterized by a plurality and diversity of idiosyncratic vocabularies as well as by a nexus between the latter and social practices.[18] Furthermore, it would be governed by a critique of dogmatism, apriorism, representationalism, and the myth of the given. Together with the Romantics and the American pragmatists, Nietzsche shows that an emphasis on the power of the imagination is central to the modern development from finding to making. "Is the world really beautified by the fact that man thinks it beautiful?," he asks in "Skirmishes of an Untimely Man" (1982b: sec. 19). And he answers his own question thus: "He has *humanized* it, that is all." The human subject, as he contends, "believes the world itself to be overloaded with beauty—and he forgets himself as the cause of this. He alone has presented the world with beauty—alas! only with a very human, all-too-human beauty" (1982b: sec. 19). A skeptic might of course advance the argument that this "all-too-human beauty" is not beautiful at all and that it might look different from the perspective of a "higher judge of beauty." However, throughout his texts, Nietzsche explains that this "all-too-human beauty" is all we will ever get and that a recognition of this fact will further the progress of mankind.

Those who believe in a true world and insist on the appearance-reality distinction, and who therefore anathematize becoming, change, contingency, and contradiction, are for Nietzsche the "unproductive." They are tired of life and unwilling to create their own world. Moreover, they believe in what has being, and their thinking is dominated by the gesture of a convergence to the antecedently real and true. They would consider the idea of seeking to become the poet of one's life to be hopelessly frivolous, and instead they focus on objectively and faithfully representing the real. "What kind of man reflects in this way? An unproductive, suffering kind, a kind weary of life" (1968: sec. 585). Nietzsche strictly opposes the "will to truth" of the metaphysicians and representationalists to the "will to create" of the experimenters and antirepresentationalists: "The belief that the world as it ought to be *is*, really exists, is a belief of the unproductive *who do not desire to create a world* as it ought to be. They posit it as already available, they seek ways and means of reaching it. 'Will to truth'—*as the impotence of the will to create*" (1968: sec. 585). However, at the same time Nietzsche argues that this will to truth still contains the power to interpret, it is still "an art of interpretation" (1968: sec. 585). As soon as the metaphysician or representationalist no longer possesses the strength to interpret and to claim that his idiosyncratic fiction corresponds to the really real, he becomes a nihilist. To Nietzsche, a nihilist "is a man who judges of the world as it is that it ought *not* to be, and of the world as it ought to be that it does not exist" (1968: sec. 585). This takes us back to Book One of *The Will to Power*, and it shows that Nietzsche's intended revaluation of values is grounded in his philosophy of creativity or creative action. The world does not speak, it does not tell us what to do, it does not confirm our beliefs and sentences, and moreover it is indifferent to (most) of our descriptions of it. Nietzsche always returns to the idea of making, to humans' creativity, to *homo poeta*. Knowing is creating, and one must never ignore "die ewige Lust des Schaffens;" that is, the subject's "eternal joy of creating" (1982b, "Ancients": sec. 4).

Nietzsche's desire to humanize the world and his emphasis on the subject's acts of creating, forming, and shaping that are central to his notions of de-deification and naturalization prepare the ground for the establishment of a genuinely postmetaphysical culture. His idea that only we have created the world that has value and that concerns humans would be central to Rorty's attempt to present his version of pragmatism as humanism. One also has to see that Nietzsche, together with Dewey, helped Rorty to develop his pragmatist humanism as a form of anti-authoritarianism; that is to say, Nietzsche prepared the ground for Rorty's critique of his fellow humans' endeavor to appeal to an outside authority (God, Truth, or Reality) in epistemology or ethics. Nietzsche and Rorty's critique of the idea of human answerability to the world, to something nonhuman, is central to their attempt to de-divinize and naturalize the world and the self.[19]

One of the main ideas that I have advanced in this book is that in order to fully grasp the significance of anti-authoritarianism, one has to consider the question of aesthetics. Both Nietzsche and the pragmatists illuminate the intimate interwovenness of art and life. According to Nietzsche, art enhances life; it is "essentially *affirmation, blessing, deification of existence*" (1968: sec. 821). Like Dewey, Nietzsche does not demand an art of metaphysical comfort, but, as he stresses in "An Attempt at Self-Criticism" in *The Birth of Tragedy*, "the art of comfort *in this world*" (1999: 12). Perhaps this this-worldly art will enable humans to "some day send all attempts at metaphysical solace to Hell—with metaphysics the first to go!" (1999: 12). While he maintains that art stimulates and enhances life, he also calls attention to its noncognitivism. Nietzsche asserts that art offers us the possibility of creating new values and new perspectives, but it does not tell us the truth about reality or the really real. In his elegant inversion of Plato, Nietzsche agrees with the latter that art is removed from truth, but he at the same time insists that this must not be regarded as an objection against art. This noncognitivism is another important parallel between Nietzsche and the pragmatists. Crucially, in contrast to the pragmatists, Nietzsche always returns to the work of aesthetic form or the practice of form-giving. As I have suggested, the Nietzschean will to power as will to creativity can also be interpreted as the will to form-giving. In other words, his notions of de-deification and naturalization and his version of anti-authoritarianism always involve the question of aesthetic form (and thus of poetic agency). As regards his insistence upon the importance of form, he goes even further than the Romantics.[20]

7.5 Conclusion

In this book, I have argued that pragmatist humanism as anti-authoritarianism is a philosophy of finitude and poetic agency.[21] In Chapter 2, I have suggested that Richard Rorty's pragmatist humanism radicalizes the project of the Enlightenment.[22] While he values the process of secularization and the anti-authoritarian tendencies that began in the Enlightenment, he simultaneously stresses that this process is incomplete. We have to go farther in order to present ourselves as truly enlightened and to develop a postmetaphysical culture. When we finally understand that "once God and his view goes, there is just us and our view" (Rorty 1998b: 54), we might be in a position to establish a "completely secularized culture" (Rorty 2021: xxxii).[23] In this new culture, the quest for the transcendent, the infinite, and the unconditioned will no longer seem necessary or attractive, and humans will realize that the conditioned and the finite are all there is. No longer seeing the necessity of getting beyond their practices to a nonhuman authority, humans will grasp the consequences of the idea that "moral and political principles should be viewed as abbreviations for narratives of successful use of tools, summaries of the results of successful experiments, rather than insights into the nature of anything large (Society, or History, or Humanity)" (Rorty 2021: xxxiii).[24]

In this chapter, I have advanced the argument that it is crucial to see that Rorty's notion of a poeticized and postmetaphysical culture as well as the idea of a pragmatist humanism have a nineteenth-century prehistory. This prehistory primarily concerns the work of the poet and his practice of form-giving as poetic agency. On the last page of *Pragmatism as Anti-Authoritarianism*, Rorty contends that pragmatists "hope to fill out the self-image sketched by the Romantic poets and partially filled in by Nietzsche and James" (2021: 191). From what I have argued in this chapter, it should be obvious that I agree with Rorty. I have sought to demonstrate that Emerson, Whitman, James, and Nietzsche are central to the modern development from finding to making and that they moreover helped prepare the ground for a humanist and anti-authoritarian culture. Telling humanist stories of progress, they show us that we must not strive to escape from our finitude by searching for the certainty, reliability, transhistoricity, immutability, and purity of what would be more than another human creation.

Conclusion

Maybe it is all very simple: "If we can rely on one another, we need not rely on anything else" (Rorty 1998b: 82). By telling a story of poeticizing and progress in this book, I have sought to demonstrate that the idea of a pragmatist enlightenment should be central to any discussion that tries to explain the significance of pragmatism in the twenty-first century. Pragmatism will play an important role in this century because of its combination of humanism and anti-authoritarianism. We have seen that the later Rorty's anti-authoritarianism is central to his brand of pragmatism as humanism. Rorty teaches us that there is no nonhuman authority whose commands humans have to obey and whose constraints they have to confront. We should reject the notion of human answerability to something nonhuman and question the gesture of a convergence to the antecedently real, true, or pure. Furthermore, we should strive to reach a position that would finally enable us to grasp that we have no duties to anything nonhuman and that would also let us realize the dangerous consequences of the desire to humble ourselves before a nonhuman authority.[1] Rorty's anti-authoritarian and antirepresentationalist story of progress and emancipation seeks to make clear that the notions of "answering" and "representing" are dominated by an image of humans as dependent on the judgment of an authority that would trump the consensus and free exchange of justifications of other human beings. Moreover, as soon as we start employing the notions of "answering" and "representing," we want to learn more about how they really work and how effective they are. This inevitably results in theoretical abstractions and a focus on epistemological problems that no longer leaves room for the endeavor to confront the problems of men and women in the Deweyan sense.

By giving up world-directedness and rational answerability to the world and by radically rejecting the hope for a noncontingent, nonhistorical, and powerful ally, humans would initiate a change with far-reaching consequences. Rorty holds that "in the long run it may make a lot of difference whether a society is regulated by its members' fear of nonhuman sanctions or by secular sentiments of pride, loyalty, and solidarity" (1998b: 76). The sentimental education whose advantages Rorty seeks to accentuate "tries to sublimate the desire to stand in suitably humble relations to nonhuman realities into a desire for free and open encounters between human beings, encounters culminating either in intersubjective agreement or in reciprocal tolerance" (Rorty 1991b: 8). Pragmatist humanism, as I have proposed in this study, is an anti-authoritarian philosophy of praxis and finitude, of *poiesis* and human freedom, which shows that progress is possible without reliance on a nonhuman power. Moreover, pragmatist humanism as anti-authoritarianism argues that talk about humans' responsibility to Truth, Reason, or Nature should be replaced with conversations about their responsibility to their fellow human beings. Replacing the verticality of firm foundations and transcendental guidance with the horizontality of contingent and historical social practices and norms, pragmatist humanists refuse to regard themselves as actors in a drama already written before they came on the scene and started to invent their practices.

After the deplorable disorientations and aberrations of antihumanist philosophies and theories, the revival of humanism in the humanities is a welcome phenomenon. Pragmatists like James, Schiller, Dewey, and Rorty offered particularly stimulating and radical versions of humanism.[2] Furthermore, they highlighted the significance of making, creating, poeticizing, and imagining. At the same time, however, these pragmatists more or less completely ignored the question of aesthetic form. One should go even further by advancing the idea that pragmatist aesthetics has never offered an adequate appreciation of the importance and the work of form. This desideratum has been central to the argument that I develop in this book. In my study, I have sought to accomplish three things. First, I have tried to contribute to the revival of humanism by elucidating the potential and the complexity of a pragmatist humanism. Second, I have argued that pragmatist humanism is a form of anti-authoritarianism. Finally, I have sought to demonstrate that there is a possibility of bringing together the revival of humanism and a renewed interest in the work of aesthetic form by suggesting that pragmatist aesthetics for too long has suffered from an insufficiently complex conception of form. Arguing that a mediation between pragmatist aesthetics and Marxist aesthetics promises interesting results and that the former can learn from the latter (particularly from Adorno's aesthetic theory), I have attempted to show that it is worthwhile to strive to stimulate pragmatist aestheticians' interest in the social register of aesthetic form.

While I agree with many of the arguments that Richard Shusterman develops in *Pragmatist Aesthetics*, I criticize his insufficient grasp of the complexity of form.[3] Shusterman's Deweyan approach, focusing on "Dewey's upbeat aesthetic of natural energies" (2000: 10), makes very clear that the notions of organic unity and aesthetic wholeness are of the utmost importance, but that pragmatist aesthetics has more to offer. Shusterman stresses "that our aesthetic concepts, including the concept of art itself, are but instruments which need to be challenged and revised when they fail to provide the best experience" (2000: 18). He does not see, however, that Dewey refuses to historicize and revise his conception of form in the confrontation with modern artworks and that this causes serious problems for his aesthetics. As we saw in Chapter 3, Shusterman strives to make Dewey's understanding of form appear more complex than it actually is. The former advances the argument that for Dewey "the permanence of experienced unity is not only impossible, it is aesthetically undesirable, for art requires the challenge of tension and disruptive novelty and the rhythmic struggle of achievement and breakdown of order" (2000: 32). According to Shusterman, Dewey's aesthetics intends to convince us that we cannot "linger in such harmony; aesthetic experience is but a temporary savored culmination, a rhythmic interval of rest, which, sharing in life's demand for variety, cannot be satisfied with order" (2000: 32). There are only a few passages in Dewey's *Art as Experience* that confirm and strengthen Shusterman's interpretation. Dewey, for instance, states that there are times when the equilibrium between the live creature and its environment is disturbed. New adjustments must be made through struggle, a new relation to the environment must be creatively established. There are disturbance, dissonance, and fragmentation. At the same time, however, Dewey maintains that the "moment of passage from the disturbance into harmony is that of intensest life" (2008a: 22). Furthermore, he contends that even through phases of conflict and dissonance "there abides the deep-seated memory of an underlying harmony" (2008a: 23). I wish to suggest that for both Dewey and Shusterman this notion of an "underlying harmony" governs their pragmatist aesthetics. In this context, one has to note that Shusterman also directs attention to the undeniable importance of fragmentation and incoherence in the work of art. In a central passage in *Pragmatist Aesthetics*, he writes:

> If our human need to perceive and experience satisfying unities in the disordered flux of experience is what motivates our interest in art, this need should not be rejected. What we should reject is the repressive limitation of art

to the expression of only such unity, the prohibition of jarring fragmentation and incoherencies which can have their own stimulating aesthetic and cognitive effect, and which can result in more complex forms of coherence. (2000: 76)

What pragmatist aesthetics needs, I submit, is not an understanding of "more complex forms of coherence," but rather an appreciation of the degree to which fragmentation and nonorganicity govern modern art and literature. Shusterman's argument suffers from the fact that he associates fragmentation and incoherence primarily with postmodern art.[4] This might be because he wrote his book in the late 1980s and early 1990s, when the phenomenon of postmodernism was still widely discussed and theorists like Baudrillard, Lyotard, and Jameson highlighted its radical novelty.

Undoubtedly, Shusterman is right in pointing out that "aesthetic inquiry would seem best served by a philosophy which treats not only art but its theory as having the highest philosophical importance and recompense for our cultural self-understanding" (2000: 11). Pragmatism is that philosophy, and there is a fairly high probability that this fact will strengthen its position in the future. It is interesting, and encouraging, that in a recent essay Roberta Dreon poses the same question that has preoccupied me in this study: "Given that pragmatist aesthetics opposes the boundaries of the fine arts, high culture or great works of art in the standard sense, does it still have adequate tools to understand contemporary artistic productions and formal issues in twentieth-century arts?" (2021: 11).[5] From what I have argued in this study, it should be clear that my answer is: "No, it does not." However, this is not a reason for despair, but rather an incentive to mediate between pragmatist aesthetics and other aesthetic approaches. While mediation as a conceptual tool is primarily associated with Marxism, one only has to think of the work of Jameson in this context, I hope that pragmatist aestheticians will profit from its use in their endeavor to make their field less rooted in Dewey's aesthetics.

We have seen that a critique of Dewey's aesthetics could focus on the idea that the practice of form-giving, as poetic agency, can be regarded as an anti-authoritarian gesture. In modernism, the idiosyncrasy and particularity of form-giving often defy aesthetic norms and standards; that is, form often is associated with nonorganicity, fragmentation, and dissonance. Form-giving urges one to confront the dialectics of wholeness (or unity) and fragment (or difference). Moreover, in modernism, the act of form-giving problematizes the link between unity, meaning, and totality.[6] I have suggested that one should use Adorno's aesthetic theory by redefining the negation of aesthetic synthesis as a radical form of anti-authoritarianism that characterizes fragmented and dissonant works of art that tend more toward nonorganicity than Adorno allowed. By grasping that the fragmented and dissonant work in a non-Adornian sense is not answerable to any external authority and that it simultaneously criticizes the semblance ("Schein") and wholeness of the traditional autonomous artwork as forms of authority, one might be in a position to regard the practice of form-giving as an anti-authoritarian act. In other words, redefining the negation of aesthetic synthesis in a non-Adornian manner will help pragmatist aestheticians to understand the practice of form-giving, the work of form, as anti-authoritarian poetic agency. This anti-authoritarianism in aesthetics might supplement the Rortyan anti-authoritarianism in epistemology and ethics.

By dialectically using Adorno's aesthetic theory, pragmatism can contribute to the development of a "positive aesthetics" (see Chapter 6). Pragmatist poetic agency demonstrates that something stimulating happens when the creativity of action comes together with the realization that the imagination goes all the way down, and it simultaneously accentuates the notion that intellectual and moral progress is not a matter of getting closer to the antecedently real or true but of creatively surpassing the past by introducing new ways of speaking and novel kinds of form-giving. As we have seen, poetic agency adds a crucial new aspect to pragmatism's story of progress and emancipation by proposing that the contingency of social practices ought to include the contingency of the work of form. New forms offer new perspectives, new constellations and relations, new symmetries and dissonances, and a new appreciation of harmony and fragmentation or linearity and nonlinearity. Form-giving is a creative practice that expands our imagination and hence may provoke new vocabularies; the novelty of forming draws attention to the indefinite expansibility of the human imagination. Like the imagination, form-giving keeps proposing new candidates for belief, new things to desire, or it may reinforce the wish to begin practical work from a radically new position and perspective.

What this signifies is that form-giving as poetic agency shows that instead of focusing on the desire for an increased access to the real, one ought to concentrate on the increased ability to creatively do things or to take part in social practices.[7] According to Rorty, it is an important feature of literature "that one can achieve success by introducing a quite new genre of poem or novel or critical essay *without* argument. It succeeds simply by its success, not because there are good reasons why poems or novels or essays should be written in the new way rather than the old" (1982: 142). From what I have argued in this book, it should be clear that in my view Rorty's suggestion that a new literary genre "succeeds simply by its success" is highly problematic. This is one of the many passages where he completely ignores the question of aesthetic form. The fact that he refrains from discussing aesthetic questions severely weakens his version of literary criticism. Pragmatist aestheticians and literary critics need more than Rorty has to offer. One of their primary future tasks should be to question the Dewey-Rorty legacy in aesthetics and literary criticism.

In this book, I have told a story of poeticizing, making, and progress, of *poiesis* and social practices, which centers around Emerson's suggestion that "the universe wear[s] our color" (1981: 286) and which uses Schiller and James's idea that "human motives sharpen all our questions, human satisfactions lurk in all our answers, all our formulas have a human twist" (James 1907: 592). This story is shaped by Nietzsche's radical proposal that "only we have created the world *that concerns man*" (1974: sec. 301) and also by Said's far-reaching idea that humanism "is the achievement of form by human will and agency" (2004: 15). In my humanist story of progress and emancipation, I have sought to elucidate to what degree pragmatists have contributed to the resurgence of humanism. Pragmatist humanism as anti-authoritarianism will play a crucial role for the attempt to create a version of humanism for the twenty-first century, and it will continue the modern development from finding to making in a thought-provoking manner.

Notes

Introduction

1 Paul Guyer comments on Hegel's idea of the end of art thus:

> If Hegel had thought that art was now something of the past on any empirical grounds, he would have been a very poor critic. But Hegel was not making a contingent claim on empirical grounds; he was asserting what he took to be a metaphysical necessity. He made this claim because he took art to be a form of cognition, one that is necessary in the development of cognition but also one that is ultimately inadequate for the complete realization of cognition and therefore ultimately has only historical significance as a stage in the development of cognition. (2014a: 119–20)

According to Guyer, Hegel's "cognitivist theory of art" rejects "the importance of art altogether as anything more than a medium for the access to the history of the development of thought" (2014a: 122). On Hegel's philosophy of art, see also William Desmond, *Art and the Absolute: A Study of Hegel's Aesthetics* (Albany: SUNY Press, 1986); Stephen Bungay, *Beauty and Truth: A Study of Hegel's Aesthetics* (Oxford: Clarendon Press, 1987); Benjamin Rutter, *Hegel on the Modern Arts* (New York: Cambridge University Press, 2010); Robert B. Pippin, *After the Beautiful: Hegel and the Philosophy of Pictorial Modernism* (Chicago: University of Chicago Press, 2013); and Stephen Houlgate, ed., *Hegel and the Arts* (Evanston: Northwestern University Press, 2007). In addition, see the chapter "Konstruktion der Moderne: Hegel, Lukács, Adorno" in Peter Bürger, *Prosa der Moderne* (Frankfurt am Main: Suhrkamp, 1988), 19–31.

2 From today's perspective, Foucault's pieces on Nietzsche are still among his most important texts: "Nietzsche, Freud, Marx" and "Nietzsche, Genealogy, History," both in *Michel Foucault: Aesthetics, Method, and Epistemology*, ed. James D. Faubion (New York: New Press, 1998), 269–78, 369–92. Antihumanism was the dominant attitude in French intellectual circles in the mid-1960s. However, this radical antihumanism had a prehistory. In his illuminating *An Atheism That Is Not Humanist Emerges in French Thought*, Stefanos Geroulanos discusses this prehistory. According to him, this reorientation of French thought took place in the period 1925 to 1950. Geroulanos's contention is that the intellectuals whom he discusses in his study, for instance, Kojève, Blanchot, Bataille, Merleau-Ponty, Malraux, and

Hyppolite, radically rejected traditional humanism: "To approach anew the codes addressing human life and significance, these thinkers developed the case for an atheist ethics not bound by humanism, rejecting Man's prominence as founder and guarantor of knowledge, thought, and ethics, and seeking to offer alternatives to the political and historical impasse they diagnosed" (2010: 3). Striving to overcome atheist anthropocentrism, the new atheism presented itself as highly critical of secular and politically transformative commitments as they were associated with the (post-Enlightenment) Left. Geroulanos maintains that "the new nonhumanist atheism came to be expressed at different times in existentialist, hyper-ethical, or cynical terms, in nondoctrinaire socialist, reactionary, ultramodernist, or even downright antipolitical principles" (2010: 3). It is probably one of the ironies of French intellectual history that after the demise of poststructuralism its prehistory seems decidedly more thought-provoking than the full-blown phenomenon of the 1960s and 1970s (not to mention the standardized and mechanistic versions one had to endure in the 1980s and 1990s, particularly in the United States). While one will most presumably never forgive Blanchot for his (temporary) political disorientation, and Bataille for the fact that he made a living as a librarian (a constant source of amusement for Breton), these authors, from today's perspective, appear more unpredictable and thus stimulating than those for whom they prepared the ground. It is interesting to see that Nietzsche, in his late text *Der Fall Wagner* (1888), describes a style and a way of thinking that remind one of (French) left Nietzscheans of the 1960s and 1970s. It is a thinking of difference and radical plurality, a rhizomatic thought that attacks any notion of totality and unity. Nietzsche's harsh critique of what he terms "literary decadence" unfortunately never registered with poststructuralists and deconstructionists, who embraced this German philosopher as one of their most important ancestors and precursors. He writes:

> What is the hallmark of all *literary* decadence? The fact that life does not reside in the totality any more. The word becomes sovereign and jumps out of the sentence, the sentence reaches out and blots out the meaning of the page, the page comes to life at the expense of the whole—the whole is not whole any more. But this is the image of every decadent style: there is always an anarchy of the atom, disintegration of the will, "freedom of the individual," morally speaking,— or, expanded into a political theory, "*equal* rights for all." Life, *equal* vitality, the vibration and exuberance of life pushed back into the smallest structures, all the rest *impoverished* of life. Paralysis everywhere, exhaustion, numbness *or* hostility and chaos: both becoming increasingly obvious the higher you climb in the forms of organization. The whole does not live at all any more: it is cobbled together, calculated, synthetic, an artifact. (2005: sec. 7)

To what degree Nietzsche's editors, Giorgio Colli and Mazzino Montinari, were appalled in the confrontation with Foucault, Derrida, and Deleuze's interpretations, or rather deformations, of Nietzsche, is described in Philipp Felsch, *Wie Nietzsche aus der Kälte kam: Geschichte einer Rettung* (München: C. H. Beck, 2022).

3   I offer a detailed discussion of Nietzsche's version of humanism and of his relationship with the American pragmatists in *Pragmatism and Poetic Agency: The Persistence of Humanism* (New York: Routledge, 2021). See also Pietro Gori, *Nietzsche's Pragmatism: A Study on [sic] Perspectival Thought* (Berlin: de Gruyter, 2020). For the latest discussion of Nietzsche's metaphilosophy, see the interesting volume *Nietzsche's Metaphilosophy: The Nature, Method, and Aims of Philosophy*, ed. Paul S. Loeb and Matthew Meyer (New York: Cambridge University Press, 2019).

4   I seek to illuminate the complexity of this modern development from finding to making in my trilogy of books: *Romanticism and Pragmatism: Richard Rorty and the Idea of a Poeticized Culture* (Basingstoke: Palgrave Macmillan, 2015); *Marxism, Pragmatism, and Postmetaphysics: From Finding to Making* (Basingstoke: Palgrave Macmillan, 2019); and *Pragmatism and Poetic Agency: The Persistence of Humanism*. Moreover, in these monographs I advance the idea that one understands the contemporary significance of pragmatism better when one realizes how pragmatism, humanism, anti-authoritarianism, and postmetaphysics are interlinked. From what I argue in the present study, it will become clear that I agree with Richard Bernstein when he maintains:

> During the past few decades, the philosophical scene has begun to change dramatically. There is a resurgence of pragmatic themes in philosophy throughout the world, and a growing interest in the works of the classical pragmatists. There are the beginnings of a more subtle, complex narrative of the development of philosophy in America that highlights the *continuity* and the *persistence* of the pragmatic legacy. (2010: 13)

5   For discussions of Nietzsche's naturalism, see Richard Schacht, *Nietzsche* (New York: Routledge, 1992); Christoph Cox, *Nietzsche: Naturalism and Interpretation* (Berkeley: University of California Press, 1999); and Brian Leiter, "Nietzsche's Naturalism Reconsidered," in *The Oxford Handbook of Nietzsche*, ed. Ken Gemes and John Richardson (Oxford: Oxford University Press, 2013), 576–98.

6   For discussions of humanism, see Alan Bullock, *The Humanist Tradition in the West* (New York: Norton, 1985); Andrew Copson and Anthony Clifford Grayling, eds., *The Wiley Blackwell Handbook of Humanism* (Oxford: Wiley Blackwell, 2015); Tony Davis, *Humanism* (New York: Routledge, 1997); Philip Kitcher, *Life After Faith: The Case for Secular Humanism* (New Haven, CT: Yale University Press, 2014); Stephen Law, *Humanism: A Very Short Introduction* (New York: Oxford University Press, 2011); and Richard Norman, *On Humanism*

(New York: Routledge, 2004). Of particular value in this context are Kate Soper, *Humanism and Anti-Humanism* (London: Hutchinson, 1986); Martin Halliwell and Andy Mousley, eds., *Critical Humanisms: Humanist/Anti-Humanist Dialogues* (Edinburgh: Edinburgh University Press, 2003); and David Alderson and Robert Spencer, eds., *For Humanism: Explorations in Theory and Politics* (London: Pluto, 2017).

7 Both the present study and *Pragmatism and Poetic Agency* try to highlight the multilayered potential of pragmatist humanism. However, in this book I focus more on aesthetics and the practice of form-giving.

8 This, of course, reminds one of James's radical gesture in *Pragmatism* (1907).

9 In its epic scope, the volume edited by Anthony B. Pinn, *The Oxford Handbook of Humanism* (Oxford: Oxford University Press, 2021) is the most recent confirmation of the urgent character and far-reaching consequences of this revival. Of particular value in this context is the first chapter, "Reclaiming the Self: Transcending Postmodern Fragmentation," in Michael Bryson, *The Humanist (Re)Turn: Reclaiming the Self in Literature* (New York: Routledge, 2020), 1–53. The renaissance of humanism in the humanities is, of course, not the only answer to the question, "What comes after poststructuralism and deconstruction?" The development of new materialisms, new formalisms, object-oriented philosophy, actor-network theory, and forms of postcritique offers new and partly stimulating perspectives on work in the humanities. My task in this book will be to show that pragmatist humanism, as a philosophy of praxis and creativity that continues the project of the Enlightenment and the process of secularization, has the potential for radically changing our ways of thinking that the other approaches and theories do not possess.

10 Peter E. Gordon comments on the significance of Adorno's aesthetic thought for the twenty-first century thus:

> It remains an unfortunate commonplace that Adorno was a man of great privilege and wealth who luxuriated in the sublime artifacts of "high" culture. That this caricature persists tells us a great deal, if not about Adorno, then about the difficulty that must confront any social theory that refuses to surrender the aesthetic ideals that were once self-evident on the political left. [...] Today, however, when a species of so-called populism has seized so much of political discourse on both the left and the right, the aspiration to aesthetic freedom as a necessary component to human freedom has grown unfamiliar, and it is often dismissed as a symptom of an intolerable elitism. It is one of the greatest distinctions of *Aesthetic Theory* that it refuses to surrender the ideal of aesthetic autonomy, even while it also honors art's deepest obligations to our common world. (2021: 144)

11 In this context, one ought to remark that Dewey, in *Reconstruction in Philosophy*, argues that theories and systems will never offer certainty. They must not

be regarded as "finalities," since they are tools that are open to modification through use:

> Here it is enough to note that notions, theories, systems, no matter how elaborate and self-consistent they are, must be regarded as hypotheses. They are to be accepted as bases of actions which test them, not as finalities. To perceive this fact is to abolish rigid dogmas from the world. It is to recognize that conceptions, theories and systems of thought are always open to development through use. It is to enforce the lesson that we must be on the lookout quite as much for indications to alter them as for opportunities to assert them. They are tools. As in the case of all tools, their value resides not in themselves but in their capacity to work shown in the consequences of their use. (1957: 145)

In *Pragmatic Naturalism*, Richard Bernstein contends that Dewey's naturalism radically rejects the idea of a transcendental philosophy and that it proposes that philosophy should always be willing to learn from scientific inquiry:

> Philosophical reflection must always be open to what we learn from scientific inquiry. This is fundamental for Dewey's pragmatic naturalism. Dewey was also critical of the quest for certainty and the spectator theory of knowing. The only certainty we achieve is a *practical* certainty that is, in principle, open to critical revision. And we never achieve a position *outside* language and the world where we can view the world *sub specie aeternitatis*. The philosophical task is never finally completed; it must be performed over and over again in light of what we learn from novel forms of scientific inquiry. (2020: 23)

While I highly value Dewey and Bernstein's approaches, my position in this book will be different insofar as I—as a pragmatist humanist—will concentrate on the following question: What can we learn from the poets (and the aestheticians)?

12 Pragmatism's future orientation always was one of this philosophy's main attractions for Rorty. In *Achieving Our Country*, for instance, he develops his interpretation of Whitman and Dewey by claiming that they bring together a profound interest in a radically different future of the United States and a clearly anti-authoritarian stance:

> Both Dewey and Whitman viewed the United States as an opportunity to see ultimate significance in a finite, human, historical project, rather than in something eternal and nonhuman. They both hoped that America would be the place where a religion of love would finally replace a religion of fear. They dreamed that Americans would break the traditional link between the religious impulse, the impulse to stand in awe of something greater than oneself, and the infantile need for security, the childish hope of escaping from time and chance. They wanted to preserve the former and discard the latter. They wanted to put

hope for a casteless and classless America in the place traditionally occupied by knowledge of the will of God. They wanted that utopian America to replace God as the unconditional object of desire. They wanted the struggle for social justice to be the country's animating principle, the nation's soul. (1998a: 17–18)

1 Humanism, Anti-Authoritarianism, and Form

1. In this context, see Richard Shusterman, *Pragmatist Aesthetics: Living Beauty, Rethinking Art*, 2nd ed. (Lanham, MD: Rowman and Littlefield, 2000); Shusterman, "Aesthetics," in *A Companion to Pragmatism*, ed. John R. Shook and Joseph Margolis (Malden, MA: Wiley-Blackwell, 2009), 352–60; and Thomas M. Alexander, *John Dewey's Theory of Art, Experience, and Nature: The Horizons of Feeling* (Albany: SUNY Press, 1987). In addition, see Leszek Koczanowicz and Katarzyna Liszka, eds., *Beauty, Responsibility, and Power: Ethical and Political Consequences of Pragmatist Aesthetics* (Leiden: Brill, 2014).
2. I seek to elucidate the crucial role of Nietzsche for the endeavor to grasp the complexity of pragmatist humanism in *Pragmatism and Poetic Agency: The Persistence of Humanism* (New York: Routledge, 2021). See the first part "Friedrich Nietzsche and the Pragmatists," 17–98.
3. This dialogue between pragmatism and Marxist aesthetics (Lukács and Adorno) was central to my study *Marxism, Pragmatism, and Postmetaphysics: From Finding to Making* (Basingstoke: Palgrave Macmillan, 2019). However, in the present book I will focus to an even higher degree on aesthetic form and the practice of form-giving.
4. For a discussion of Renaissance humanism, see Jill Kraye, ed., *The Cambridge Companion to Renaissance Humanism* (New York: Cambridge University Press, 1996); Mario A. Di Cesare, ed., *Reconsidering the Renaissance* (Binghamton: SUNY Press, 1992); Charles G. Nauert, *Humanism and the Culture of Renaissance Europe* (New York: Cambridge University Press, 2006); and Patrick Baker, *Italian Renaissance Humanism in the Mirror* (New York: Cambridge University Press, 2015). While Rorty and I have begun our respective intellectual histories centering on the development of pragmatism or pragmatist humanism with the attempt to illuminate the significance of Romanticism, a discussion of the role of Renaissance humanism for the establishment of a pragmatist poeticized culture promises interesting results.
5. In *Studies in the History of the Renaissance*, Walter Pater writes about the significance of Pico della Mirandola as regards the idea of man's "reassertion" as follows:

> For this high dignity of man thus bringing the dust under his feet into sensible communion with the thoughts and affections of the angels was supposed to belong to him not as renewed by a religious system, but by his own natural right; and it was a counterpoise to the increasing tendency of mediaeval religion to depreciate man's nature, to sacrifice this or that element in it, to make it ashamed of itself, to keep the degrading or painful accidents of it always in view. It helped man onward to that reassertion of himself, that rehabilitation of human nature, the body, the senses, the heart, the intelligence, which the Renaissance fulfils. (2010: 23–4)

6 See the following chapters: "F. C. S. Schiller: Pragmatism, Humanism, and Postmetaphysics," in *Romanticism and Pragmatism: Richard Rorty and the Idea of a Poeticized Culture* (Basingstoke: Palgrave Macmillan, 2015), 19–30; "'Only We Have Created the World *That Concerns Man*!': Nietzsche, Naturalism, and the Idea of Creativity" and "'The Humanistic State of Mind': James and Nietzsche" in *Pragmatism and Poetic Agency*, 19–50.

7 Brennan expands on this reading of Nietzsche as follows: "And yet, in the end all modern antihumanism is Nietzschean, expanding on or adapting his philosophy's central principles that free choice is an illusion; that knowledge, even if it were possible, has no 'use'; that ethics constrain Man's [sic] life-enhancing instincts; and that 'truth' is rhetorical, language a means of artful deception" (2017: 6). In this context, see also the chapter "Nietzsche and the Colonies," in Timothy Brennan, *Borrowed Light: Vico, Hegel, and the Colonies* (Stanford, CA: Stanford University Press, 2014), 133–95.

8 See Alan D. Schrift, "Nietzsche's French Legacy," in *The Cambridge Companion to Nietzsche*, ed. Bernd Magnus and Kathleen M. Higgins (New York: Cambridge University Press, 1996), 323–55; and Alan D. Schrift, *Nietzsche and the Question of Interpretation: Between Hermeneutics and Deconstruction* (London: Routledge, 1990).

9 In "The Apotheosis of the Romantic Will," Berlin directs attention to how important the notion of the fragmented or nonorganic work of art is when one seeks to grasp what Romanticism means. In his opinion, for the Romantic writers

> the tidy regularities of daily life are but a curtain to conceal the terrifying spectacle of true reality, which has no structure, but is a wild whirlpool, a perpetual *tourbillon* of the creative spirit which no system can capture: life and motion cannot be represented by immobile, lifeless concepts, nor the infinite and unbounded by the finite and the fixed. A finished work of art, a systematic treatise, are attempts to freeze the flowing stream of life; only fragments, intimations, broken glimpses can begin to convey the perpetual movement of reality. (2000: 575)

The notion of the fragmented artwork will play a crucial role in my discussion of Marxist aesthetics in Chapter 5. Adorno's aesthetics, in particular, cannot be adequately understood without analyzing the meaning of the nonorganic, avant-garde artwork (the same goes for Walter Benjamin—one only has to think of his concept of allegory as he develops in the *Trauerspielbuch*).

10 In this context, one should also think of the significance of Adorno's thought and style for the argument that Edward Said develops in the essays collected in *On Late Style: Music and Literature Against the Grain* (New York: Bloomsbury, 2006).

11 For a detailed discussion of the similarities and differences between Said and Rorty's versions of humanist literary criticism, see the chapter "'All Anybody Ever Does with Anything Is Use It': Edward Said, Richard Rorty, and the Task of Humanist Criticism," in Ulf Schulenberg, *Pragmatism and Poetic Agency*, 182–209.

12 In his conclusion, Hammer observes "that Adorno's philosophical presuppositions simply did not allow him to address the post-auratic, often essentially conceptual art practices that arose in the wake of the avant-garde movements of the 1960s and their critique of the value of aesthetic autonomy" (2015: 211). In this context, see also the chapters "Models of Mediation" and "Politics of Postmodernism" in Lambert Zuidervaart, *Adorno's Aesthetic Theory: The Redemption of Illusion* (Cambridge: MIT Press, 1991), 217–47, 248–74. In addition, see the chapter "Reading Mass Culture" in Peter Uwe Hohendahl, *Prismatic Thought: Theodor W. Adorno* (Lincoln: University of Nebraska Press, 1995), 119–48.

2 "We Have No Duties to Anything Nonhuman": Richard Rorty's Anti-Authoritarianism

1 For discussions of Rorty's anti-authoritarianism, see David Rondel, "Anti-authoritarianism, Meliorism, and Cultural Politics: On the Deweyan Deposit in Rorty's Pragmatism," *Pragmatism Today* 2 (1) (2011): 56–67; and David Rondel's "Introduction: The Unity of Richard Rorty's Philosophy," in *The Cambridge Companion to Rorty*, ed. Rondel (New York: Cambridge University Press, 2020), 1–18. It is interesting to note that Rorty even speaks of his "militant anti-authoritarianism" (2000b: 376). In *Reconstructing Pragmatism: Richard Rorty and the Classical Pragmatists*, Christopher Voparil makes the interesting suggestion that Rortyan irony "is best read as an ethical form of antiauthoritarian fallibilism" (2022: 22). For Voparil's understanding of Rorty's anti-authoritarianism, his "Introduction: Learning from Rorty's Reconstructed Pragmatism" and chapter 2 ("Rorty and James: The Ethics and Epistemology of Belief") are of particular significance.

2 I have sought to elucidate the implications and consequences of Rorty's antifoundationalist and antirepresentationalist story of progress and emancipation in my trilogy of books: *Romanticism and Pragmatism: Richard Rorty and the Idea of a Poeticized Culture* (Basingstoke: Palgrave Macmillan, 2015); *Marxism, Pragmatism, and Postmetaphysics: From Finding to Making* (Basingstoke: Palgrave Macmillan, 2019); and *Pragmatism and Poetic Agency: The Persistence of Humanism* (New York: Routledge, 2021).

3 For a detailed discussion of pragmatism as humanism, see Ulf Schulenberg, *Pragmatism and Poetic Agency*.

4 The posthumously published *Pragmatism as Anti-Authoritarianism* once again highlights the significance of anti-authoritarianism for the later Rorty's thought. In the preface, he states that his lectures

> offer a way of thinking about the human situation which abjures both eternity and sublimity, and is finitistic through and through. The lectures try to sketch the result of putting aside the cosmological, epistemological, and moral versions of the sublime: God as immaterial first cause, Reality as utterly alien to our epistemic subjectivity, and moral purity as unreachable by our inherently sinful empirical selves. I follow Dewey in suggesting that we build our philosophical reflections around our political hopes: around the project of fashioning institutions and customs which will make human life, finite and mortal life, more beautiful. (2021: xxix)

5 As far as the relation between secularism and pragmatism is concerned, Rorty points out: "But I suspect people become pragmatists only because they are first secularists: I cannot imagine anyone adopting James's view of truth who was not already convinced that human beings are responsible only to one another. Pragmatism stands on the shoulders of the Enlightenment" (2010b: 548).

6 In "Towards Rehabilitating Objectivity," John McDowell gives an excellent summary of Rorty's Deweyan narrative that concentrates on Western culture's coming to maturity:

> What Rorty takes to parallel authoritarian religion is the very idea that in everyday and scientific investigations we submit to standards constituted by the things themselves, the reality that is supposed to be the topic of the investigation. Accepting that idea, Rorty suggests, is casting the world in the role of the non-human Other before which we are to humble ourselves. Full human maturity would require us to acknowledge authority only if the acknowledgement does not involve abasing ourselves before something non-human. The only authority that meets the requirement is that of human consensus. If we conceive inquiry and judgment in terms of making ourselves answerable to the world, as opposed to being answerable to our fellows, we are merely postponing the completion of

the humanism whose achievement begins with discarding authoritarian religion. (2000: 109–10)

7 For a discussion of this notion of a pragmatist enlightenment, see the chapter "Naturalizing Kant?: Constructivism and Pragmatism," in Ulf Schulenberg, *Pragmatism and Poetic Agency*, 81–97. For Rorty's use and critique of Brandom, see "Robert Brandom on Social Practices and Representations," in Rorty (1998b: 122–37).

8 In "Ethics without Principles," Rorty summarizes his understanding of imagination as follows: "We see imagination as the cutting edge of cultural evolution, the power which—given peace and prosperity—constantly operates so as to make the human future richer than the human past" (1999: 87). In the first chapter of *Philosophy as Poetry*, he underlines that too many (analytic) philosophers are still reluctant to fully accept the power of the imagination:

> My hypothesis about why ontology remains so popular is that we are still reluctant to admit that the poetic imagination sets the bounds for human thought. At the heart of philosophy's quarrel with poetry is the fear that the imagination goes all the way down—that there is nothing we talk about that we might not have talked of differently. This fear causes philosophers to become obsessed by the need to achieve *direct* access to reality. (2016: 3)

9 For a detailed discussion of Rorty's reading of Romanticism and of the significance of Emerson and Whitman in this context, see the chapters "'Toolmakers Rather than Discoverers': Richard Rorty's Reading of Romanticism" and "'Strangle the Singers Who Will Not Sing You Loud and Strong': Ralph Waldo Emerson, Walt Whitman, and the Idea of a Literary Culture," in Ulf Schulenberg, *Romanticism and Pragmatism*, 120–33, 80–92.

10 Berlin's *The Roots of Romanticism* had a profound influence on Rorty's understanding of Romanticism.

11 Although I cannot discuss this in detail, I would like to mention that an analysis of the relationship between Romanticism and pragmatism as anti-authoritarianism should also consider Rorty's notion of polytheism. In "Pragmatism as Romantic Polytheism," he writes:

> The substitution of poetry for religion as a source of ideals, a movement that began with the Romantics, seems to me usefully described as a return to polytheism. [...] Different poets will perfect different sides of human nature, by projecting different ideals. A romantic utilitarian will probably drop the idea of diverse immortal persons, such as the Olympian deities, but she will retain the idea that there are diverse, conflicting, but equally valuable forms of human life. (2007: 29)

Later in his essay, Rorty shows that polytheism is also linked with his idea of anti-authoritarianism:

> To be a polytheist in this sense you do not have to believe that there are non-human persons with power to intervene in human affairs. All you need do is abandon the idea that we should try to find a way of making everything hang together, which will tell all human beings what to do with their lives, and tell all of them the same thing. (2007: 30)

12 For a reading of Nietzsche that in a thought-provoking manner differs from Rorty's and mine, see Peter Poellner, *Nietzsche and Metaphysics* (Oxford: Oxford University Press, 1995). The most convincing discussion of Nietzsche's naturalism still is Richard Schacht's *Nietzsche* (New York: Routledge, 1995). For a stimulating recent interpretation of how Nietzsche's naturalism shapes his conception of truth, see Christian J. Emden, "Nietzsche, Truth, and Naturalism," in *The New Cambridge Companion to Nietzsche*, ed. Tom Stern (New York: Cambridge University Press, 2019), 273–301.

13 For a detailed discussion of the relationship between Nietzsche and pragmatism, see the first part "Friedrich Nietzsche and the Pragmatists," in Ulf Schulenberg, *Pragmatism and Poetic Agency*, 17–98.

14 The Rortyan formulation that "nature itself is a poem that we humans have written," of course, goes back to Nietzsche who refers to "the whole eternally growing world of valuations, colors, accents, perspectives, scales, affirmations, and negations" as "this poem that we have invented" ["Diese von uns erfundene Dichtung"] (1974: sec. 301). To those who choose to ignore our poem or who simply cannot see it, Nietzsche says: "One is much more of an artist than one realizes" (2003: sec. 192).

15 In this context, see chapter 11, "Sainte-Beuve and Balzac," in Marcel Proust's *Contre Sainte-Beuve*, in *Marcel Proust on Art and Literature*, trans. Sylvia Townsend Warner (New York: Carroll and Graf, 1997), 157–89. For illuminating discussions of *Contre Sainte-Beuve*, see chapter 18 in William C. Carter, *Marcel Proust: A Life* (New Haven, CT: Yale University Press, 2013), 463–86; and chapter 12 in Jean-Yves Tadié, *Marcel Proust: Biographie* (Frankfurt am Main: Suhrkamp, 2008), 605–70.

16 In this context, see the chapter "Kunst und Erkenntnis," in Ernst Robert Curtius, *Marcel Proust* (Frankfurt am Main: Schöffling, 2021 [1925]), 17–20.

17 See Alexander Nehamas, *Nietzsche: Life as Literature* (Cambridge, MA: Harvard University Press, 1985). In addition, see Duncan Large's interesting *Nietzsche and Proust: A Comparative Study* (Oxford: Oxford University Press, 2001).

18 Concerning this notion of a possible plurality of worlds, Proust writes:

> Thanks to art, instead of seeing one world only, our own, we see that world multiply itself and we have at our disposal as many worlds as there are original artists, worlds more different one from the other than those which revolve in infinite space, worlds which, centuries after the extinction of the fire from which their light first emanated, whether it is called Rembrandt or Vermeer, send us still each one its special radiance. (2000: 254)

In this context, it is interesting to see how David Ellison comments on the narrator's suggestion that "the writer's task and duty are those of a translator" (2000: 247). Ellison convincingly combines this emphasis on translation with Proust's use of metaphors or metaphorical language:

> One could say that the entirety of Proust's aesthetic project, as contained in the seven volumes of the *Recherche* we have just read, is a vast, continually renewed exercise in translation conveyed in metaphorical terms. Whether it is the narrator attempting to translate his sensual impressions into an evocative descriptive language; whether it is Elstir, through the "metaphors" of his seascapes attempting to connect the disparate realms of water and land; or whether it is the reader attempting to find, underlying the human comedy of the *Recherche*, the general social laws upon which it is based—in each case, the efforts to uncover relations and to bridge gaps depend upon a properly translational movement, whereby the evidence of our sense and the meanings we impute to the world are transported from one place to another. (2010: 179)

19 In *The Quest for Certainty*, Dewey not only stresses that philosophy in its worldliness has a social mission, he also shows how important an antifoundationalist and anti-authoritarian story of progress is when one seeks to grasp the task that a pragmatist or naturalistic humanism has to confront. Concerning the foundations of knowledge, the first two chapters of *Quest*, "Escape from Peril" and "Philosophy's Search for the Immutable," tell a story that illuminates the cause and the consequences of a sharp division between theory and practice, intellect and action, or knowing and doing. While both religion and philosophy offer the subject the possibility of self-transcendence, it is philosophy that is characterized by the connection between rationality, logic, immutability, and eternal truth:

> Telling the story of the universe in the form of rational discourse instead of emotionalized imagination signified the discovery of logic as a rational science. Conformity on the part of supreme reality to the requirements of logic conferred upon its constitutive objects necessary and immutable characteristics. Pure contemplation of these forms was man's highest and most divine bliss, a communion with unchangeable truth. (1988: 13)

20　For a detailed discussion of Dewey's story of progress, see the chapter "John Dewey's Antifoundationalist Story of Progress," in Ulf Schulenberg, *Romanticism and Pragmatism*, 106–19.
21　For a discussion of Rorty's highly problematic understanding of aesthetic form, see Chapter 3.
22　As regards Rorty's dichotomous understanding of the function of literature, see the chapter "The Politics of the Novel," in Christopher J. Voparil, *Richard Rorty: Politics and Vision* (Lanham, MD: Rowman and Littlefield, 2006), 61–88. In addition, see Serge Grigoriev, "Rorty and Literature," in *A Companion to Rorty*, ed. Alan Malachowski (Hoboken, NJ: Wiley Blackwell, 2020), 413–26.
23　In this context, one should note that Rorty in many texts argues that in Western liberal societies moral progress is in the direction of greater human solidarity. However, faithful to his Deweyan anti-Platonism as antiessentialism, he stresses that solidarity must not be

> thought of as recognition of a core self, the human essence, in all human beings. Rather, it is thought of as the ability to see more and more traditional differences (of tribe, religion, race, customs, and the like) as unimportant when compared with similarities with respect to pain and humiliation—the ability to think of people wildly different from ourselves as included in the range of "us." (1989: 192)

24　In "Remarks on Deconstruction and Pragmatism," Derrida clearly states that he does not accept, and has no use for, Rorty's private-public distinction. While Rorty insists that deconstruction does not have political consequences, Derrida thinks that deconstruction is "hyper-politicizing in following paths and codes which are clearly not traditional" (1996: 85). Moreover, the latter underscores his hope "that certain elements of deconstruction will have served or—because the struggle continues, particularly in the United States—*will* serve to politicize or repoliticize the left with regard to positions which are not simply academic" (1996: 85). For Bernstein's reading of Derrida, see the chapter "Serious Play: The Ethical-Political Horizon of Derrida," in *The New Constellation: The Ethical-Political Horizons of Modernity/Postmodernity* (Cambridge: Polity, 1991), 172–98.
25　For a discussion of Rorty's critique of Martha Nussbaum's interpretation of the relation between literature and morality, see Ulf Schulenberg, *Romanticism and Pragmatism*, 163–6. Rorty's contention is that Nussbaum is too reluctant "to switch from a Platonic rhetoric of discovery to a Nietzschean rhetoric of creation" (2010a: 404).
26　In *The Ethics of Theory*, Robert Doran offers a particularly illuminating analysis of Rorty's "Redemption from Egotism." Doran argues that together with the preface to his final volume of essays, the "Redemption" essay marks a new position for Rorty.

Leaving behind his ironist framework, he now urges his readers to regard novel reading as a form of "cultural politics." Doran writes:

> Along with the 2007 preface to *Philosophy as Cultural Politics*, this is the closest that Rorty comes to breaking out of his ironist cage: a declaration that, generally speaking, reading ironist novels can have/should have a real-world, socio-political impact. That is, insofar as these novels are uniquely calibrated to effect an escape from "egotism," ironist literature allows for a reconsideration of our final vocabularies and, through this effort, a reconsideration of collective purposes and ideas of justice. In short, novel reading is a practice of "cultural politics." (2017: 92)

27 Maybe I should differentiate this judgment. I think that Rorty's reading of Proust in *Contingency* is truly stimulating and convincing, particularly the way he opposes Nietzsche and Proust. His interpretation of James and Proust in "Redemption from Egotism" is neither stimulating nor convincing. Rorty's reading of a form-obsessed writer like Nabokov, which focuses on the latter's attitude toward "cruel incuriosity" (Rorty 1989: 158), also is problematic. In this chapter on Nabokov, Rorty advances the following idea: "Literary art, the nonstandard, nonpredictable use of words, cannot, indeed, be gauged in terms of accuracy of representation. For such accuracy is a matter of conformity to convention, and the point of writing well is precisely to break the crust of convention" (1989: 167). There are two problems with this passage. First, Rorty favors literary texts for which "the accuracy of representation" *is* important; namely, nineteenth-century realist novels, naturalist novels, and nineteenth- and twentieth-century novels of social protest. Second, breaking "the crust of convention," whether in literature, painting, or music, at the beginning of the twentieth century becomes primarily a question of form. Modern artworks, in other words, show the severe limitations of Rorty's understanding of the Deweyan endeavor to break "the crust of convention." In modernism, it is the idiosyncrasy and contingency of form-giving that demonstrate the problematic consequences of Rorty's radical dismissal of the moral-aesthetic distinction. The apodictic nature of his claim that "literary interest will always be parasitic on moral interest" (1989: 167) confirms that his analyses of literature are of only limited use for the development of a pragmatist literary criticism. Another point is worth mentioning in this context. Rorty is very critical of how the so-called cultural Left has politicized work in the humanities. In literary studies, this has led to an almost complete neglect of formal questions. Hence, Rorty and his sworn enemies have at least this rejection of aesthetic form in common.

28 It is interesting to note that Rorty also uses the term "poeticized culture" in his essay "Inquiry as Recontextualization" (1991b: 110), which he wrote in the late 1980s.

29   One ought to see that the idea of a post-philosophical culture preoccupied Rorty since his introduction to *The Linguistic Turn* (1967). It was central to many of the essays collected in *Consequences of Pragmatism* (1982), and it played a decisive role in the final chapter ("Philosophy Without Mirrors") of *Philosophy and the Mirror of Nature* (1979). For a detailed discussion, see the chapter "Richard Rorty's Notion of a Poeticized Culture," in Ulf Schulenberg, *Romanticism and Pragmatism*, 31–41.

30   One of the most interesting aspects of Rorty's posthumously published *Philosophy as Poetry* is that he now regrets having ever used the terms literary culture and poeticized culture. He writes:

> In the past I have sometimes described such a culture as one in which literature and the arts have replaced science and philosophy as sources of wisdom. But that description now seems to me misguided. I think it would be better to say that it would be a culture in which the meaning of the word "wisdom" had reverted to its pre-Platonic sense. (2016: 58)

This pre-Platonic sense was "something like 'skill,' something that could be gained only through the accumulation of experience" (2016: 59). Rorty also directs attention to the fact that *philosophia*, before Plato and Socrates, had meant something like "intellectual culture" (2016: 59). In a post-Platonic culture, whose members no longer strove to escape from finitude and who no longer needed the certainty and profundity of something that would be more than another human creation, "it would be history rather than science, philosophy, art, or literature that would be central to intellectual life" (2016: 59). Although I do understand Rorty's wish to put an even stronger emphasis on the significance of history, I think that his refusal to continue using the terms literary culture or poeticized culture is truly unfortunate. "Poeticized culture" offers everything that he needs, and it also highlights the central role literature and the novel play for his pragmatist humanism.

31   Rorty's most detailed discussion of the beauty-sublimity distinction can be found in *Die Schönheit, die Erhabenheit und die Gemeinschaft der Philosophen* (2000a). This text is only available in German. He writes about the role of the Romantics and their „Wende vom Schönen zum Erhabenen" ("turn from the beautiful to the sublime"):

> Ich werde Kapital schlagen aus der wohlbekannten Behauptung, daß die Bewegung, die wir "Romantik" nennen, eine Bewegung, die sich in der Politik und in der Philosophie so gut wie in den bildenden Künsten, der Dichtung und der Musik findet, eine Wende vom Schönen zum Erhabenen darstellte. Das heißt, statt vertraute Dinge in eine neue, erfreuliche Ordnung bringen zu wollen, strebte man nach etwas anderem als der Umordnung oder Neubeschreibung vertrauter Dinge; nach etwas, das sich kaum in Worte fassen läßt. (2000a: 22)

32 In *Marxism, Pragmatism, and Postmetaphysics*, I argued that Rorty always was highly critical of the longing for radical revolution as it is typical of many Marxists. A leftist liberal like him is rather in favor of piecemeal reforms and gradual persuasion in the public sphere. Concerning political thought that is governed by the notion of sublimity, Rorty points out:

> Moralisches und politisches Denken, das auf Erhabenheit gerichtet ist, unterstellt dagegen, daß unsere Nachkommen das moralische Analogon zur Korrespondenz mit der immanenten Struktur der Wirklichkeit oder das politische Analogon zur himmlischen Vision schaffen werden: vollkommene Freiheit, vollkommene Autonomie, eine Welt, in der keine Kompromisse zwischen widerstreitenden Interessen mehr nötig sind, weil die Menschheit das Bedürfnis, das beste dem besseren zu opfern, überwunden hat. Revolution und Emanzipation werden total sein. (2000a: 35)

33 How important these questions are becomes clear when one considers that Rorty speaks of his utopia "in which all metaphysical problems have been dissolved, and religion and science have yielded their places to poetry" (1995b: 35). What form does poetry have? What exactly is the significance of this form, and what can it perform? It should be noted that Rorty, already in the mid-1990s, stresses that he sees "cultural politics, rather than metaphysics, as the context in which to place everything else" (1995b: 35). This emphasis on cultural politics would dominate his final collection of philosophical papers that was published in 2007. For a discussion of the development of Rorty's cultural criticism, see Colin Koopman, "Challenging Philosophy: Rorty's Positive Conception of Philosophy as Cultural Criticism," in *Richard Rorty: From Pragmatist Philosophy to Cultural Politics*, ed. Alexander Gröschner, Colin Koopman, and Mike Sandbothe (New York: Bloomsbury, 2013), 75–106.

3 Pragmatism, Humanism, and Form

1 For stimulating recent discussions of humanism, see Anthony B. Pinn, ed., *The Oxford Handbook of Humanism* (Oxford: Oxford University Press, 2021); Andrew Copson and Anthony Clifford, eds., *The Wiley-Blackwell Handbook of Humanism* (Oxford: Wiley-Blackwell, 2015); Martin Halliwell and Andy Mousley, eds., *Critical Humanisms: Humanist/Anti-Humanist Dialogues* (Edinburgh: Edinburgh University Press, 2003); and David Alderson and Robert Spencer, eds., *For Humanism: Explorations in Theory and Politics* (London: Pluto, 2017). For intellectual histories of humanism, see Edward Craig, *The Mind of God and*

the *Works of Men* (Oxford: Clarendeon Press, 1987); and David E. Cooper, *The Measure of Things: Humanism, Humility, and Mystery* (Oxford: Clarendon Press, 2002). See my discussion of Craig and Cooper in Chapter 1. In addition, see Ulf Schulenberg, *Pragmatism and Poetic Agency: The Persistence of Humanism* (New York: Routledge, 2021).

2 In this context, see Ulf Schulenberg, *Romanticism and Pragmatism: Richard Rorty and the Idea of a Poeticized Culture* (Basingstoke: Palgrave Macmillan, 2015).

3 Regarding the relation between Nietzsche and aestheticism, see Sebastian Gardner, "Nietzsche's Philosophical Aestheticism," in *The Oxford Handbook of Nietzsche*, ed. Ken Gemes and John Richardson (Oxford: Oxford University Press, 2013), 599–628. In addition, see Alexander Nehamas, *Nietzsche: Life as Literature* (Cambridge, MA: Harvard University Press, 1985).

4 For a discussion of the relationship between Romanticism and pragmatism, see Russell B. Goodman, *American Philosophy and the Romantic Tradition* (New York: Cambridge University Press, 1990); Kathleen Wheeler, *Romanticism, Pragmatism, and Deconstruction* (Oxford: Blackwell, 1993); and Ulf Schulenberg, *Romanticism and Pragmatism*.

5 It is, of course, difficult to understand the idea of a pragmatist humanism without considering the significance of Kant's Copernican revolution in epistemology. In this context, see Tom Rockmore, *In Kant's Wake: Philosophy in the Twentieth Century* (Oxford: Blackwell, 2006); and the chapter "Naturalizing Kant?: Constructivism and Pragmatism," in Ulf Schulenberg, *Pragmatism and Poetic Agency*, 81–98.

6 For a discussion of the relation between James and Nietzsche, see Jason M. Boffetti, "Rorty's Nietzschean Pragmatism: A Jamesian Response," *The Review of Politics* 66 (4) (2004): 605–31; and Neil Sinhababu, "Nietzschean Pragmatism," *The Journal of Nietzsche Studies* 48 (1) (2017): 56–70.

7 For a discussion of Schiller's version of humanism, see Reuben Abel, *The Pragmatic Humanism of F.C.S. Schiller* (New York: King's Crown Press, 1955).

8 I openly admit that I do not have a problem with the idea of a radical anthropocentrism. I define the latter either as pragmatist humanism or, in Nietzsche's case, as a stimulating mixture of naturalism and aestheticism. This also signifies, of course, that I am strongly disinclined to argue for the necessity of developing forms of posthumanism.

9 In this context, see the chapter "Rorty's Notion of a Poeticized Culture," in Ulf Schulenberg, *Romanticism and Pragmatism*, 31–41.

10 For the most recent discussion of Rorty's humanism, see Emil Visnovsky, "Rorty's Humanism: Making It Explicit," *European Journal of Pragmatism and American*

Philosophy XII-1 (2020), http//journals.openedition.org/ejpap/1878 (accessed June 26, 2020).

11 For the latest discussions of Dewey's understanding of art, see Mary Jane Jacob, *Dewey for Artists* (Chicago: University of Chicago Press, 2018); and Scott R. Stroud, *John Dewey and the Artful Life: Pragmatism, Aesthetics, and Morality* (University Park: Pennsylvania State University Press, 2011).

12 Regarding Dewey's aesthetics, see Richard Eldridge, "Dewey's Aesthetics," in *The Cambridge Companion to Dewey*, ed. Molly Cochran (New York: Cambridge University Press, 2010), 242–64; Paul Guyer, *A History of Modern Aesthetics, Vol. 3*, 309–34; and David L. Hildebrand, *Dewey* (Oxford: Oneworld, 2008), 146–82. For a discussion of Dewey's "idealist" aesthetics, see Stephen C. Pepper, "Some Questions on Dewey's Esthetic," in *The Philosophy of John Dewey*, ed. Paul Arthur Schilpp and Lewis Edwin Hahn (La Salle, IL: Open Court, 1989), 369–90; and the chapter "The Pepper-Croce Thesis," in Thomas Alexander, *John Dewey's Theory of Art, Experience, and Nature*, 1–13. Richard Bernstein discusses to what degree Dewey was influenced by Hegel's critique of modern fragmentation. According to Bernstein, this "early appeal of Hegelianism is reflected in Dewey's frequent use of organic metaphors and his reliance on the theory of the 'social organism'" (2010: 144). Bernstein's argument is important since it convincingly shows how Dewey's notion of organicity links his aesthetics and his idea of creative democracy:

> Dewey's approach to the emotional and aesthetic sense of fulfillment also has the utmost significance for his vision of creative democracy. Like the early Marx (and Hegel), Dewey was distressed by the fragmentation and alienation characteristic of so much of modern life. Dewey's vision of the good society is aesthetic insofar as he calls for the type of education and social reform that can enrich experience—fund it with consummatory meaning. (2010: 148)

13 Illuminating recent analyses of the question of aesthetic form can be found in Angela Leighton, *On Form*; and Caroline Levine, *Forms: Whole, Rhythm, Hierarchy, Network* (Princeton, NJ: Princeton University Press, 2015).

14 Paul Guyer's discussions of the Bloomsbury critics are particularly valuable (2014b: 108–28). For a useful overview of analytic aesthetics, see the chapter "On Analytic Aesthetics: From Empiricism to Metaphysics," in Richard Shusterman, *Surface and Depth: Dialectics of Criticism and Culture* (Ithaca, NY: Cornell University Press, 2002), 15–33. In addition, see the "General Introduction," in *Aesthetics and the Philosophy of Art: The Analytic Tradition*, ed. Peter Lamarque and Stein Haugom Olsen (Hoboken; NJ: Wiley Blackwell, 2019), xiii–xvi.

15 In the chapter "Post-Impressionism, Quantum Mechanics, and the Triumph of Phenomenal Experience," in *John Dewey: Dilemmas of a Philosopher and Naturalist*

(2002: 149–74), Thomas Dalton offers an interesting discussion of the influence of Albert Barnes on Dewey's understanding of (visual) art. While Dalton sees Dewey's conception of aesthetic form in a more positive light than I do, he also speaks of "Barnes's realist sensibilities" and his strong aversion to "abstract form" and cubist paintings (155). Thus, Dewey's "teacher" had obvious problems with the radically new forms of modern art. See particularly the parts "Explaining the Origins of Modern Art" and "Matisse and the Birth and Tragedy of Art" in the chapter mentioned earlier. For another discussion of Dewey and formalism that differs from mine in a thought-provoking manner, see David Granger, "The Science of Art: Aesthetic Formalism in John Dewey and Albert Barnes, Part II," *The Journal of Aesthetic Education* 52 (2) (2018): 53–70.

16 See also Thomas Alexander, "The Art of Life: Dewey's Aesthetics," in *Reading Dewey: Interpretations for a Postmodern Generation*, ed. Larry A. Hickman (Bloomington: Indiana University Press, 1998), 1–22.

17 See particularly the chapters "Placing Pragmatism" (3–33) and "Art and Theory between Experience and Practice" (34–61) in Shusterman, *Pragmatist Aesthetics*.

18 For a discussion of Adorno's concept of aesthetic form within a pragmatist framework, see the chapter "'Kunst hat soviel Chance wie die Form': Theodor W. Adorno and the Idea of a Poeticized Culture," in Ulf Schulenberg, *Marxism, Pragmatism, and Postmetaphysics: From Finding to Making* (Basingstoke: Palgrave Macmillan, 2019), 69–96. In addition, see Peter Bürger, *Prosa der Moderne* (Frankfurt am Main: Suhrkamp, 1987). I offer a detailed discussion of the question of what pragmatist humanism can learn from materialist aesthetic theories in Chapter 5.

19 For Bürger's thought-provoking analysis of the problematics of the neo-avant-garde (e.g., minimal and conceptual art), see *Nach der Avantgarde* (Weilerswist: Velbrück, 2014). For a critique of Bürger's interpretation of the avant-garde, see Hal Foster, *The Return of the Real* (Cambridge: MIT Press, 1996).

20 In this context, see the chapter "Richard Rorty's 'cultural politics': Ironist philosophy and the ethics of reading," in Robert Doran, *The Ethics of Theory: Philosophy, History, Literature* (New York: Bloomsbury, 2017), 79–95; and the chapter "The Politics of the Novel," in Christopher J. Voparil, *Richard Rorty: Politics and Vision* (Lanham, MD: Rowman and Littlefield, 2006), 61–88. In addition, see Simon Stow, *Republic of Readers?: The Literary Turn in Political Thought and Analysis* (Albany: SUNY Press, 2007).

21 In this context, see Chapters 2 and 5 in this book.

22 The volume *Reading for Form* (Seattle: University of Washington Press, 2006), edited by Susan J. Wolfson and Marshall Brown, prepared the ground for an intensive discussion of a new formalism, whereas the essays collected in John J.

Joughin and Simon Malpas, eds., *The New Aestheticism* (Manchester: Manchester University Press, 2003) called attention to the complexity of a new aestheticism.

23 For the latest discussion of Lukács, see Timothy Bewes and Timothy Hall, eds., *Georg Lukács: The Fundamental Dissonance of Existence* (New York: Bloomsbury, 2011); and Michael J. Thompson, ed., *Georg Lukács Reconsidered: Critical Essays in Politics, Philosophy, and Aesthetics* (New York: Bloomsbury, 2011). For what is still the most wide-ranging analysis of the question of Marxism and form, see Fredric Jameson, *Marxism and Form: Twentieth-Century Dialectical Theories of Literature* (Princeton, NJ: Princeton University Press, 1971).

24 Even Rorty sometimes had tame moments. In one of those, he made clear that pragmatism was not necessarily synonymous with a radical rejection of theory. However, he simultaneously underlines that theory does not come first: "The need to have a general theory [...] is the sort of need which James and Dewey tried to put in perspective by insisting, with Hegel, that theory follows after, rather than being presupposed by, concrete accomplishment" (1991b: 79). The degree to which early analytic aesthetics was critical of the idea of developing a theory of art became obvious in Morris Weitz's influential "The Role of Theory in Aesthetics," which was published in 1956 in the *Journal of Aesthetics and Art Criticism*. Influenced by the later Wittgenstein, and particularly his notion of family resemblance, Weitz suggested that instead of posing the question "What is art?," one should rather focus on how the concept of art is actually used in our language. According to him, seeking to illuminate the necessary and sufficient qualities of art is a pointless endeavor because it does not possess any necessary and sufficient qualities or characteristics.

4 "… and the Practice Has to Speak for Itself": Wittgenstein, Pragmatism, and Anti-Authoritarianism

1 For a detailed discussion of the relation between the later Wittgenstein and the pragmatists, see Anna Boncompagni, *Wittgenstein and Pragmatism: On Certainty in the Light of Peirce and James* (Basingstoke: Palgrave Macmillan, 2016). In spite of his critique of Rorty's reading of Wittgenstein, Hilary Putnam contends that the latter "tells us that the traditional enterprises of metaphysics and epistemology have failed; and not just that they have failed at the end of the day, but that they failed, so to speak, at the beginning of the day, that they were stillborn, that the questions which are supposed to generate metaphysics and epistemology are, as they are traditionally formulated, nonsensical" (1995: 31).

2   For stimulating recent readings of the *Tractatus*, see Thomas Ricketts, "Pictures, Logic, and the Limits of Sense in Wittgenstein's *Tractatus*," in *The Cambridge Companion to Wittgenstein*, ed. Hans Sluga and David G. Stern, 2nd ed. (New York: Cambridge University Press, 2018), 54–95; and Cora Diamond, "The *Tractatus* and the Limits of Sense," in *The Oxford Handbook of Wittgenstein*, ed. Oskari Kuusela and Marie McGinn (New York: Oxford University Press, 2011), 240–75. An illuminating book-length discussion is Michael Morris's *Wittgenstein and the* Tractatus Logico-Philosophicus (New York: Routledge, 2008).

3   In this context, see Stanley Cavell, The Availability of Wittgenstein's Later Philosophy," in *Must We Mean What We Say?: A Book of Essays*, updated ed. (New York: Cambridge University Press, 2002), 41–67; Cavell, "Declining Decline: Wittgenstein as a Philosopher of Culture," in *This New Yet Unapproachable America: Lectures after Emerson after Wittgenstein* (Chicago: University of Chicago Press, 2013 [1989]), 29–76; and Toril Moi, *Revolution of the Ordinary*. For discussions of the role Wittgenstein plays for literary studies and aesthetics, see John Gibson and Wolfgang Huemer, eds., *The Literary Wittgenstein* (London: Routledge, 2004); Anat Matar, ed., *Understanding Wittgenstein: Understanding Modernism* (New York: Bloomsbury, 2017); and Garry L. Hagberg, ed., *Wittgenstein and Aesthetic Understanding* (Basingstoke: Palgrave Macmillan, 2017).

4   For thought-provoking discussions of *On Certainty*, see Andy Hamilton, *Wittgenstein and* On Certainty (New York: Routledge, 2014); Rush Rhees, *Wittgenstein's* On Certainty: *There—Like Our Life*, ed. D. Z. Phillips (Oxford: Blackwell, 2003); Danièle Moyal-Sharrock, *Understanding Wittgenstein's* On Certainty; and Danièle Moyal-Sharrock and W. H. Brenner, eds., *Readings of Wittgenstein's* On Certainty (Basingstoke: Palgrave Macmillan, 2005).

5   My argument in *Pragmatism and Poetic Agency* ought to be seen in connection with the ones developed in my monographs *Romanticism and Pragmatism: Richard Rorty and the Idea of a Poeticized Culture* (Basingstoke: Palgrave Macmillan, 2015) and *Marxism, Pragmatism, and Postmetaphysics: From Finding to Making* (Basingstoke: Palgrave Macmillan, 2019).

6   For a discussion of the Rortyan idea of a poeticized culture, see the chapter "Richard Rorty's Notion of a Poeticized Culture" in Ulf Schulenberg, *Romanticism and Pragmatism*, 31–41. For an analysis of Nietzsche's role in the humanist and anti-authoritarian story of progress and emancipation, see the first part, "Friedrich Nietzsche and the Pragmatists," in Ulf Schulenberg, *Pragmatism and Poetic Agency*, 17–98.

7   Crucially, a discussion of the relation between pragmatism and the later Wittgenstein could also play an important role for the attempt to argue for a

"Third Wittgenstein." In this context, see Danièle Moyal-Sharrock, ed., *The* Third *Wittgenstein: The Post-*Investigations *Works* (Aldershot: Ashgate, 2004).

8   In this context, see Rorty's important pieces "Solidarity or Objectivity?" and "The Priority of Democracy to Philosophy," both in *Objectivity, Relativism, and Truth: Philosophical Papers, Vol. 1*, 21–34, 175–96. In addition, see James T. Kloppenberg, "Rorty's Insouciant Social Thought," in *The Cambridge Companion to Rorty*, ed. David Rondel (New York: Cambridge University Press, 2021), 201–21.

9   For Misak's understanding of pragmatism, see also her *The American Pragmatists* (New York: Oxford University Press, 2013).

10 In this context, see also Rorty's "Pragmatism Without Method," in *Objectivity, Relativism, and Truth*, 63–77.

11 For the latest discussion of the relation between Wittgenstein and Rorty, see Alan Malachowski, "Common Understanding Without Uncommon Certainty: Rorty's Wittgenstein Revisited," in *A Companion to Rorty*, ed. Malachowski (Hoboken, NJ: Wiley Blackwell, 2020), 357–69.

12 In "Wittgenstein, Heidegger, and the Reification of Language," Rorty comments on Wittgenstein's development thus: "The direction in which Wittgenstein was going led him to radical doubts about the very notion of philosophy as a provider of knowledge, and to a detranscendentalized, naturalized conception of philosophy as a form of therapy, as a *techne* rather than as the achievement of *theoria*" (1991a: 52).

13 For stimulating analyses of Wittgenstein's version of foundationalism, see Avrum Stroll, "Wittgenstein's Foundational Metaphors," and Dan Hutto, "Two Wittgensteins Too Many: Wittgenstein's Foundationalism," both in *The* Third *Wittgenstein: The Post-*Investigations *Works*, ed. Danièle Moyal-Sharrock, 13–42.

14 In this context, see also Moyal-Sharrock, "*On Certainty* and the Grammaticalization of Experience," in *The* Third *Wittgenstein*, 43–62; and "Wittgenstein: No Linguistic Idealist," in *Wittgenstein and the Creativity of Language*, ed. Sebastian Sunday Grève and Jakub Mácha (Basingstoke: Palgrave Macmillan, 2016), 117–38.

15 According to Hilary Putnam, Rorty's antirepresentationalism is grounded in a highly problematic understanding of metaphysical realism. Putnam argues that Rorty so much craves for a guarantee that our words are capable of representing things outside themselves that when he eventually finds out that there will never be such a guarantee he reacts in too radical a fashion by apodictically claiming that our language does not represent anything at all (it is not a medium of representation but a tool). Whereas other philosophers have called Rorty a disappointed Platonist, Putnam holds that "one detects the trace of a disappointed metaphysical realist impulse" (1994: 299) in Rorty's position. The vehemence of

Rorty's antirepresentationalist gesture shows that metaphysical realism still has a hold on him.

16 In this context, see the chapter "John Dewey's Antifoundationalist Story of Progress," in Ulf Schulenberg, *Romanticism and Pragmatism*, 106–19.

17 From what I have said in this chapter it should be obvious that I disagree with Toril Moi when she explains Wittgenstein's understanding of use as follows: "Use is not a ground. Use is a practice grounded on nothing. Use is simply what we do. Nothing—no essences, no built-in referential power—obliges us to continue using language as we do now. In fact, we don't always continue: language is a constantly changing practice" (2017: 29). Moi's argument in her book suffers from the fact that she too much concentrates on the *Investigations* and too often ignores the insights in *On Certainty*. Had she considered the latter, she would have noticed that the sentence "Use is a practice grounded on nothing" is too undifferentiated as a characterization of the later Wittgenstein's position. For Moi, it seems, Wittgenstein is clearly an antifoundationalist:

> We don't pay attention to use, because we keep looking for something firmer, deeper, something that can *ground* use itself, something like the ultimate explanation of meaning as such. Wittgenstein's most fundamental conviction—and the hardest to follow—is that the request for such an ultimate explanation is meaningless precisely because it presupposes a picture in which meaning, or use, has a ground. (2017: 35)

As we have seen, *On Certainty* is of particular value, since it offers a multilayered discussion of the relation between epistemological ground and the plurality of linguistic practices.

5 Marxism, Form, and the Negation of Aesthetic Synthesis

1 For the first full-scale discussion of the relationship between these two philosophies of praxis, see Ulf Schulenberg, *Marxism, Pragmatism, and Postmetaphysics: From Finding to Making* (Basingstoke: Palgrave Macmillan, 2019).

2 In *Pragmatist Aesthetics*, Richard Shusterman talks about his decision, in the late 1980s, to "trade Adorno's austere, gloomy, and haughtily elitist Marxism for Dewey's more earthy, upbeat, and democratic pragmatism" (2000: xvii). He does not offer an extensive discussion of Adorno's conception of form or of his modernist aesthetics in general. However, Adorno's critique of popular art of course plays a crucial role for Shusterman's Deweyan approach. It serves as a negative foil. Throughout his monograph, Shusterman stresses that in his opinion

there is nothing wrong with the avant-garde impulse of high art. However, he thinks that the "problem is the exclusionary presumption that this tradition exhausts the realm of legitimate art and aesthetic experience" (2000: 51).

3   As regards the relation between art and knowledge, Mann, in "Death in Venice," radicalizes the position he sketched in "Tonio Kröger" (1903). One only has to think of the famous dialogue between Tonio and the painter Lisaweta in the latter's studio.

4   For Lukács's reading of Mann, see part III in *Faust und Faustus: Ausgewählte Schriften II* (Reinbek bei Hamburg: Rowohlt, [1967] 2018), 211–308.

5   In this context, see Katie Terezakis "Afterword: The Legacy of Form," in Georg Lukács, *Soul and Form*, ed. John T. Sanders and Katie Terezakis (New York: Columbia University Press, 2010), 215–34. For another discussion of the Lukácsian understanding of form, see Yoon Sun Lee, "Temporalized Invariance: Lukács and the Work of Form," in *Georg Lukács: The Fundamental Dissonance of Existence*, ed. Timothy Bewes and Timothy Hall (New York: Bloomsbury, 2011), 17–35.

6   Peter Uwe Hohendahl correctly points out:

> As much as *The Theory of the Novel* examines the formal structure of the novel and its historical transformation from Cervantes to Dostoyevsky, the ultimate point is a deeper one. The form of the novel is the precise literary expression of the transcendental homelessness of the modern individual. Differently put, Lukács insists on the philosophical meaning of the form and it is this meaning that legitimizes the genre. The Lukácsian dialectic relates the literary form to the "given historico-philosophical realities" and interprets the world in order to express this *Gegebenheit*. (2011: 84)

I wish to use this opportunity to draw attention to the fact that Hohendahl's essay is particularly valuable as regards his comments on the high degree to which Adorno's discussion of the novel relied on the early Lukács. Hohendahl writes: "In structural terms, Adorno's essays on the novel and individual novelists (Balzac, Kafka, Proust, and Joyce) rest on *The Theory of the Novel* seen through the lens of the later *History and Class Consciousness* (1923). They represent a Marxist rearticulation of the narrative developed in *The Theory of the Novel*" (2011: 83). In addition, see Timothy Hall, "Adorno's Aesthetic Theory and Lukács's *Theory of the Novel*," in *Adorno and Literature*, ed. David Cunningham and Nigel Mapp (New York: Continuum, 2006), 145–58; and J. M. Bernstein, *The Philosophy of the Novel: Lukács, Marxism, and the Dialectics of Form* (Minneapolis: University of Minnesota Press, 1984).

7   For an illuminating reading of *History and Class Consciousness*, see the chapter "Georg Lukács and the Origins of the Western Marxist Paradigm," in Martin Jay, *Marxism and Totality: The Adventures of a Concept from Lukács to Habermas* (Berkeley: University of California Press, 1984), 81–127. In addition, see "Part

Two: Lukács and Brecht," in Eugene Lunn, *Marxism and Modernism: An Historical Study of Lukács, Brecht, Benjamin, and Adorno* (Berkeley: University of California Press, 1982), 75–145. See also the essays in "Part II: Life, History, Social Theory," in *Georg Lukács: The Fundamental Dissonance of Existence*, ed. Bewes and Hall, 81–153.

8   In "Marx and Engels on Aesthetics," Lukács defines dialectics as follows: "Dialectics reject the existence of any purely one-sided, cause-and-effect relationships; it recognizes in the simplest facts a complicated interaction of causes and effects. And historical materialism insists that in a process so multileveled and multifaceted as the evolution of society, the total process of the social and historical development emerges in the form of an intricate complex of interactions" (1978: 64).

9   In this context, see the chapter "Stories of Emancipation and the Idea of Creative Praxis: Karl Marx and John Dewey," in Ulf Schulenberg, *Marxism, Pragmatism, and Postmetaphysics*, 191–206; and the chapter "Pragmatism, Marxism, and Humanism," in Ulf Schulenberg, *Pragmatism and Poetic Agency: The Persistence of Humanism* (New York: Routledge, 2021), 143–81.

10 In *The Meaning of Contemporary Realism*, Lukács claims that in modern literature the "disintegration of personality is matched by a disintegration of the outer world." Moreover, it is characterized by the "attenuation of actuality" (2006: 25). In Lukács's opinion, in modern literature "distortion becomes as inseparable a part of the portrayal of reality as the recourse to the pathological" (2006: 33). In contrast to realist writers, modernist writers assert "the unalterability of outward reality." Consequently, "human activity is, a priori, rendered impotent and robbed of meaning" (2006: 36). In modern fiction, as Lukács maintains, "the unity of the world is broken up, since an essentially subjective vision is identified with reality itself. The terror generated by the world of imperialist capitalism (anticipatory of its later fascist progeny), where human beings are degraded to mere objects—this fear, originally a subjective experience, becomes an objective entity. The reflection of a distortion becomes a distorted reflection" (2006: 52–3). It is crucial to realize, however, that Lukács, despite his severe critique of modernism in *Meaning*, does not show an aversion to "new forms," these are "intimately related to this active, unceasing exploration of reality" (2006: 97–8). In this context, I want to draw attention to the fact that Lukács's theoretical framework prevents him from fully appreciating the significance of what Adorno terms "realism on the basis of a loss of reality." In "Balzac-Lektüre," the latter writes:

> Balzac's oddness sheds light on something that characterizes nineteenth century prose as a whole after Goethe. The realism with which even those who are idealistically inclined are preoccupied is not primary but derived: realism on the basis of a loss of reality. The epic that is no longer in command of the material

concreteness it attempts to protect has to exaggerate it in its demeanor, has to describe the world with exaggerated precision precisely because it has become alien, can no longer be kept in physical proximity. (1991: 128)

Later in the same essay, Adorno repeats an argument that is also central to his piece, "Standort des Erzählers im zeitgenössischen Roman," and that goes back to Benjamin's notion of the waning of experience ("Erfahrungsschwund") in (late-) capitalist society: "It is precisely because in the bourgeois world one can no longer tell stories about the things that are decisive that storytelling is dying out. The deficiencies inherent in Balzacian realism already represent, in latent form, the verdict on the realistic novel" (1991: 133).

11   Regarding the autonomy of aesthetic form, Lukács contends:

> Marxist aesthetics combats with equal vehemence another false extreme in the theory and practice of art, the conception which holds that since copying reality is to be rejected and artistic forms are independent of this superficial reality, artistic forms therefore possess their own autonomy, that perfection of form and striving after perfection are ends in themselves abstracted from reality and that artistic perfection is independent of reality; and thus the artist has the right to transform and stylize reality at will. (1978: 75)

12   One of the central questions that preoccupy Lukács in one of his most famous essays, "Es geht um den Realismus" (1938), is the role and function of the "real" avant-garde. When expressionism, impressionism, surrealism, or modernism in general have not only distorted reality but also the meaning of the term "avant-garde," the question arises as to how one can reinterpret this term from the perspective of a Marxist realist. Lukács expands on this point thus:

> Great realism, therefore, does not portray an immediately obvious aspect of reality but one which is permanent and objectively more significant, namely man in the whole range of his relations to the real world, above all those which outlast mere fashion. Over and above that, it captures tendencies of development that only exist incipiently and so have not yet had the opportunity to unfold their entire human and social potential. To discern and give shape to such underground trends is the great historical mission of the true literary avant-garde. Whether a writer really belongs to the ranks of the avant-garde is something that only history can reveal, for only after the passage of time will it become apparent whether he has perceived significant qualities, trends, and the social functions of individual human types, and has given them effective and lasting form. […] / So what really matters is not the subjective belief, however sincere, that one belongs to the avant-garde and is eager to march in the forefront of literary developments. Nor is it essential to have been the first to discover

some technical innovation, however dazzling. What counts is the social and human content of the avant-garde, the breadth, the profundity, and the truth of the ideas that have been "prophetically" anticipated. (2007: 48)

13 The appearance-reality dichotomy also plays a critical role in "Realism in the Balance." Modernist works, to Lukács, are governed by "an abstraction away from reality;" they are static, devoid of inner tension, and incapable of breaking through the surface to "a living dialectic of appearance and essence" (2007: 39). He elaborates on this dialectic as follows:

> This, then, is the artistic dialectic of appearance and essence. The richer, the more diverse, complex and "cunning" (Lenin) this dialectic is, the more firmly it grasps hold of the living contradictions of life and society, then the greater and the more profound the realism will be. / In contrast to this, what does it mean to talk of an abstraction away from reality? When the surface of life is only experienced immediately, it remains opaque, fragmentary, chaotic, and uncomprehended. Since the objective mediations are more or less consciously ignored or passed over, what lies on the surface is frozen and any attempt to see it from a higher intellectual vantage-point has to be abandoned. (2007: 39)

14 For a discussion of the significance of narrative for Lukács, see Ulf Schulenberg, "Marxism, Pragmatism, and Narrative," *New Literary History* 48 (1) (2017): 149–70.

15 Concerning Lukács's contemporary significance, particularly in the context of debates pro and contra formalism, Judith Butler asserts:

> Lukács's text [*Soul and Form*] precedes these debates by several decades. It has no inkling of the formalisms, historicisms, or Marxisms to come. Historically, though, it might be said that his time has come around again. Reading Lukács now, one realizes that his own approach to form is both more subtle and complicated than either the advocates or the detractors of formalism could or can imagine. Moreover, form is always in a bind with life, with soul, and with experience; life gives rise to form, but form is understood to distill life; life wrecks the distillation, only to open us to the ideal that form itself seeks to approach, but cannot. Form is never static. (2010: 5)

16 For interesting discussions of Adorno's concept of form, see Josh Robinson, *Adorno's Poetics of Form* (Albany: SUNY Press, 2018); the chapter "An Aesthetics of Negativity," in Hammer, *Adorno's Modernism*, 180–207; "Part Three: Modes of Theory," in Peter Uwe Hohendahl, *Prismatic Thought: Theodor W. Adorno* (Lincoln: University of Nebraska Press, 1995), 185–253; and the chapter "Reality, Realism, and Representation," in Hohendahl, *The Fleeting Promise of Art: Adorno's Aesthetic Theory Revisited* (Ithaca, NY: Cornell University Press, 2013), 103–28.

Concerning the relation between Adorno's conception of form and the new formalism, Eva Geulen correctly points out:

> The centrality Adorno affords to form is what makes him interesting at the present moment. Yet for Adorno, aesthetic form is what distinguishes and separates the artwork from the social world. The new concept of form ignores this fundamental distinction. Instead, everything now turns out to be form. The expanded concept of form absorbs its other so completely that in the current New Formalist discussion, old debates about art as autonomous and as *fait social* (as Adorno called it) are repeated *within* the new paradigm of form—as it were, form-immanently. (2021: 7)

The following volume is still indispensable for an understanding of Adorno's aesthetic theory: *Materialien zur ästhetischen Theorie Th. W. Adornos: Konstruktion der Moderne*, ed. Burkhard Lindner and W. Martin Lüdke (Frankfurt am Main: Suhrkamp, 1980). For a discussion of the relation between form and the truth-content of the artwork in Adorno, see the chapter "'Kunst hat soviel Chance wie die Form': Theodor W. Adorno and the Idea of a Poeticized Culture," in Ulf Schulenberg, *Marxism, Pragmatism, and Postmetaphysics*, 69–96.

17 For thought-provoking analyses of the relation between Lukács and Adorno, see the chapter "The Debate between Adorno and Lukács," in Peter Bürger, *Theory of the Avant-Garde*, 83–92; the chapter "Aesthetic Debates," in Lambert Zuidervaart, *Adorno's Aesthetic Theory: The Redemption of Illusion* (Cambridge, MA: MIT Press, 1991), 28–43; and Hohendahl, "The Theory of the Novel and the Concept of Realism in Lukács and Adorno," in *Georg Lukács Reconsidered*, ed. Michael J. Thompson, 75–98. In addition, see Titus Stahl, "Lukács and the Frankfurt School," in *The Routledge Companion to the Frankfurt School*, ed. Peter E. Gordon, Espen Hammer, and Axel Honneth (New York: Routledge, 2019), 237–50.

18 On the occasion of the fiftieth anniversary of *Ästhetische Theorie* the following volumes were published: *Adorno's Aesthetic Theory at Fifty*, ed. Peter E. Gordon, special issue of *New German Critique* 143 (August 2021); and *Eros und Erkenntnis: 50 Jahre* Ästhetische Theorie, ed. Martin Endres, Axel Pichler, and Claus Zittel (Berlin: de Gruyter, 2019). In addition, see *Theodor W. Adorno: Ästhetische Theorie*, ed. Anne Eusterschulte and Sebastian Tränkle (Berlin: de Gruyter, 2021).

19 In this context, see J. M. Bernstein, "Negative Dialectic as Fate: Adorno and Hegel," in *The Cambridge Companion to Adorno*, ed. Thomas Huhn (New York: Cambridge University Press, 2004), 19–50.

20 In this context, see the essay "Über den Fetischcharakter in der Musik und die Regression des Hörens," in Theodor W. Adorno, *Dissonanzen: Musik in der verwalteten Welt* (Göttingen: Vandenhoeck and Ruprecht, 1991 [1956]), 9–45.

21 In "Engagement," Adorno speaks of the "rücksichtslose Autonomie der Werke" (1981: 425; "the reckless autonomy of the works") and of "a thoroughgoing articulation, to the point of worldlessness" (1992: 90). At the end of "Presuppositions," he maintains that the hermetic work "forms within itself the discontinuity that is the discontinuity between the world and the work" (1992: 108).

22 Consider also the following passage:

> Even the Lukács of *The Theory of the Novel* had to admit that the artworks that came after the end of the supposedly meaning-filled age had gained infinitely in richness and depth. What speaks for the survival of the concept of harmony as an element is that artworks that remonstrate against the mathematical ideal of harmony and the requirement of symmetrical relations, striving rather for absolute asymmetry, fail to slough off all symmetry. In terms of its artistic value, asymmetry is only to be comprehended in its relation to symmetry. (Adorno 1997: 159)

23 Notoriously enough, Adorno's negative critique of surrealism differs from Benjamin's decidedly more positive approach. According to the former, "after the European catastrophe the Surrealist shocks lost their force" (1991: 87). Moreover, Adorno argues that "the montages of Surrealism are the true still lives [sic]. In making compositions out of what is out of date, they create *nature morte*" (1991: 89). If one thinks of Breton's fascination with movement, activity, contingency, and agility, this is indeed a devastating judgment.

24 In *Theory of the Avant-Garde*, Bürger contends "that the historical avant-garde movements negate those determinations that are essential in autonomous art: the disjunction of art and the praxis of life, individual production, and individual reception as distinct from the former. The avant-garde intends the abolition of autonomous art by which it means that art is to be integrated into the praxis of life" (1984: 53–4).

25 In "Adorno's Anti-Avant-Gardism," Bürger pointedly formulates: "Modern art is autonomous. It defends the demarcations first defined by idealist aesthetics and interprets it even more strictly than the theoreticians of aesthetic autonomy" (1991: 52). In this context, see also Peter Bürger's *The Decline of Modernism*, trans. Nicholas Walker (University Park: Pennsylvania State University Press, 1992). His most detailed discussion of aesthetic modernism can be found in *Prosa der Moderne* (Frankfurt am Main: Suhrkamp, 1988). Admittedly, my argument that Adorno holds onto the idea of organicity, in contrast to the historical avant-gardists, and moreover refuses to reject harmony and formal coherence might seem problematic. There are passages in his oeuvre that let one conclude the exact opposite. In the chapter on Schönberg in *Philosophie der neuen Musik*, for instance,

he advances a critique of the closed work of art ("das geschlossene Kunstwerk") and how it stands for subject-object identity. By contrast, the radically dissonant and fragmented artwork ("das zerrüttete Kunstwerk") dismisses the notion of subject-object identity, and by doing so is capable of reaching a position from which it can tell the truth about late-capitalist society in which the relation between subject and object is severely disturbed and talk about subject-object identity a lie:

> Das geschlossene Kunstwerk erkannte nicht, sondern ließ in sich Erkenntnis verschwinden. Es machte sich zum Gegenstand bloßer "Anschauung" und verhüllte alle Brüche, durch welche Denken der unmittelbaren Gegebenheit des ästhetischen Objekts entweichen könnte. […] Daß es anschaulich sein soll, täuscht bereits die Überwindung des Bruches von Subjekt und Objekt vor, in deren Artikulation Erkenntnis besteht: die Anschaulichkeit der Kunst selber ist ihr Schein. Erst das zerrüttete Kunstwerk gibt mit seiner Geschlossenheit die Anschaulichkeit preis und den Schein mit dieser. […] Das geschlossene Kunstwerk nimmt den Standpunkt der Identität von Subjekt und Objekt ein. In seinem Zerfall erweist sich die Identität als Schein und das Recht der Erkenntnis, die Subjekt und Objekt einander kontrastiert, als das größere, als das moralische. (1978: 118)

It is undoubtedly tempting to call Adorno's aesthetics an "Ästhetik des Bruchs," but, as I try to show in this chapter, while this underscores the radical nature of his aesthetic thought it inevitably reduces its complexity.

26 In *Theory of the Avant-Garde*, Peter Bürger makes unequivocally clear that he is very critical of the "neo-avant-garde." He offers a detailed critique of neo-avant-garde artists such as Daniel Buren, Jeff Wall, and Tacita Dean in *Nach der Avantgarde* (Weilerswist: Velbrück, 2014). In this context, see also his *Das Altern der Moderne* (Frankfurt am Main: Suhrkamp, 2001). The latter study also contains "Der Anti-Avantgardismus Adornos" (31–47).

27 André Breton's "récit" *Nadja* (1928) could function as an example of a text to which the idea of a negation of aesthetic synthesis can be applied and where the positive connotations of this idea would clearly dominate. It is a nonorganic and formally demanding artwork, partly using the technique of montage, which emphasizes the meaning of contingency (the search for "la trouvaille," chance encounters with Nadja and Fanny Beznos, and the contingency of seemingly incoherent associations ["Les mots BOIS-CHARBONS," Breton 1964: 29]). It would be interesting to ask what role Breton's idea of "la beauté convulsive" (1964: 190), which would be central to his *L'Amour fou* (1937), could play for a theorization of the negation of aesthetic synthesis. For a stimulating reading of *Nadja*, see the chapter "Bretons *Nadja*" in Peter Bürger, *Der französische Surrealismus: Studien zur avantgardistischen Literatur*, expanded ed. (Frankfurt am Main: Suhrkamp, 1996),

119–33; for background information, see the chapter "Revolution by Any Means" in Mark Polizzotti, *Revolution of the Mind: The Life of André Breton*, rev. and updated ed. (Boston: Black Widow Press, 2009), 214–45. In addition, see the parts that discuss the relation between Breton and Bataille in Michel Surya's interesting intellectual biography *Georges Bataille, la mort à l'oeuvre* (Paris: Gallimard, 2012 [1992]).

28   I am aware that my remarks concerning the negation of aesthetic synthesis will seem inadequate and antiquated to those theorists who focus on the allegedly radical gestures of the neo-avant-garde or on conceptual and postconceptual art (and who are thus interested, among other things, in how the dissonant modern artwork was replaced by the open and hybrid work that uses multiple media and conceptual frameworks and radically redefines the role of the spectator as participant—one only has to think of Nicolas Bourriaud's relational aesthetics). However, it is interesting to note that Adorno still plays a crucial role for sophisticated attempts to map contemporary art and art theory. See, for instance, Peter Osborne, *Anywhere or Not At All: Philosophy of Contemporary Art* (New York: Verso, 2013); Juliane Rebentisch, *Theorien der Gegenwartskunst* (Hamburg: Junius, 2013); and *Die Kunst und die Künste: Ein Kompendium zur Kunsttheorie der Gegenwart*, ed. Georg W. Bertram, Stefan Deines, and Daniel Martin Feige (Berlin: Suhrkamp, 2021).

29   Regarding Jameson's understanding of the complexity of a late or multinational capitalism, he openly admits that Ernest Mandel's *Late Capitalism* (1975) enabled him to theorize this new form of capitalism and its cultural logic.

30   The latest studies of Jameson's work are: Robert T. Tally Jr., *Fredric Jameson: The Project of Dialectical Criticism* (London: Pluto, 2014); Phillip E. Wegner, *Periodizing Jameson: Dialectics, the University, and the Desire for Narrative* (Evanston, IL: Northwestern University Press, 2014); and Clint Burnham, *Fredric Jameson and the Wolf of Wall Street* (New York: Bloomsbury, 2015). In addition, see Sean Homer, *Fredric Jameson: Marxism, Hermeneutics, Postmodernism* (Malden, MA: Polity, 1998); Adam Roberts, *Fredric Jameson* (New York: Routledge, 2000); and Ian Buchanan, *Fredric Jameson: Live Theory* (New York: Continuum, 2006).

31   I offer a more detailed discussion of cognitive mapping and the idea of a new realism in the chapter "Fredric Jamesons Theorie der Postmoderne" in *Zwischen Realismus und Avantgarde: Drei Paradigmen für die Aporien des Entweder-Oder* (Frankfurt am Main: Peter Lang, 2000), 58–83.

32   By studying together Jameson's *A Singular Modernity: Essay on the Ontology of the Present* (2002) and *The Modernist Papers* (2007), one will be in a position to approach the complexity of his understanding of modern art and literature. It is in the latter volume that Jameson comments on the form-content dichotomy as

follows: "I have felt, here and throughout, that the opposition between form and content is only to be overcome (that is to say, made productive) by complicating it, and not by doing away with one of its terms" (2007: xiii). This is indeed valuable advice, and I have tried to follow it in the present study.

33 In this context, see the chapter "Cognitive Mapping and Globalization," in Tally Jr., *Fredric Jameson*, 100–19; and the chapter "Cognitive Mapping and Utopia" in Buchanan, *Fredric Jameson*, 106–19.

34 See, for instance, the following passage in *Postmodernism*:

> The new political art (if it is possible at all) will have to hold to the truth of postmodernism, that is to say, to its fundamental object—the world space of multinational capital—at the same time at which it achieves a breakthrough to some as yet unimaginable new mode of representing this last, in which we may again begin to grasp our positioning as individual and collective subjects and regain a capacity to act and struggle which is at present neutralized by our spatial as well as our social confusion. The political form of postmodernism, if there ever is any, will have as its vocation the invention and projection of a global cognitive mapping, on a social as well as a spatial scale. (1991: 54)

35 However, even if he does not explicitly mention the idea of cognitive mapping anymore in his later texts, it still plays a crucial role in his analyses of the phenomenon of globalization (see *Valences of the Dialectic* [2009]). In this context, one has to see that it is only on the very last page of *Postmodernism* that Jameson, in a Lukácsian manner, shows that for him totality ought to be understood as a code word for class consciousness, but he also states that cognitive mapping "was in reality nothing but a code word for 'class consciousness'—only it proposed the need for class consciousness of a new and hitherto undreamed of kind, while it also inflected the account in the direction of that new spatiality implicit in the postmodern" (1991: 418).

36 In this context, see Christopher Pawling, "The American Lukács?: Fredric Jameson and Dialectical Thought," in *Fredric Jameson: A Critical Reader*, ed. Douglas Kellner and Sean Homer (New York: Palgrave Macmillan, 2004), 22–41. For Jameson's reading of Lukács, see also Homer, *Fredric Jameson*, 152–64; Tally Jr, *Fredric Jameson*, 47–9, 131–4; and Wegner, *Periodizing Jameson*, 27–37.

37 For a detailed discussion of Rorty's attitude toward Marxism, see Ulf Schulenberg, "Zwischen Liberalismus und Marxismus: Rortys Pragmatismus im politischen Kontext," in *Soziale Hoffnung, liberale Ironie: Zur Aktualität von Richard Rortys politischem Denken*, ed. Veith Selk, Christoph Held, and Torben Schwuchow (Baden-Baden: Nomos, 2021), 25–48; and Ulf Schulenberg, "Zwei Philosophien der Praxis: Rorty und der Marxismus," in *Handbuch Richard Rorty*, ed. Martin Müller (Berlin: Springer) (forthcoming). Using a term coined by Todd Gitlin,

Rorty refers to himself as a "red-diaper anticommunist baby" (1998a: 58). He repeatedly tried to explain to his students and readers what it meant "to grow up on the anticommunist reformist Left in mid-century" (1998a: 58). This reformist Left was characterized by the fact that American patriotism, anticommunism, Deweyan pragmatism, and the notion of redistributionist economics naturally went together. The mid-Sixties, as Rorty argues in *Achieving Our Country*, constituted a radical break with the politically active progressive Left. They marked the beginning of the end of a tradition of leftist reformism that could be traced back to the Progressive Era. Rorty seeks to oppose the post-Sixties Left's semi-conscious anti-Americanism, its inverted exceptionalism, by elaborating on the close connection between Americanism and pragmatism. In this context, see his autobiographical essay, "Trotsky and the Wild Orchids," in *Philosophy and Social Hope* (New York: Penguin, 1999), 3–20. In addition, see the part "Rorty's Life" (4–11) in Christopher Voparil's "General Introduction," in *The Rorty Reader*, ed. Voparil and Richard J. Bernstein (Malden, MA: Wiley-Blackwell, 2010), 1–52. See also the first two chapters in Neil Gross, *Richard Rorty: The Making of an American Philosopher* (Chicago: University of Chicago Press, 2008), 29–83.

38   Whereas Dewey and Rorty accentuate the incompatibility between pragmatism and Marxism, the relation between these two philosophies appears in a different light in the writings of Sidney Hook and Cornel West. In this context, see the chapter "Early Encounters: Sidney Hook, Richard J. Bernstein, and George Novack," in Ulf Schulenberg, *Marxism, Pragmatism, and Postmetaphysics*, 21–46; and the chapter "Love and Resistance: Cornel West's Prophetic Pragmatism as Oppositional Cultural Criticism," in Ulf Schulenberg, *Lovers and Knowers: Moments of the American Cultural Left* (Heidelberg: Universitätsverlag Winter, 2007), 187–221.

39   Barbara Epstein gives a very useful definition of socialist humanism:

> Socialist humanism made the question of what kind of society we want to live in central. It criticised any form of socialism that would set social solidarity against freedom of expression and the right to dissent, and more broadly it stressed the need to create the conditions under which individual creativity could flourish. Socialist humanism challenged dogmatism by insisting that the future remains open and that no theory can predict it with certainty. (2017: 20–1)

At the end of her piece, Epstein writes that socialist humanism

> contributes a conception of human nature, and of the kinds of relations that human nature calls for, that points to the positive capacities of humans, individually and collectively. The environmental crisis, human responsibility for it, and the narrowing chances of reversing it make it much more difficult than it once was to sustain a positive view of the human race or hope for the future. But

it remains the case that humans are capable of constructive behaviour. Socialist humanism builds on this possibility. (2017: 64)

In this context, see also Jean-Marie Harribey, "Ecological Marxism or Marxian Political Ecology?" in *Critical Companion to Contemporary Marxism*, ed. Jacques Bidet and Stathis Kouvelakis (Chicago, IL: Haymarket Books, 2009), 189–208. For the resurgence of Marxism, see Alex Callinicos, Stathis Kouvelakis, and Lucia Pradella, eds., *Routledge Handbook of Marxism and Post-Marxism* (New York: Routledge, 2022).

40 Admittedly, in this chapter—and in this book—I often refer to the process of establishing relations. It is crucial to note that despite my critique of Dewey's aesthetics, this insistence upon the significance of establishing links between hitherto isolated aspects is a Deweyan gesture. Highlighting the importance of Dewey's "continuity thesis," Shusterman correctly points out: "In contrast to analytic philosophy (and perhaps again reflecting the Kant/Hegel opposition), Dewey was intent on making connections rather than distinctions. He was keen to connect aspects of human experience and activity which had been divided by specialist, compartmentalizing thought and then more brutally sundered by specialist, compartmentalizing institutions in which such fragmented disciplinary thinking is reinscribed and reinforced" (2000: 12).

6 "Nothing Is Known—Only Realized": Postcritique, Bruno Latour, and the Idea of a Positive Aesthetics

1 Important postcritical texts are Eve Kosofsky Sedgwick, "Paranoid Reading and Reparative Reading, or, You're So Paranoid, You Probably Think This Essay Is about You," in *Touching Feeling: Affect, Pedagogy, Performativity* (Durham, NC: Duke University Press, 2003), 123–58; Heather Love, "Close but not Deep: Literary Ethics and the Descriptive Turn," *New Literary History* 42 (2) (2010): 371–92; and Steven Best and Sharon Marcus, "Surface Reading: An Introduction," *Representations* 108 (2009): 1–21. In addition, see Amanda Anderson, *The Way We Argue Now* (Princeton, NJ: Princeton University Press, 2006).
2 In this context, see the chapter "Marxism, Pragmatism, and Postcritique," in Ulf Schulenberg, *Marxism, Pragmatism, and Postmetaphysics: From Finding to Making* (Basingstoke: Palgrave Macmillan, 2019), 141–59.
3 Important texts regarding Felski's understanding of postcritique are also the introduction, with Elizabeth Anker, to *Critique and Postcritique*, 1–28; and her introduction to the volume *Latour and the Humanities*, ed. Felski and Muecke, 1–27.

4 For a discussion of *The Limits of Critique*, see *PMLA* 132 (2) (2017): 331–91.
5 It is interesting to see Felski's idea of a positive aesthetics together with the argument Christopher Castiglia develops in "Hope for Critique?," in *Critique and Postcritique*, ed. Anker and Felski, 211–29. Even if one is inclined to agree with most of what the postcritics write, I think one at the same time should consider what Jeffrey Di Leo proposes in the introduction to *What's Wrong with Anti-Theory?*:

> Theory can no more die than philosophy or literature or rhetoric. Ultimately, the discontentment of antitheorists is not so much from outside of theory but from within. While some might be inclined to view postcritique or speculative realism as battles "against theory," as we have seen, others view them as local struggles within theory for institutional dominance. Whether we regard theory as the legacies of antifoundationalism or the rise of alternatives to it, the dialectics of theory must be regarded as an essential aspect of its rise and dominance in the academy over the past fifty years. (2020: 20)

In "Critique Unlimited," Robert Tally Jr. criticizes Felski for not really engaging with the work of a single critic:

> The reader of *The Limits of Critique* will search in vain for what surely must have been the missing section in which Felski engages with a particular work of criticism, showing how its rhetoric and tone belied its baleful project. Much as she paraphrases or imagines critics making suspicious arguments about cultural artifacts, Felski does not really present a clear example of a critic or work of criticism to support the argument. (2020: 124)

Tally is right in advancing this critique. However, it is actually even worse, since one has to see that Felski continues her superficial and undifferentiated discussions of individual theorists in *Hooked*. Even a postcritic should have more to say about, for instance, Althusser, Jameson, Foucault, or Derrida than Felski does in her books. Undoubtedly, it is difficult to take postcritique seriously when most postcritics criticize Jameson for being a master theorist but obviously have never studied anything but *The Political Unconscious*. In this context, see also Jeffrey R. Di Leo, ed., *Criticism after Critique: Aesthetics, Literature, and the Political* (Basingstoke: Palgrave Macmillan, 2014); and Di Leo, ed., *The Bloomsbury Handbook of Literary and Cultural Theory* (New York: Bloomsbury, 2021).
6 As regards the future development of the humanities, Felski poses the question of whether Latour's work can "inspire an alternative vision of what humanists do? One that is less invested in the iconoclasm of critique and more invested in forms of making and building?" (2020b: 13). Further on she expands on the potential of Latour's vision of composition as follows: "Interpretation becomes an act of co-making that brings new things to light rather than a deciphering of repressed

meaning or an endless rumination on the deficits or opacities of language. / The language of composition can draw humanists closer to others who are invested in making, building, and constructing" (2020b: 13).

7   In this context, Antoine Hennion's following statement is much too undifferentiated; it might apply to James's radical empiricism as panrelationism, but not to other pragmatists: "It is *pragmata*—thing-relations, plural and extended—that are at the heart of pragmatism, not practice, which doesn't require anyone to challenge the grand divide between human actions and the things they act upon" (2020: 66).

8   There has not yet been a detailed discussion of the commonalities and the differences between ANT and pragmatism. Furthermore, Latour does not play a role in the latest volumes on Richard Rorty's version of pragmatism: Alan Malachowski, ed., *A Companion to Rorty* (Hoboken, NJ: Wiley Blackwell, 2020); and David Rondel, ed., *The Cambridge Companion to Rorty* (New York: Cambridge University Press, 2021).

9   For introductions to Latour's oeuvre, see Gerard de Vries, *Bruno Latour* (Malden, MA: Polity, 2016); and Graham Harman, *Prince of Networks: Bruno Latour and Metaphysics*. Harman's volume is of particular value since he reads Latour as a philosopher. In addition, see Georg Kneer, Markus Schroer, and Erhard Schüttpelz, eds., *Bruno Latours Kollektive* (Frankfurt am Main: Suhrkamp, 2008).

10 As Latour shows in numerous texts, iconoclasm and antifetishism are an essential part of modern critique. His notion of the "factish" paves the way for a nonmodern way of thinking. He writes in *Pandora's Hope*:

> The factish suggests an entirely different move: it is *because* it is constructed that it is so very real, so autonomous, so independent of our own hands. As we have seen over and over, attachments do not decrease autonomy, but foster it. Until we understand that the terms "construction" and "autonomous reality" are *synonyms*, we will misconstrue the factish as yet another form of social constructivism rather than seeing it as the modification of the entire theory of *what it means to construct*. (1999: 275)

Latour describes the modern constellation as follows: "High above them, watching like protective goddesses, the sharp-cut distinctions between subject and object, science and politics, facts and fetishes, render forever invisible the complicated and rather bizarre means by which all of these categories are mixed" (1999: 277–8). Concerning the Latourian understanding of factishes, see also his *On the Modern Cult of the Factish Gods* (Durham, NC: Duke University Press, 2010).

11 This idea is, of course, central to *We Have Never Been Modern*. In his most famous text, which can also serve as a useful introduction to his thought, Latour advances the argument

that the word "modern" designates two sets of entirely different practices which must remain distinct if they are to remain effective, but have recently begun to be confused. The first set of practices, by "translation," creates mixtures between entirely new types of beings, hybrids of nature and culture. The second, by "purification," creates two entirely distinct ontological zones: that of human beings on the one hand; that of nonhumans on the other. (1993: 10–11)

As we have seen, Latour's contention is that it is typical of the modern critic to strictly separate between two practices: that of translation or mediation or proliferation, on one side, and that of purification and the use of the appearance-reality distinction, on the other. Consequently, as he submits, as soon as

we direct our attention simultaneously to the work of purification and the work of hybridization, we immediately stop being wholly modern, and our future begins to change. At the same time we stop having been modern, because we become retrospectively aware that the two sets of practices have always already been at work in the historical period that is ending. Our past begins to change. (1993: 11)

12 In *Philosophy and the Mirror of Nature*, Rorty tells a different story about the necessity of getting out from under Platonism. He does this by combining pragmatism with the insights of analytic philosophers such as Wilfrid Sellars, W. V. O. Quine, and Donald Davidson.

13 In "How the 'True World' Finally Became a Fable," Nietzsche writes about the apparent or illusory world in the final stage of detranscendentalization: "The true world is gone: which world is left? The illusory one, perhaps? ... But no! *we got rid of the illusory world along with the true one!*" (2005: 171).

14 In *We Have Never Been Modern*, Latour writes about postmodernism (and this negative judgment can also be found in some of his other texts): "Postmodernism is a symptom, not a fresh solution. It lives under the modern Constitution, but it no longer believes in the guarantees the Constitution offers. It senses that something has gone awry in the modern critique, but it is not able to do anything but prolong that critique, though without believing in its foundations" (1993: 46).

15 Graham Harman's reading of *Irréductions* is particularly suggestive. See the respective chapter in his *Prince of Networks*, 11–32.

16 In the introduction to *Truth and Progress*, Rorty, for instance, describes a future "post-truth" culture as follows (in *Contingency, Irony, and Solidarity* he termed this kind of culture a "poeticized culture" [1989: 53]):

For in such a culture we would be more sensitive to the marvelous diversity of human languages, and of the social practices associated with those languages, because we shall have ceased asking whether they "correspond to" some

> nonhuman, eternal reality. Instead of asking "Are there truths out there that we shall never discover?" we would ask "Are there ways of talking and acting that we have not yet explored?" Instead of asking whether the intrinsic nature of reality is yet in sight (the secular counterpart of asking whether things are *dis aliter visum*), we should ask whether each of the various descriptions of reality employed in our various cultural activities is the best we can imagine—the best means to the ends served by those activities. (1998b: 6)

In this context, see also Richard Rorty and Pascal Engel, *What's the Use of Truth?* (New York: Columbia University Press, 2007); and Engel, "Are Pragmatists About Truth True Democrats?," in *A Companion to Rorty*, ed. Alan Malachowski, 149–62. In addition, see Akeel Bilgrami, "Is Truth a Goal of Inquiry?: Rorty and Davidson on Truth," in *Rorty and His Critics*, ed. Robert B. Brandom (Malden, MA: Blackwell, 2000), 242–61.

17 For Graham Harman's interpretation of Latour, see also *Bruno Latour: Reassembling the Political* (London: Pluto, 2014); and his essay "Demodernizing the Humanities with Latour," in *Latour and the Humanities*, ed. Felski and Muecke, 76–106.

18 In this context, see Aaron Ridley's illuminating study *The Deed Is Everything: Nietzsche on Will and Action* (New York: Oxford University Press, 2018).

19 Latour clearly and unequivocally rejects the traditional understanding of humanism. In *We Have Never Been Modern*, he states: "Yet the human, as we now understand, cannot be grasped and saved unless that other part of itself, the share of things, is restored to it. So long as humanism is constructed through contrast with the object that has been abandoned to epistemology, neither the human nor the nonhuman can be understood" (1993: 136).

20 In a thought-provoking manner, Richard Schacht expands on the possibility of bringing together Nietzsche's idea that only we have created the world that concerns us as human beings and his understanding of art as the good will to appearance:

> Without a sensibility enabling us to take satisfaction in that which we ourselves have created, we could not but be deeply dismayed upon recognizing the extent to which everything transpiring in our lives is and inescapably will continue to be a merely contingently established human affair, answering to nothing written into the fundamental nature of reality. It may be a mere prejudice we were better to dispense with (as Nietzsche elsewhere urges) to think of human reality and experience as mere "appearance" for this reason. Given certain of our deep-seated intellectual predilections, however, the grip of this prejudice upon us is not easily broken. The emergence of "art as the good will to

appearance" constitutes an important step in that direction, and points the way to a reassessment of what we have made and might further make of ourselves. (1992: 526)

Concerning the idea of *l'art pour l'art*, Nietzsche points out in *Twilight of the Idols*: "Once you exclude the purposes of sermonizing and improving people from art, it does not follow even remotely that art is totally purposeless, aimless, senseless, in short, *l'art pour l'art*—a worm swallowing its own tail" ("Skirmishes," sec. 24). His rejection of *l'art pour l'art* becomes even more obvious later in the same aphorism, when he asks the following questions: "Is the artist's most basic instinct bound up with art, or is it bound up much more intimately with *life*, which is the meaning of art? Isn't it bound up with the *desirability of life?*—Art is the great stimulus to life: how could art be understood as purposeless, pointless, *l'art pour l'art*?" As we have seen, what makes Nietzsche's position special is that his critique of *l'art pour l'art* and his insistence upon the intimate relation between art and life come together with his endeavor to highlight the meaning of form and the practice of form-giving.

21 Kant's Copernican Revolution, according to Latour, "offers a perfected model for modernizing explanations, [...] but nothing obliges us to take that revolution as a decisive event that sets us for ever [sic] on the sure path of science, morality and theology" (1993: 79). Latour calls his own approach a "Copernican counter-revolution": "I call this reversed reversal—or rather this shift of the extremes centreward and downward, a movement that makes both object and subject revolve around the practice of quasi-objects and mediators—a Copernican counter-revolution" (1993: 79).

7 "I Turned to the Poets": Humanist Stories of Progress

1 In *Contingency, Irony, and Solidarity*, Rorty writes about his use of the term "poet": "I assume that Bloom would be willing to extend the reference 'poet' beyond those who write verse, and to use it in the large, generic sense in which I am using it—so that Proust and Nabokov, Newton and Darwin, Hegel and Heidegger, also fall under the term" (1989: 24 n. 1).
2 For a discussion of the role that Emerson played for the development of pragmatism, see the chapter "The Emersonian Prehistory of American Pragmatism" in Cornel West, *The American Evasion of Philosophy: A Genealogy of Pragmatism*, 9–41.
3 For a discussion of the complexity of Emersonian self-reliance, see chapter 2 "Emersonian Self-Reliance in Theory and Practice," in Lawrence Buell, *Emerson* (Cambridge, MA: Belknap Press, 2003), 59–106. In addition, see Wesley T.

Mott, "'The Age of the First Person Singular': Emerson and Individualism," in *A Historical Guide to Ralph Waldo Emerson*, ed. Joel Myerson (New York: Oxford University Press, 2000), 61–100. Valuable regarding the question of self-reliance is also Stephen E. Whicher, "The Dream of Greatness," in *Ralph Waldo Emerson: A Collection of Critical Essays*, ed. Lawrence Buell (Upper Saddle River, NJ: Prentice Hall, 1993), 61–76.

4   In this context, see Richard Shusterman, "Emerson's Pragmatist Aesthetics," *Revue Internationale de Philosophie* 53 (207) (1999): 87–99.

5   For stimulating readings of the relation between Emerson and Nietzsche, see George J. Stack, *Nietzsche and Emerson: An Elective Affinity* (Athens: Ohio University Press, 1992); Stanley Cavell, "Old and New in Emerson and Nietzsche," in Cavell, *Emerson's Transcendental Etudes* (Stanford, CA: Stanford University Press, 2003), 224–33; and the chapter "Emerson as a Philosopher?" in Buell's *Emerson*, 199–241.

6   In this context, see the chapter "Getting Rid of the Appearance-Reality Distinction" in Richard Rorty, *Philosophy as Poetry*, 1–22.

7   In his discussion of Emerson, Dewey repeatedly underscores that in his opinion the former, in a paradigmatic manner, makes the question "poet or philosopher?" look pointless. Dewey writes: "Perhaps those are nearer right, however, who deny that Emerson is a philosopher, because he is more than a philosopher. He would work, he says, by art, not by metaphysics, finding truth 'in the sonnet and the play'" (1903: 366). Further on, Dewey points out: "It is significant irony that the old quarrel of philosopher and poet was brought off by one who united in himself more than has another individual the qualities of both artist and metaphysician" (1903: 367). In this context, one should also consider Cornel West's proposal that the Emersonian evasion of philosophy "views poetry and philosophy neither as identical nor as antagonistic but as different metaphor-deploying activities to achieve—by means of agon and struggle—specific aims" (1989: 73). Emerson in this sense is a strong poet as mediator, a mediator in a strictly non-Hegelian sense who does not seek to achieve a synthesis of poetry and philosophy, but who rather elegantly uses different vocabularies for different purposes.

8   For a discussion of Rorty's attitude toward religion, see Jacob L. Goodson and Brad Elliott Stone, eds., *Rorty and the Religious: Christian Engagements with a Secular Philosopher* (Eugene, OR: Cascade Books, 2012); and Charley D. Hardwick and Donald A. Crosby, eds., *Pragmatism, Neo-Pragmatism, and Religion: Conversations with Richard Rorty* (New York: Peter Lang, 1997). See also Emil Visnovsky, "Rorty's Philosophy of Religion," in *A Companion to Rorty*, ed. Alan Malachowski (Hoboken, NJ: Wiley Blackwell, 2020), 456–66; and Stephen S. Bush, "Rorty on Religion," in *The Cambridge Companion to Rorty*, ed. David Rondel (New York: Cambridge University Press, 2021), 243–60.

9 For a discussion of the question of Whitman and pragmatism, see Stephen John Mack, *The Pragmatic Whitman* (Iowa City: University of Iowa Press, 2002); and Daniel Malachuk, "Walt Whitman and the Culture of Pragmatism," *Walt Whitman Quarterly Review* 17 (1) (1999): 60–8.
10 That this tension between metaphysical need and postmetaphysical desire is characteristic of Romanticism becomes obvious in Meyer H. Abrams, *Natural Supernaturalism: Tradition and Revolution in Romantic Literature* (New York: Norton, 1971); and Isaiah Berlin, *The Roots of Romanticism* (Princeton, NJ: Princeton University Press, 1999).
11 For a discussion of Whitman's attitude toward religion, see David Reynolds, *Walt Whitman's America: A Cultural Biography*, 251–9; and Stephen John Mack, *The Pragmatic Whitman*, 135–59.
12 David Reynolds suggests that *Democratic Vistas* should be considered "in several ways a radical document" (1996: 483). Of particular interest is his attempt to explain the significance of the combination of Darwin and Hegel in this context. Reynolds points out:

> Torn between a lost ideal, the war, and an increasingly sordid present, Whitman turned hopefully to the future. No longer able to rely upon an all-absorbing poetic "I," he looked now to outside systems for consolation. Despite everything pushing him toward cynicism, he actually gained a new source of optimism after the war in what might be termed "progressive evolution," a combination post-Darwinian thought and Hegelian idealism. (1996: 480)

Further on he writes: "For Whitman, as for many other spiritual-minded postbellum Americans, neither Hegel nor Darwin was inconsistent with religious belief. Both offered large, overarching systems that, in his mind, made history a long-developing process slowly separating the evil from the good, the unfit from the fit, the imperfect from the perfect" (1996: 481). In addition, see the parts that discuss Whitman's work in Reynolds's *Beneath the American Renaissance: The Subversive Imagination in the Age of Emerson and Melville* (Cambridge, MA: Harvard University Press, 1988).
13 In this context, see Ulf Schulenberg, "William James, Romanticism, and the 'Humanistic Principle,'" in *The Jamesian Mind*, ed. Sarin Marchetti (New York: Routledge, 2022), 365–74; and the chapter "'The Humanistic State of Mind': James and Nietzsche" in Ulf Schulenberg, *Pragmatism and Poetic Agency: The Persistence of Humanism* (New York: Routledge, 2021), 36–50.
14 For stimulating analyses of James's impact on American culture, see Ross Posnock, "The Influence of William James on American Culture," in *The Cambridge Companion to William James*, ed. Ruth Anna Putnam (New York: Cambridge University Press, 1997), 322–42; and James T. Kloppenberg, "James's *Pragmatism* and American Culture, 1907–2007," in *100 Years of Pragmatism: William James's*

Revolutionary Philosophy, ed. John J. Stuhr (Bloomington: Indiana University Press, 2010), 7–40. See also Deborah Whitehead, *William James, Pragmatism, and American Culture* (Bloomington: Indiana University Press, 2015). George Cotkin discusses James's function as a public philosopher in *William James, Public Philosopher* (Baltimore, MD: Johns Hopkins University Press, 1990).

15 Concerning James's conception of pluralism, see the chapter "Radical Empiricism and Pluralism," in James Campbell's *Experiencing William James: Belief in a Pluralistic World* (Charlottesville: University of Virginia Press, 2017), 160–99; and Barry Allen, "'Ever Not Quite!': William James's *A Pluralistic Universe*," in *Understanding James, Understanding Modernism*, ed. David H. Evans (New York: Bloomsbury, 2017), 75–92.

16 For a detailed discussion of the relationship between Nietzsche and pragmatism, see the first part, "Friedrich Nietzsche and the Pragmatists," in Ulf Schulenberg, *Pragmatism and Poetic Agency*, 17–98.

17 As regards Nietzsche's understanding of the function and enormous importance of art, see section 853 in *The Will to Power*: "Art and nothing but art! It is the great means of making life possible, the great seduction to life, the great stimulant of life. / Art as the only superior counterforce to all will to denial of life, as that which is anti-Christian, anti-Buddhist, antinihilist *par excellence*."

18 As far as Nietzsche's aestheticism is concerned, the following texts are useful: Alexander Nehamas, *Nietzsche: Life as Literature* (Cambridge, MA: Harvard University Press, 1985); Nehamas, "Nietzsche, Modernity, Aestheticism," in *The Cambridge Companion to Nietzsche*, ed. Bernd Magnus and Kathleen M. Higgins (New York: Cambridge University Press, 1996), 223–51; and Sebastian Gardner, "Nietzsche's Philosophical Aestheticism," in *The Oxford Handbook of Nietzsche*, ed. Ken Gemes and John Richardson (Oxford: Oxford University Press, 2013), 599–628. In *Nietzsche*, Richard Schacht offers a convincing and stimulating analysis of Nietzsche's naturalism. Of particular value in this context is Christoph Cox, *Nietzsche: Naturalism and Interpretation* (Berkeley: University of California Press, 1999).

19 For my discussion of Rorty's reading of Nietzsche, see Section 2.2. In addition, see the chapter "'But the Answer to a Great Poem Is a Still Better Poem': Rorty and Nietzsche," in Ulf Schulenberg, *Pragmatism and Poetic Agency*, 68–80.

20 One should consider the final paragraph of the "Preface for the Second Edition" of *The Gay Science*, where Nietzsche writes about the ancient Greeks:

> Oh, those Greeks! They knew how to live. What is required for that is to stop courageously at the surface, the fold, the skin, to adore appearance, to believe in forms, tones, words, in the whole Olympus of appearance. Those Greeks were

superficial—*out of profundity*. [...] Are we not, precisely in this respect, Greeks? Adorers of forms, of tones, of words? And therefore—*artists*? (1974: 38)

In this context, see the chapter "Art, Truth, and Woman: The Raging Discordance" in Matthew Rampley, *Nietzsche, Aesthetics, and Modernity* (New York: Cambridge University Press, 2000), 190–214. In addition, see Philip Pothen, *Nietzsche and the Fate of Art* (New York: Routledge, 2018 [2002]). While Nietzsche puts a premium on the activity of form-giving, it would be interesting to ask whether he also sees the necessity of thinking the idea of a dissonant or fragmented form. This also means that it would be stimulating to discuss whether there is a connection between the will to power and dissonance. Is Nietzsche clearly a nineteenth-century aesthetician who holds that existence and the world are chaotic, without structure, and meaningless, and who therefore associates aesthetic form exclusively with organicity and harmony? According to Aaron Ridley, form "is conceived by Nietzsche along traditional (perhaps Romantic) organicist lines: because parts acquire their 'meaning' from their 'relation to the whole', the resultant structure 'lives'" (2013: 420). I think that Ridley does have a point. However, I am also inclined to surmise that a more detailed analysis of the Nietzschean notions of form and form-giving might present a more "modern" Nietzsche, who leaves room for the idea that artworks might be fragmented, nonlinear, and as governed by contingency as the arts of self-creation or self-stylization.

21 At the beginning of *Philosophy as Poetry*, Rorty submits that if we were to get rid of the appearance-reality distinction,

> we should no longer wonder whether the human mind, or human language, is capable of representing reality accurately. We should stop thinking that some parts of our culture are more in touch with reality than other parts. We would express our sense of finitude not by comparing our humanity with something nonhuman but by comparing our way of being human with other, better, ways that may someday be adopted by our descendants. (2016: 1)

22 As we saw in Chapter 2, Robert Brandom correctly points out that Rorty "wholly applauds the Enlightenment's secular, humanistic, critical, and emancipatory commitments and accomplishments, as theoretically articulating the progressive transformation of traditional institutions and forms of life into distinctively modern ones" (2021: xxv).

23 It ought to be noted that Rorty somewhat modified his attitude toward religion in his final years. One can detect a development from his notorious piece "Religion as Conversation-Stopper" (1994) to his conversations with the Catholic philosopher Gianni Vattimo. The latter were published as *The Future of Religion* (2005). Still counting himself among the "contemporary secularists" (2005: 33), Rorty

underlines that "anticlericalism" (2005: 33) would describe his position better than atheism.

24 In the "Epilogue" to *Pragmatism as Anti-Authoritarianism*, Eduardo Mendieta offers a concise definition of Rorty's version of anti-authoritarianism:

> Anti-authoritarianism in epistemology and ethics is what we get when we let pragmatism carry forward the unfinished project of the Enlightenment, when we let the vocabularies of pragmatism help us slough off metaphors of depth and altitude for metaphors of expansion and inclusion, when we stop looking to and talking to a silent authority and start looking around us and talking to each other in more expansive and inspirational vocabularies. Anti-authoritarianism is what we get when all we have is the horizontality of human linguistic and social practices. (2021: 197)

In chapter 6 ("Against Depth") in *Pragmatism as Anti-Authoritarianism*, Rorty explains why pragmatists as panrelationalists have no use for metaphors of verticality:

> No relation between things is higher or deeper than any other, and linguistic descriptions of the world are just more such relations. There is no dimension in which we can move in order to get above, or below, language. There is neither a God's-eye view, nor a Ground of Being, nor a Way the World Is independent of how it is described. Because panrelationalists cannot use the notion of intrinsic properties lurking below merely relational properties, all metaphors of depth look suspect to them. Nor, of course, can we retain metaphors of higher, purer, isolated things getting stained with relational accretions when they descend into, or are exemplified by, other realms of being. All metaphors of verticality must be eschewed. (2021: 105)

For Rorty's understanding of panrelationalism, see also the chapter "A World without Substances or Essences" in *Philosophy and Social Hope* (New York: Penguin, 1999), 47–71.

Conclusion

1 In "Science and Solidarity," Rorty directs attention to the important question of "whether notions like 'unforced agreement' and 'free and open encounter'—descriptions of social situations—can take the place in our moral lives of notions like 'the world,' 'the will of God,' 'the moral law,' 'what our beliefs are trying to represent accurately,' and 'what makes our beliefs true'" (1991b: 42).

2   In this context, see Ulf Schulenberg, *Pragmatism and Poetic Agency: The Persistence of Humanism* (New York: Routledge, 2021).
3   It is interesting to note that Shusterman terms his version of pragmatism, including his experimental work in performance and his literary work, a "poetic pragmatism" (Shusterman and Dreon 2021: 2). Writing the history of poetic pragmatism, which would also focus on the crucial differences between Shusterman and Rorty, is still a desideratum. I have begun this work in my previous three monographs. For interesting discussions of Shusterman's *Pragmatist Aesthetics*, see the *European Journal of Pragmatism and American Philosophy* 4 (1) (2012), "A Symposium on R. Shusterman, *Pragmatist Aesthetics* 20 Years later." Richard Shusterman discusses and critiques Rorty's work in numerous pieces. See, for instance, the chapter "Reason and Aesthetics between Modernity and Postmodernity: Habermas and Rorty" in his *Practicing Philosophy: Pragmatism and the Philosophical Life* (New York: Routledge, 1997), 113–30; the chapter "Pragmatism and Culture: Margolis and Rorty" in his *Surface and Depth: Dialectics of Criticism and Culture* (Ithaca, NY: Cornell University Press, 2002), 191–207; and "Rorty's Aesthetics," in *Archives de philosophie* 82 (3) (2019): 557–72.
4   In the chapter "The Fine Art of Rap," Shusterman offers a convincing discussion of the formal aspects of rap. He is, for instance, right in contending that rap

> refutes the dogma that concern for form and formal experimentation cannot be found in popular art. Moreover, it displays the thematized attention to artistic medium and method often regarded as the hallmark of contemporary high art. Sampling is not only rap's most radical formal innovation (since some earlier pop songs also experimented with speech rather than singing), it is also the one most concerned with rap's artistic medium—recorded music. (2000: 232)

At the end of his discussion, he explicates that rap's formal innovation of sampling is intimately linked to fragmentation and ought to be seen as an attack on traditional notions of formal coherence. There is indeed "a tension between rap's claims of formal innovation and its satisfaction of the formal coherence required of art. For rap's artistic innovation, particularly its technique of sampling, is closely connected with elements of fragmentation, dislocation, and breaking of forms" (2000: 235). Since there is no room for this gesture of radically breaking traditional forms in Dewey's aesthetics, Shusterman's argument becomes particularly interesting as soon as he indirectly questions his Deweyan framework.

5   In her "Introduction to Pragmatist Legacies in Aesthetics," Dreon correctly maintains that pragmatism has played a crucial role as regards the development of everyday aesthetics, environmental aesthetics, social aesthetics, and, of course, somaesthetics. However, the essays that she has gathered for her special issue on "Pragmatist Legacies in Aesthetics" do not answer the question of how useful

pragmatist aesthetics is when one seeks to understand and analyze modern and postmodern art and literature (not to mention minimal art, conceptual art, and postconceptual art). Does a Deweyan approach to aesthetics necessarily have to exclude this question? When Shusterman's pragmatist aesthetics and Rorty's pragmatist literary criticism fail to appreciate the complexity of modern art and literature, pragmatist aesthetics and literary criticism have a problem.

6 In *Experience and Nature*, Dewey asserts that "wherever there is art the contingent and ongoing no longer work at cross purposes with the formal and recurrent but commingle in harmony" (2008b: 269). Dewey here and elsewhere works with the dichotomy "the contingent and the formal." The latter seems to be the general and universal; it transcends the practical life that is governed by contingencies, and hence it is reliable. As I have argued in this book, Dewey ignores the question of what would happen if one considered the formal as dominated by contingency. Whereas he states that the contingent and the formal "commingle in harmony," I have advanced the idea that harmony is decidedly more difficult to establish when one regards form-giving as poetic agency and hence as a contingent and historical practice. Asking "Where is the formal in Romanticism and modernism?" must not be misunderstood as another paean to aesthetic nominalism, but rather as a reminder that the pragmatist insistence upon the contingency and historicity of social practices should also be of primary importance for one's appreciation of the practice of aesthetic form-giving.

7 In this context, one should also consider one of the central passages in Caroline Levine's *Forms*: "Literary forms and social formations are equally real in their capacity to organize materials, and equally *un*real in being artificial, contingent constraints. Instead of seeking to reveal the reality suppressed by literary forms, we can understand sociopolitical life as itself composed of a plurality of different forms, from narrative to marriage and from bureaucracy to racism" (2015: 14).

References

Adorno, Theodor W. (1973), *Ästhetische Theorie*, Frankfurt am Main: Suhrkamp.
Adorno, Theodor W. (1977), "Reconciliation under Duress," in Theodor W. Adorno, Walter Benjamin, Ernst Bloch, Bertolt Brecht, and Georg Lukács, *Aesthetics and Politics*, 151–76, London: Verso.
Adorno, Theodor W. (1978), *Philosophie der neuen Musik*, Frankfurt am Main: Suhrkamp.
Adorno, Theodor W. (1981), *Noten zur Literatur*, Frankfurt am Main: Suhrkamp.
Adorno, Theodor W. (1991), *Notes to Literature, Vol. 1*, trans. Shierry Weber Nicholsen, New York: Columbia University Press.
Adorno, Theodor W. (1992), *Notes to Literature, Vol. 2*, trans. Shierry Weber Nicholsen, New York: Columbia University Press.
Adorno, Theodor W. (1997), *Aesthetic Theory*, trans. Robert Hullot-Kentor, Minneapolis: University of Minnesota Press.
Alexander, Thomas M. (1987), *John Dewey's Theory of Art, Experience, and Nature: The Horizons of Feeling*, Albany: State University of New York Press.
Anker, Elizabeth S., and Rita Felski (2017), "Introduction," in Elizabeth S. Anker and Rita Felski (eds.), *Critique and Postcritique*, 1–28, Durham, NC: Duke University Press.
Bell, Clive ([1914] 1958), *Art*, New York: Capricorn Books.
Berlin, Isaiah (1999), *The Roots of Romanticism*, Princeton, NJ: Princeton University Press.
Berlin, Isaiah (2000), "The Apotheosis of the Romantic Will," in Isaiah Berlin, *The Proper Study of Mankind: An Anthology of Essays*, ed. Henry Hardy and Roger Hausheer, 553–80, New York: Farrar, Straus and Giroux.
Bernstein, Richard J. (2010), *The Pragmatic Turn*, Malden, MA: Polity.
Bernstein, Richard J. (2020), *Pragmatic Naturalism: John Dewey's Living Legacy*, New York: Graduate Faculty Philosophy Journal.
Brandom, Robert B. (2000a), "Introduction," in Robert B. Brandom (ed.), *Rorty and His Critics*, ix–xx, Malden, MA: Blackwell.
Brandom, Robert B. (2000b), "Vocabularies of Pragmatism: Synthesizing Naturalism and Historicism," in Robert B. Brandom (ed.), *Rorty and His Critics*, 156–82, Malden, MA: Blackwell.
Brandom, Robert B. (2011), *Perspectives on Pragmatism: Classical, Recent, and Contemporary*, Cambridge, MA: Harvard University Press.

Brandom, Robert B. (2021), "Foreword: Achieving the Enlightenment," in Richard Rorty, *Pragmatism as Anti-Authoritarianism*, ed. Eduardo Mendieta, vii–xxvi, Cambridge, MA: Belknap Press of Harvard University Press.

Brennan, Timothy (2017), "Introduction: Humanism's Other Story," in David Alderson and Robert Spencer (eds.), *For Humanism: Explorations in Theory and Politics*, 1–16, London: Pluto Press.

Breton, André (1964), *Nadja*, Paris: Gallimard.

Bürger, Peter (1984), *Theory of the Avant-Garde*, trans. Michael Shaw, Minneapolis: University of Minnesota Press.

Bürger, Peter (1991), "Adorno's Anti-Avant-Gardism," *Telos* 86: 49–60.

Butler, Judith (2010), "Introduction," in György Lukács, *Soul and Form*, ed. John T. Sanders and Katie Terezakis, trans. Anna Bostock, 1–15, New York: Columbia University Press.

Cooper, David E. (2002), *The Measure of Things: Humanism, Humility, and Mystery*, Oxford: Clarendon Press.

Craig, Edward (1987), *The Mind of God and the Works of Man*, Oxford: Clarendon Press.

Dalton, Thomas C. (2002), *John Dewey: Dilemmas of a Philosopher and Naturalist*, Bloomington: Indiana University Press.

Derrida, Jacques (1996), "Remarks on Deconstruction and Pragmatism," in Chantal Mouffe (ed.), *Deconstruction and Pragmatism*, 77–88, New York: Routledge.

Dewey, John (1903), "Emerson – The Philosopher of Democracy," in Larry A. Hickman and Thomas M. Alexander (eds.), *The Essential Dewey: Vol. 2 Ethics, Logic, Psychology*, 366–70, Bloomington: Indiana University Press, 1998.

Dewey, John (1917), "The Need for a Recovery of Philosophy," in Larry A. Hickman and Thomas M. Alexander (eds.), *The Essential Dewey: Vol. 1 Pragmatism, Education, Democracy*, 46–70, Bloomington: Indiana University Press, 1998.

Dewey, John (1925), "The Development of American Pragmatism," in Larry A. Hickman and Thomas M. Alexander (eds.), *The Essential Dewey: Vol. 1 Pragmatism, Education, Democracy*, 3–13, Bloomington: Indiana University Press, 1998.

Dewey, John ([1948] 1957), *Reconstruction in Philosophy*, enlarged ed., Boston: Beacon.

Dewey, John ([1929] 1988), *The Quest for Certainty*, in John Dewey, *The Later Works 1925–1953, Vol. 4*, ed. Jo Ann Boydston, Carbondale: Southern Illinois University Press.

Dewey, John (1989), *Freedom and Culture*, Amherst, NY: Prometheus Books.

Dewey, John ([1934] 2008a), *Art as Experience*, in John Dewey, *The Later Works 1925–1953, Vol. 10*, ed. Jo Ann Boydston, Carbondale: Southern Illinois University Press.

Dewey, John ([1925] 2008b), *Experience and Nature*, in John Dewey, *The Later Works 1925–1953, Vol. 1*, ed. Jo Ann Boydston, Carbondale: Southern Illinois University Press.

Di Leo, Jeffrey R. (2020), "Introduction: Anti-Theory and Its Discontents," in Di Leo (ed.), *What's Wrong with Anti-Theory?*, 1–22, New York: Bloomsbury.

Doran, Robert (2017), *The Ethics of Theory: Philosophy, History, Literature*, New York: Bloomsbury.

Dreon, Roberta (2021), "Introduction to Pragmatist Legacies in Aesthetics," *European Journal of Pragmatism and American Philosophy* XIII-1, http://journals.openedition.org/ejpap/2259 (accessed April 4, 2022).

Ellison, David (2010), *A Reader's Guide to Proust's* In Search of Lost Time, New York: Cambridge University Press.

Emerson, Ralph Waldo (1836), "Nature," in Carl Bode (ed.), *The Portable Emerson*, 7–50, New York: Penguin, 1981.

Emerson, Ralph Waldo (1837), "The American Scholar," in Carl Bode (ed.), *The Portable Emerson*, 51–71, New York: Penguin, 1981.

Emerson, Ralph Waldo (1841a), "Circles," in Carl Bode (ed.), *The Portable Emerson*, 228–40, New York: Penguin, 1981.

Emerson, Ralph Waldo (1841b), "Self-Reliance," in Carl Bode (ed.), *The Portable Emerson*, 138–64, New York: Penguin, 1981.

Emerson, Ralph Waldo (1844), "The Poet," in Carl Bode (ed.), *The Portable Emerson*, 241–65, New York: Penguin, 1981.

Emerson, Ralph Waldo (1981), *The Portable Emerson*, ed. Carl Bode. New York: Penguin.

Emerson, Ralph Waldo (2000), *The Essential Writings of Ralph Waldo Emerson*, ed. Brooks Atkinson, New York: Modern Library.

Epstein, Barbara (2017), "The Rise, Decline and Possible Revival of Socialist Humanism," in David Alderson and Robert Spencer (eds.), *For Humanism: Explorations in Theory and Politics*, 17–67, London: Pluto Press.

Felski, Rita (2008), *Uses of Literature*, Malden, MA: Blackwell.

Felski, Rita (2015), *The Limits of Critique*, Chicago, IL: University of Chicago Press.

Felski, Rita (2020a), *Hooked: Art and Attachment*, Chicago, IL: University of Chicago Press.

Felski, Rita (2020b), "Introduction," in Rita Felski and Stephen Muecke (eds.), *Latour and the Humanities*, 1–27, Baltimore, MD: Johns Hopkins University Press.

Geroulanos, Stefanos (2010), *An Atheism That Is Not Humanist Emerges in French Thought*, Stanford, CA: Stanford University Press.

Geulen, Eva (2021), "'The Primacy of the Object': Adorno's *Aesthetic Theory* and the Return of Form," in Peter E. Gordon (ed.), *Adorno's* Aesthetic Theory *at Fifty*, special issue of *New German Critique* 143: 5–19.

Gordon, Peter E. (2021), "Social Suffering and the Autonomy of Art," in Peter E. Gordon (ed.), *Adorno's* Aesthetic Theory *at Fifty*, special issue of *New German Critique* 143: 125–46.

Guyer, Paul (2014a), *A History of Modern Aesthetics: Vol. 2 The Nineteenth Century*, New York: Cambridge University Press.

Guyer, Paul (2014b), *A History of Modern Aesthetics: Vol. 3 The Twentieth Century*, New York: Cambridge University Press.

Hall, David L. (1994), *Richard Rorty: Prophet and Poet of the New Pragmatism*, Albany: SUNY Press.

Hammer, Espen (2015), *Adorno's Modernism: Art, Experience, and Catastrophe*, New York: Cambridge University Press.

Harman, Graham (2009), *Prince of Networks: Bruno Latour and Metaphysics*, Melbourne: re.press.

Hegel, Georg Wilhelm Friedrich (2004), *Introductory Lectures on Aesthetics*, ed. Michael Inwood, trans. Bernard Bosanquet, New York: Penguin.

Hennion, Antoine (2020), "From ANT to Pragmatism: A Journey with Bruno Latour at the CSI," in Rita Felski and Stephen Muecke (eds.), *Latour and the Humanities*, 52–75, Baltimore: Johns Hopkins University Press.

Hohendahl, Peter Uwe (2011), "The Theory of the Novel and the Concept of Realism in Lukács and Adorno," in Michael J. Thompson (ed.), *Georg Lukács Reconsidered: Critical Essays in Politics, Philosophy, and Aesthetics*, 75–98, New York: Bloomsbury.

James, William (1880), "Great Men and Their Environment," in William James, *The Will to Believe and Other Essays in Popular Philosophy*, 216–54, New York: Dover, 1956.

James, William (1891), "The Moral Philosopher and the Moral Life," in William James, *Pragmatism and Other Writings*, ed. and with an introduction by Giles Gunn, 242–63, New York: Penguin, 2000.

James, William (1907), *Pragmatism*, in Bruce Kuklick (ed.), *William James, Writings 1902-1910*, 479–624, New York: Library of America, 1987.

James, William (1909a), *The Meaning of Truth*, in Bruce Kuklick (ed.), *William James, Writings 1902–1910*, 821–978, New York: Library of America, 1987.

James, William (1909b), *A Pluralistic Universe*, in Bruce Kuklick (ed.), *William James, Writings 1902–1910*, 625–819, New York: Library of America, 1987.

James, William (1911), *Some Problems of Philosophy*, in Bruce Kuklick (ed.), *William James, Writings 1902–1910*, 979–1106, New York: Library of America, 1987.

Jameson, Fredric (1971), *Marxism and Form: Twentieth-Century Dialectical Theories of Literature*, Princeton: Princeton University Press.

Jameson, Fredric (1975), "Beyond the Cave: Demystifying the Ideology of Modernism," in Fredric Jameson, *The Ideologies of Theory*, 415–33, New York: Verso, 2008.

Jameson, Fredric (1976), "The Ideology of the Text," in Fredric Jameson, *The Ideologies of Theory*, 20–76, New York: Verso, 2008.

Jameson, Fredric (1977), "Reflections on the Brecht-Lukács Debate," in Fredric Jameson, *The Ideologies of Theory*, 434–50, New York: Verso, 2008.

Jameson, Fredric (1988), "Cognitive Mapping," in Cary Nelson and Lawrence Grossberg (eds.), *Marxism and the Interpretation of Culture*, 347–60, Chicago: University of Illinois Press.

Jameson, Fredric ([1981] 1989), *The Political Unconscious: Narrative as a Socially Symbolic Act*, New York: Routledge.

Jameson, Fredric (1990), *Late Marxism: Adorno, or, The Persistence of the Dialectic*, New York: Verso.

Jameson, Fredric (1991), *Postmodernism, or, The Cultural Logic of Late Capitalism*, New York: Verso.

Jameson, Fredric (1998), "History and Class Consciousness as an Unfinished Project," in Fredric Jameson, *Valences of the Dialectic*, 201–22, New York: Verso, 2009.

Jameson, Fredric (2007), *The Modernist Papers*, New York: Verso.

Jameson, Fredric (2008), *The Ideologies of Theory*, New York: Verso.

Jameson, Fredric (2009), *Valences of the Dialectic*, New York: Verso.

Kundera, Milan (2003), *The Art of the Novel*, trans. Linda Asher, New York: Harper.

Kundera, Milan (2007), *The Curtain: An Essay in Seven Parts*, trans. Linda Asher, New York: Harper.

Latour, Bruno (1988), *The Pasteurization of France, Part II: Irreductions*, trans. John Law, Cambridge, MA: Harvard University Press.

Latour, Bruno (1993), *We Have Never Been Modern*, trans. Catherine Porter, Cambridge, MA: Harvard University Press.

Latour, Bruno (1999), *Pandora's Hope: Essays on the Reality of Science Studies*, Cambridge, MA: Harvard University Press.

Latour, Bruno (2004), "Why Has Critique Run Out of Steam?: From Matters of Fact to Matters of Concern," *Critical Inquiry* 30 (2): 225–48.

Latour, Bruno (2010), "An Attempt at a 'Compositionist Manifesto,'" *New Literary History* 41 (3): 471–90.

Leighton, Angela (2007), *On Form: Poetry, Aestheticism, and the Legacy of a Word*, New York: Oxford University Press.

Levine, Caroline (2015), *Forms: Whole, Rhythm, Hierarchy, Network*, Princeton, NJ: Princeton University Press.

Lukács, Georg (1971), *The Theory of the Novel: A Historico-Philosophical Essay on the Forms of Great Epic Literature*, trans. Anna Bostock, Cambridge: MIT Press.

Lukács, Georg (1978), *Writer and Critic*, ed. and trans. Arthur Kahn, London: Merlin Press.

Lukács, Georg (1994), *Die Theorie des Romans: Ein geschichtsphilosophischer Versuch über die Formen der großen Epik*, Munich: DTV.

Lukács, Georg (2002), *Studies in European Realism: Balzac, Stendhal, Tolstoy, Zola, Gorky*, trans. Edith Bone, New York: Howard Fertig.

Lukács, Georg (2006), *The Meaning of Contemporary Realism*, trans. John and Necke Mander, London: Merlin Press.

Lukács, Georg (2007), "Realism in the Balance," trans. Rodney Livingstone, in Theodor W. Adorno, Walter Benjamin, Ernst Bloch, Bertolt Brecht, and Georg Lukács, *Aesthetics and Politics*, 28–59, London: Verso, 1977.

Lukács, Georg (2010), *Soul and Form*, ed. John T. Sanders and Katie Terezakis, trans. Anna Bostock, New York: Columbia University Press.

Lukács, Georg (2011), *History and Class Consciousness: Studies in Marxist Dialectics*, trans. Rodney Livingstone, London: Merlin Press.

Mann, Thomas (1992), *Der Tod in Venedig*, Frankfurt am Main: Fischer.

Mann, Thomas (2006), *Death in Venice and Other Stories*, trans. David Luke, New York: Vintage.

McDowell, John (2000), "Towards Rehabilitating Objectivity," in Robert B. Brandom (ed.), *Rorty and His Critics*, 109–23, Malden, MA: Blackwell.

McGinn, Marie (2013), *Wittgenstein's Philosophical Investigations*, London: Routledge.

Mendieta, Eduardo (2021), "Epilogue," in Richard Rorty, *Pragmatism as Anti-Authoritarianism*, ed. Mendieta, 192–8, Cambridge, MA: Belknap Press.

Misak, Cheryl (2016), *Cambridge Pragmatism*, New York: Oxford University Press.

Moi, Toril (2017), *Revolution of the Ordinary: Literary Studies after Wittgenstein, Austin, and Cavell*, Chicago: University of Chicago Press.

Moyal-Sharrock, Danièle (2004), *Understanding Wittgenstein's On Certainty*, Basingstoke: Palgrave Macmillan.

Nietzsche, Friedrich (1968), *The Will to Power*, ed. Walter Kaufmann, trans. Kaufmann and R. J. Hollingdale, New York: Vintage.

Nietzsche, Friedrich (1974), *The Gay Science*, trans. Walter Kaufmann, New York: Vintage.

Nietzsche, Friedrich (1982a), *Thus Spoke Zarathustra*, in *The Portable Nietzsche*, ed. and trans. Walter Kaufmann, 103–439, New York: Penguin.

Nietzsche, Friedrich (1982b), *The Twilight of Idols*, in *The Portable Nietzsche*, ed. and trans. Walter Kaufmann, 463–563, New York: Penguin.

Nietzsche, Friedrich (1988), *Die fröhliche Wissenschaft*, Kritische Studienausgabe Band 3, ed. Giorgio Colli and Mazzino Montinari, Berlin: de Gruyter.

Nietzsche, Friedrich (1999), *The Birth of Tragedy and Other Writings*, ed. Raymond Geuss and Ronald Speirs, trans. Ronald Speirs, Cambridge: Cambridge University Press.

Nietzsche, Friedrich (2003), *Beyond Good and Evil: Prelude to a Philosophy of the Future*, trans. R. J. Hollingdale, New York: Penguin.

Nietzsche, Friedrich (2005), *The Anti-Christ, Ecce Homo, Twilight of the Idols*, ed. Aaron Ridley and Judith Norman, trans. Judith Norman, New York: Cambridge University Press.

Nietzsche, Friedrich (2011), *Dawn: Thoughts on the Presumptions of Morality*, trans. Brittain Smith, Stanford, CA: Stanford University Press.

Nietzsche, Friedrich (2017), *The Will to Power: Selections from the Notebooks of the 1880s*, ed. R. Kevin Hill, trans. R. Kevin Hill and Michael A. Scarpitti, New York: Penguin.

Pater, Walter (2010), *Studies in the History of the Renaissance*, ed. Matthew Beaumont, New York: Oxford University Press.

Plato (2003), *The Last Days of Socrates*, trans. Hugh Tredennick and Harold Tarrant, New York: Penguin.

Proust, Marcel (2000), *Time Regained*, trans. A. Mayor and T. Kilmartin, rev. D. J. Enright, New York: Vintage.

Putnam, Hilary (1994), *Words and Life*, ed. James Conant, Cambridge, MA: Harvard University Press.

Putnam, Hilary (1995), *Pragmatism: An Open Question*, Cambridge, MA: Blackwell.

Putnam, Hilary, and Ruth Anna Putnam (2017), *Pragmatism as a Way of Life: The Lasting Legacy of William James and John Dewey*, ed. David Macarthur, Cambridge, MA: Belknap Press.

Reynolds, David S. (1996), *Walt Whitman's America: A Cultural Biography*, New York: Vintage.

Ridley, Aaron (2013), "Nietzsche and the Arts of Life," in Ken Gemes and John Richardson (eds.), *The Oxford Handbook of Nietzsche*, 415–31, New York: Oxford University Press.

Rondel, David (2021), "Introduction: The Unity of Richard Rorty's Philosophy," in David Rondel (ed.), *The Cambridge Companion to Rorty*, 1–18, New York: Cambridge University Press.

Rorty, Richard (1979), *Philosophy and the Mirror of Nature*, Princeton, NJ: Princeton University Press.

Rorty, Richard (1982), *Consequences of Pragmatism: Essays 1972–1980*, Minneapolis: University of Minnesota Press.

Rorty, Richard (1989), *Contingency, Irony, and Solidarity*, New York: Cambridge University Press.

Rorty, Richard (1991a), *Essays on Heidegger and Others: Philosophical Papers, Vol. 2*, New York: Cambridge University Press.

Rorty, Richard (1991b), *Objectivity, Relativism, and Truth: Philosophical Papers, Vol. 1*, New York: Cambridge University Press.

Rorty, Richard (1995a), "Philosophy and the Future," in Herman J. Saatkamp Jr. (ed.), *Rorty and Pragmatism: The Philosopher Responds to His Critics*, 197–205, Nashville, TN: Vanderbilt University Press.

Rorty, Richard (1995b), "Response to Hartshorne," in Herman J. Saatkamp Jr. (ed.), *Rorty and Pragmatism: The Philosopher Responds to His Critics*, 29–36, Nashville, TN: Vanderbilt University Press.

Rorty, Richard (1998a), *Achieving Our Country: Leftist Thought in Twentieth-Century America*, Cambridge, MA: Harvard University Press.

Rorty, Richard (1998b), *Truth and Progress: Philosophical Papers, Vol. 3*, New York: Cambridge University Press.
Rorty, Richard (1999), *Philosophy and Social Hope*, New York: Penguin.
Rorty, Richard (2000a), *Die Schönheit, die Erhabenheit und die Gemeinschaft der Philosophen*, trans. Christa Krüger and Jürgen Blasius, Frankfurt am Main: Suhrkamp.
Rorty, Richard (2000b), "Response to Bjorn Ramberg," in Robert B. Brandom (ed.), *Rorty and His Critics*, 370–7, Malden, MA: Blackwell.
Rorty, Richard (2001), "Response to Richard Shusterman," in Matthew Festenstein and Simon Thompson (eds.), *Richard Rorty: Critical Dialogues*, 153–7, Cambridge: Polity.
Rorty, Richard (2004), "Philosophy as a Transitional Genre," in Seyla Benhabib and Nancy Fraser (eds.), *Pragmatism, Critique, Judgment: Essays for Richard J. Bernstein*, 3–28, Cambridge: MIT Press.
Rorty, Richard (2007), *Philosophy as Cultural Politics: Philosophical Papers, Vol. 4*, New York: Cambridge University Press.
Rorty, Richard (2009), "Pragmatism as Anti-Authoritarianism," in John R. Shook and Joseph Margolis (eds.), *A Companion to Pragmatism*, 257–66, Malden, MA: Wiley-Blackwell.
Rorty, Richard (2010a), "Redemption from Egotism: James and Proust as Spiritual Exercises," in Christopher J. Voparil and Richard J. Bernstein (eds.), *The Rorty Reader*, 389–406, Malden, MA: Wiley-Blackwell.
Rorty, Richard (2010b), "Reply to Jeffrey Stout," in Randall E. Auxier and Lewis Edwin Hahn (eds.), *The Philosophy of Richard Rorty*, 546–9, Chicago, IL: Open Court.
Rorty, Richard (2016), *Philosophy as Poetry*, Charlottesville: University of Virginia Press.
Rorty, Richard (2021), *Pragmatism as Anti-Authoritarianism*, ed. Eduardo Mendieta, Cambridge, MA: Belknap Press of Harvard University Press.
Rorty, Richard, and Gianni Vattimo (2005), *The Future of Religion*, ed. Santiago Zabala, New York: Columbia University Press.
Said, Edward W. (2000), *Reflections on Exile and Other Literary and Cultural Essays*, London: Granta Books.
Said, Edward W. (2004), *Humanism and Democratic Criticism*, New York: Columbia University Press.
Schacht, Richard (1992), *Nietzsche*, New York: Routledge.
Schiller, F. C. S. (1903), *Humanism: Philosophical Essays*, New York: Macmillan.
Schiller, F. C. S. (1907), *Studies in Humanism*, New York: Macmillan.
Schulenberg, Ulf (2007), *Lovers and Knowers: Moments of the American Cultural Left*, Heidelberg: Universitätsverlag Winter.
Schulenberg, Ulf (2015), *Romanticism and Pragmatism: Richard Rorty and the Idea of a Poeticized Culture*, Basingstoke: Palgrave Macmillan.

Schulenberg, Ulf (2019), *Marxism, Pragmatism, and Postmetaphysics: From Finding to Making*, Basingstoke: Palgrave Macmillan.

Schulenberg, Ulf (2021), *Pragmatism and Poetic Agency: The Persistence of Humanism*, New York: Routledge.

Sellars, Wilfrid (1997), *Empiricism and the Philosophy of Mind*, with an Introduction by Richard Rorty and a Study Guide by Robert Brandom, Cambridge, MA: Harvard University Press.

Shusterman, Richard (2000), *Pragmatist Aesthetics: Living Beauty, Rethinking Art*, 2nd ed., Lanham, MD: Rowman and Littlefield.

Shusterman, Richard, and Roberta Dreon (2021), "Pragmatist Aesthetics: Histories, Questions, and Consequences: An Interview with Richard Shusterman," *European Journal of Pragmatism and American Philosophy* XIII-1, http://journals.openedition.org/ejpap/2261 (accessed April 4, 2022).

Tally, Jr., Robert T. (2020), "Critique Unlimited," in Jeffrey R. Di Leo (ed.), *What's Wrong with Anti-Theory?*, 115–33, New York: Bloomsbury.

Trilling, Lionel (2000), *The Moral Obligation to Be Intelligent: Selected Essays*, ed. and with an Introduction by Leon Wieseltier, New York: Farrar, Straus and Giroux.

Voparil, Christopher J. (2010), "General Introduction," in Christopher J. Voparil and Richard J. Bernstein (eds.), *The Rorty Reader*, 1–52, Malden, MA: Wiley-Blackwell.

Voparil, Christopher (2022), *Reconstructing Pragmatism: Richard Rorty and the Classical Pragmatists*, New York: Oxford University Press.

West, Cornel (1989), *The American Evasion of Philosophy: A Genealogy of Pragmatism*, Madison: University of Wisconsin Press.

Whitman, Walt (1855), "Preface to *Leaves of Grass*," in Mark Van Doren (ed.), *The Portable Walt Whitman*, 5–27, New York: Penguin, 1977.

Whitman, Walt (1856), "Prefatory Letter to Ralph Waldo Emerson – *Leaves of Grass* 1856," in Michael Moon (ed.), *Leaves of Grass and Other Writings*, 638–46, New York: Norton, 2002.

Whitman, Walt (1871), *Democratic Vistas*, in Mark Van Doren (ed.), *The Portable Walt Whitman*, 317–82, New York: Penguin, 1977.

Whitman, Walt (1872), "Preface 1872 – As a Strong Bird on Pinions Free," in Michael Moon (ed.), *Leaves of Grass and Other Writings*, 647–52, New York: Norton, 2002.

Whitman, Walt (1876), "Preface 1876 – *Leaves of Grass* and *Two Rivulets*," in Michael Moon (ed.), *Leaves of Grass and Other Writings*, 652–61, New York: Norton, 2002.

Whitman, Walt (1888), "A Backward Glance O'er Travel'd Roads," in Mark Van Doren (ed.), *The Portable Walt Whitman*, 295–312, New York: Penguin, 1977.

Wittgenstein, Ludwig ([1969] 1972), *On Certainty*, ed. G. E. M. Anscombe and G. H. von Wright, trans. Denis Paul and Anscombe, New York: Harper & Row.

Wittgenstein, Ludwig (1979), *Tagebücher 1914–1916*, Werkausgabe Band 1, Frankfurt am Main: Suhrkamp, 2006.

Wittgenstein, Ludwig ([1953] 2009), *Philosophical Investigations*, ed. P. M. S. Hacker and Joachim Schulte, trans. G. E. M. Anscombe, P. M. S. Hacker, and Joachim Schulte, Malden, MA: Wiley-Blackwell.

Wolfson, Susan J. (2006), "Introduction: Reading for Form," in Susan J. Wolfson and Marshall Brown (eds.), *Reading for Form*, 3–24, Seattle: University of Washington Press.

Index

(Note: Page numbers followed by "n" refer to notes)

Adorno, Theodor W. 5, 8, 13–14, 77, 89, 120–9, 137, 139, 184
    art's autonomy 122–3, 125, 127
    the avant-garde 120, 122–3, 124–8
    coherence 121, 126–7
    dissonance 121, 123, 127–8
    form 8, 24, 84, 120–2
    form and truth 122–3
    idealist aesthetics 123–5
    Jameson and 24
    Lukács and 121–2
    montage 8, 125–6
    negation of aesthetic synthesis 8, 108, 126–9, 137, 186–7
    nonorganic artwork 123, 125, 127, 187
    Said and 23
    semblance 124, 127–8, 187
aestheticism 37, 70, 89, 160, 178
aesthetics 23, 67, 77–92, 107–38, 180. *See also* form
Alexander, Thomas M. 83–4
analytic philosophy 80, 95
Anker, Elizabeth 142–3
anthropocentrism 15, 73, 75, 97
anti-authoritarianism 4, 13, 14, 27–32, 93, 154, 180. *See also* Dewey, John; Nietzsche, Friedrich; Rorty, Richard; Wittgenstein, Ludwig
    humanism and 3, 4, 6, 10, 13, 18, 24, 32, 63–4, 94, 96–7, 105, 181, 184
antiessentialism 15, 27–8, 53, 63, 96
antifoundationalism 103, 147, 172
antifoundationalist story of progress 2, 3, 6, 14, 28, 32, 48, 63–4, 66, 70–1, 87, 153, 157, 178. *See also* humanism
antihumanism 1, 18, 69, 184, 189–90 n.2
anti-Platonism 33, 40–1, 180. *See also* Platonism

antirepresentationalism 20, 30, 34, 70, 96, 106, 179, 183
appearance-reality distinction 2, 41–2, 64, 87, 89, 115, 146–7, 169
apriorism 158, 178
Aristotle 103
the avant-garde 7, 8, 67–8, 70, 78, 83–5, 122–6. *See also* Adorno, Theodor W.

Balzac, Honoré de 43, 60, 89, 117, 131
Barthes, Roland 18, 77, 147
Bataille, Georges 18, 147
Baudelaire, Charles 177
Baudrillard, Jean 186
Beckett, Samuel 115, 123
Bell, Clive 82
Benjamin, Walter 85
Bennington, Geoffrey 58
Berlin, Isaiah 6, 15, 18–19, 34
Bernstein, Richard J. 11, 59, 70
Blanchot, Maurice 147
Bloom, Harold 64–5, 154–5
Booth, Wayne C. 61
Bradley, F. H. 73
Brandom, Robert B. 31, 51, 94, 98–9
Braque, Georges 125
Brennan, Timothy 15, 17–18
Breton, André 84, 122, 218–19 n.27
Bruno, Giordano 15
Bürger, Peter 84–5, 126–7, 217–18 n.25
Butler, Judith 111

Chase, Richard 61
Coleridge, Samuel T. 40, 53, 89
contingency 4, 41, 47, 87, 140, 142, 175
convergence to the antecedently real 2, 27, 70, 74, 93, 142, 158, 160, 167, 179, 183, 187. *See also* human answerability

Cooper, David E. 6, 15–16
Craig, Edward 6, 15, 16–18
creativity of action 74, 76, 87, 92, 142, 158, 174–5, 179. *See also* practice/praxis
Cubism 125
Culler, Jonathan 58

Darwin, Charles 28, 30
deconstruction 1, 24, 58, 69, 132, 147
Deleuze, Gilles 148, 159
depth 35, 112, 118, 140
Derrida, Jacques 2, 18, 57–9, 77, 147
Descartes, René 16, 27, 98
Dewey, John 2, 4, 10, 34, 67–8, 74–5. *See also* pragmatism; Rorty, Richard
  aesthetic experience 78, 81
  anti-authoritarianism 48–52
  antidualism 81, 88
  Emerson and 160–2
  form 7, 67, 70, 78–85, 87–92, 152, 234 n.6
  knowledge 74–5, 104
  Marxism 135–6
  naturalist aesthetics 70, 78–80, 89, 185–6
  organicity 80, 83
  quest for certainty 11, 66, 103–4
  spectator theory of knowledge 17, 104
  task of philosophy 48–9, 68
Dickens, Charles 53, 60, 86
Dreiser, Theodore 60
Dreon, Roberta 186
Du Bois, W. E. B. 172
Duchamp, Marcel 125

Eliot, T. S. 78
emancipation 16, 62, 76, 183, 187–8
  Marxism 134
  social 11
Emerson, Ralph Waldo 10, 34, 40, 71, 153, 154–62, 168, 188
  appearance-reality distinction 159–60
  contingency 155, 159
  Dewey and 160–2
  Emersonian poet 154–6, 159, 162
  form 160–2
  language 156
  poetic agency 157–60
  progress 159

redescription 155, 159
Romanticism 157, 162
Rorty and 155–6, 160–1
self-reliance 155, 159, 164
the Enlightenment 4, 27. *See also* pragmatism
  completing the project of 4, 6, 29, 31, 48, 51, 76, 181
epistemology 2, 51, 74, 81, 100, 104, 134, 143, 147–8, 172, 183
experience 78–82
experiment 42, 75, 148, 161

Faulkner, William 84–5, 115
Felski, Rita 9, 139–44, 150
  critique 139–40
  form 143
  Latour and 9, 141–3
  positive aesthetics 140–4, 150, 187
  postcritique 141–4
Fichte, Johann Gottlieb 20
finding. *See also* making
  from finding to making 2, 22, 34, 39, 70, 98, 129, 142, 157, 181, 188
  metaphors of 14, 112
Fish, Stanley 20
Flaubert, Gustave 43, 78, 84, 85, 113
form 5, 14, 61, 68. *See also* aesthetics; idealist aesthetics; Marxist aesthetics; pragmatist aesthetics
  anti-authoritarianism and 9, 13, 19, 92, 128–9, 166, 186–8
  form-content dialectics 1, 8, 61, 77, 80–3, 129
  Marxism 107–38
  pragmatism 7, 61, 77–92, 128–9
formalism 25, 67, 79–80, 89, 119, 129, 151, 160
Foucault, Michel 18, 58, 147
foundationalism 8, 34, 93, 96–8, 102–3, 105, 142, 164, 177. *See also* antifoundationalism
Frege, Gottlob 95
Freud, Sigmund 150
Fry, Roger 82

Gadamer, Hans-Georg 2
Galilei, Galileo 16

Gasché, Rodolphe 58
Genet, Jean 59
Gide, André 85
God's-eye view 2
God-substitutes 64, 70, 92
Goethe, Johann Wolfgang von 17
Green, T. H. 73

Habermas, Jürgen 35, 58
Hall, David L. 154
Hammer, Espen 24, 126
Harman, Graham 148
Hegel, G. W. F. 1, 17, 24, 55, 58–9, 62–3, 111, 116, 120
Heidegger, Martin 35, 37, 58–9
historicism 15, 22, 50
human answerability 4, 7, 13–14, 27, 37, 70, 93, 158, 180, 183
humanism 13–26, 69, 183–4. *See also* pragmatism
   antifoundationalist story of progress and 4, 27–9, 183
   humanist story of progress 33–4, 93–4, 153–81, 188
   liberal humanism 69
   Marxism 136–7
   Nietzsche 175–9
   pragmatism 4, 69–77, 97
   Renaissance humanism 15–16
   revival of 5, 184, 188
   socialist humanism 120, 221 n.39

idealist aesthetics 80, 123–5
imagination 32, 44, 55, 65, 74, 87, 154, 187
instrumentalism 88
intellectual history 5
interpretation 140–4, 179

James, Henry 59–60
James, William 2, 10, 34, 69, 71–3, 93, 96, 142, 144, 153, 171–5, 184, 188. *See also* pragmatism
   Kant and 158
   knowledge 72, 172
   monism 72–3
   Nietzsche and 71, 177
   pluralism 72, 174
   poet 172–4
   postmetaphysical culture and 172–5
   public philosopher 171–2
   relations 142
   religion 60
   subject as maker 71–2
   theory 72
   truth 34
Jameson, Fredric 5, 8–9, 77, 107–8, 129–35, 137, 186
   Adorno and 24, 129
   cognitive mapping 131–3
   form 9, 131, 133–5
   Lukács and 9, 130, 133–5, 137
   narrative 133–5
   new realism 129–30
   postmodernism 129–33
   realism 129–30, 134
   totality 130, 132, 134
Joyce, James 78, 84–5, 115, 131

Kafka, Franz 78, 88, 113, 131
Kandinsky, Wassily 78
Kant, Immanuel 4, 8, 16, 21, 27, 40, 55, 111, 117, 119, 129, 151
Kuhn, Thomas S. 2, 165
Kundera, Milan 54–5

Latour, Bruno 9, 139–52. *See also* Felski, Rita
   actor-network theory 144–5
   agency 143, 152
   compositionism 145–6
   contingency 142
   critique 144–6
   epistemology 143, 147–9
   form 9–10, 143, 151–2
   immanence 148
   metaphysics 146
   panrelationalism 142, 144
   posthumanism 143, 149
   pragmatism 147, 149, 151–2
Leighton, Angela 89
literary culture. *See under* poeticized culture
Locke, Alain 172
Love, Heather 139
Lukács, Georg 5, 8, 108–20, 133–8

Adorno and 114
appearance-reality distinction 117–19
authoritarianism 119–20
the avant-garde 214 n.12
the early Lukács 110–13
form 89–90, 110–17, 119
formal redemption 111, 119
form-content dialectics 115
Hegel and 111, 113
Jameson and 108, 130, 133–5
metaphysics 112
middle period of 110, 115–19
modernism 112, 116, 118, 213 n.10
narrative 119, 133–5
pragmatism 119–20
realism 110, 113, 116–18, 134–5
reflection theory 114–15, 118
totality 112–13, 117–19
Lyotard, Jean-François 136, 186

McGinn, Marie 95–6
Machiavelli, Niccolò 15
making 74, 146, 149, 158, 180, 184. *See also* finding; creativity of action
poetic achievements 14, 65, 159, 178
Mallarmé, Stéphane 88, 111, 139
Man, Paul de 58, 77
Mann, Thomas 108–10
Marx, Karl 16, 150
Marxism 14, 59, 107, 133–7
practice 113–15
pragmatism and 8, 107–8, 137–8
Marxist aesthetics 8, 14, 90, 107–38
form 8–9, 24, 108–20, 120–9
materialism 170
mediation 91, 111, 137, 148, 184, 186
meliorism 172
metaphysics 3, 18, 58, 70, 104, 112, 136, 170, 178. *See also* postmetaphysics
mimesis 43, 71, 130, 164
Mirandola, Pico della 15
Misak, Cheryl 99–100
modernism 7, 68, 78, 80, 83–4, 87–8, 130, 186. *See also* Adorno, Theodor W.; Lukács, Georg
Montaigne, Michel de 15
Moore, G. E. 95
Moyal-Sharrock, Danièle 97, 101–3

Nabokov, Vladimir 86, 129
Nagel, Thomas 143
naturalism 50, 79, 118
Nehamas, Alexander 44
New Criticism 80
Nietzsche, Friedrich 1, 10, 13–14, 17, 58, 69, 71, 97, 140, 146–7, 153, 175–81, 188. *See also* James, William; Rorty, Richard
aesthetics 150–1
anti-authoritarianism 37–40, 175, 180
appearance 146–7
art 1–2, 38, 150–1, 177, 180, 226–7 n.20
contingency 149, 175, 179
critique of metaphysics 37, 45, 178
death of God 2–3, 37, 39
form 20–1, 149–51, 180, 230–1 n.20
God's shadows 2, 38
Heidegger and 37
humanism 1–3, 13–14, 18, 21, 175–9
knowledge 38
naturalism 2–3, 176, 178
nihilism 150
philosophy of creativity 178
poets 175, 177–8
postcritique 149–51
postmetaphysics 37, 176, 178, 180
pragmatism 38, 180
Romanticism 157–8, 176, 179
self-creation 177
as theorist 45–7
truth 149–50, 179
will to power 149–50, 180
nominalism 46, 76, 93, 96, 119, 158
normativity 4, 27, 98–9, 148, 177
Nussbaum, Martha 61

ordinary language philosophy 95
Orwell, George 53, 86

panrelationalism 45, 142, 144, 232 n.24
particularity 90
perspectivism 2, 45, 47, 72
philosophy of creativity 2, 178
philosophy of praxis 113–15, 134
Picasso, Pablo 78, 88, 125
Plato 3, 103, 109, 153, 180

Platonism 2, 22, 36, 37, 41, 87, 98, 111, 117, 148. *See also* anti-Platonism
poetic agency 16, 21, 71, 77, 87, 90, 128, 140, 144, 152, 157, 160, 181, 186–7
poeticized culture 62–5. *See also* postmetaphysics; Rorty, Richard
poiesis 5, 6, 13, 19, 21, 28, 38, 71, 184, 188
postcritique 9, 139–52
posthumanism 7, 69, 143, 149
postmetaphysics 10, 154. *See also* Rorty, Richard
  postmetaphysical culture 4, 21, 29, 33, 66–7, 69, 91, 171, 178
postmodernism 9, 24, 147, 186. *See also* Jameson, Fredric
post-philosophy 31
poststructuralism 1, 7, 18, 24, 69, 147
practice/praxis 17, 72, 96, 134, 148, 151
pragmatism. *See also* Dewey, John; humanism; James, William; Rorty, Richard; Schiller, F.C.S.
  pragmatist enlightenment 64, 66
  pragmatist humanism 3–4, 5, 10, 25, 48, 66, 69–77, 87, 137, 143, 152–4, 166, 171, 181, 184, 188
  pragmatist-humanist literary criticism 9–10, 52–5, 61, 86, 129, 152
  Romanticism and 63–4, 154–62, 163–71
pragmatist aesthetics 8–9, 61, 87, 90–1, 135, 137, 149, 185–8. *See also* Dewey, John; Rorty,Richard
  form 6, 13, 77–92, 128–9, 152, 160–2, 184
Protagoras 175
Proust, Marcel 29, 32, 43–7, 53, 59–60, 78, 86, 131
purity 50, 89, 111, 169, 181
Putnam, Hilary 208 n.1, 210 n.15

quest for certainty 4, 17, 30, 98, 111, 143, 151, 158. *See also* Dewey, John
Quine, W. V. O. 35, 99

realism 43–4. *See also* Jameson, Fredric; Lukács, Georg
religion 1, 16, 63, 150
representationalism 30, 35, 178
Ricoeur, Paul 150

Romanticism 19–20, 62, 87, 153–81. *See also* Emerson, Ralph Waldo; Nietzsche, Friedrich; pragmatism; Rorty, Richard; Whitman, Walt
Rondel, David 5
Rorty, Richard 2, 4, 15, 27–68, 107, 137–8, 147. *See also* pragmatism
  anti-authoritarianism 6, 15, 27–32, 34, 43, 48, 65–8, 154, 180–1, 183–4
  contingency 45, 56, 65
  Derrida and 57–9
  Dewey and 47–52
  form 61, 65–6, 77, 85–6, 129, 143, 188, 202 n.27
  imagination 33, 76
  ironism 64–5
  justification 30, 76, 183
  knowledge 30
  on Kundera 54–5
  literary criticism 23, 61, 86, 91, 129, 143, 188
  Marxism 136, 220–1 n.37
  morality and literature 52–5, 60–1, 86
  Nietzsche and 7, 37–43, 180
  on Nietzsche and James 36
  the novel 44–7, 52–61, 86
  Platonism 40–1
  poeticized culture 7, 10, 28, 32–3, 36, 55, 62–5, 75–6, 86, 153–4, 164, 174–5
  private-public distinction 52–3, 58–60, 66–7, 86
  progress 28, 33, 36, 63
  on Proust 7, 43–7, 60–1
  public irony 61
  redemptive truth 56, 60
  redescription 32–4, 76, 155
  Romanticism 7, 21, 32–7, 40, 55, 63, 66
  self-creation 40, 64, 154
  sentimental education 52–3, 86, 184

Said, Edward W. 6, 13, 15, 21–3, 25, 171, 188
Sainte-Beuve, Charles Augustin 61
Sartre, Jean-Paul 122
Schiller, F. C. S. 2, 13, 16, 51, 70, 73–4, 158, 184, 188. *See also* pragmatism
Schönberg, Arnold 78, 123
Sedgwick, Eve 139

self-creation 20, 32, 39, 154, 177
Sellars, Wilfrid 30, 99
Shelley, P. B. 34, 166, 168
Shklar, Judith 53
Shusterman, Richard 83, 185–6
Snow, C. P. 62
Socrates 153
Stowe, Harriet Beecher 53, 60
Stroll, Avrum 102

theory 18, 20, 91, 95, 100, 144, 151
    theory and practice 91, 104, 172
Thoreau, Henry David 168
Tolstoy, Leo 89
totality 63, 108. *See also* Jameson, Fredric;
    Lukács, Georg
Trilling, Lionel 52, 61
truth 34, 42, 54, 56, 63–4, 148, 154, 180
    correspondence theory of truth 2, 70, 74,
        104, 142

Vico, Giambattista 2, 6, 21–2, 134
Voparil, Christopher J. 5, 154

West, Cornel 171
Whitman, Walt 10, 34, 153, 163–71
    American poet 163, 166
    anti-authoritarianism 167, 169, 171
    contingency 163, 170

democracy 163, 169–70
Emerson and 163, 166
form 166, 171
idealism 168, 170
literature 165
pragmatism 170
religion 168–71
Romanticism 163, 168, 171
Rorty and 164–5, 167–8, 170
Whitehead, Alfred North 144
wholeness, 8, 67, 80, 83, 108, 116, 124,
    134, 186
Wittgenstein, Ludwig 68, 93–106,
    147
    anti-authoritarianism 93–4, 99, 105–6
    foundationalism 94, 96–8, 102–3, 105
    human certainty 95, 98, 101, 104–5
    metaphysics 97, 99, 103
    normativity 98–9, 99
    pragmatism 7–8, 93–5, 98–105
    Rorty and 93–4, 98, 100–1
    social practice 94, 96–7, 102, 105
    theory 100
    therapy 96, 100
Woolf, Virginia 78, 85, 115, 131
Wordsworth, William 168
Wright, Richard 53, 60

Zola, Emile 53, 115

www.ingramcontent.com/pod-product-compliance
Lightning Source LLC
Chambersburg PA
CBHW050324020526
44117CB00031B/1775